This book deals with the 'credit view' and its main theoretical assumptions. First, banks' decisions concerning their assets are seen as at least as relevant as their decisions concerning their liabilities. Second, securities and bank credit are highly imperfect substitutes. In this regard, it is important to investigate the way industrial and financial sectors interact. In particular, how is the macroeconomy affected by the phenomenon of 'securitization' and by exogenous changes in the industrial structure of the credit market. The interactions between real and financial sectors are also analysed from the point of view of the industrial firm, in a model where the investment and financial decisions of the firm are taken simultaneously. This book constitutes an interesting attempt to relate the literatures of finance, industrial economics and investment to the theoretical framework of the 'credit view'.

Credit, investments and the macroeconomy

Credit, investments and the macroeconomy

MARCO MAZZOLI

Università di Modena
Facoltà di Giurisprudenza

CAMBRIDGE
UNIVERSITY PRESS

PUBLISHED BY THE PRESS SYNDICATE OF THE UNIVERSITY OF CAMBRIDGE
The Pitt Building, Trumpington Street, Cambridge CB2 1RP, United Kingdom

CAMBRIDGE UNIVERSITY PRESS
The Edinburgh Building, Cambridge CB2 2RU, United Kingdom
40 West 20th Street, New York, NY 10011–4211, USA
10 Stamford Road, Oakleigh, Melbourne 3166, Australia

First published 1998

Printed in the United Kingdom at the University Press, Cambridge

Typeset in 10/12pt Times New Roman   [SE]

A catalogue record for this book is available from the British Library

Library of Congress Cataloguing-in-Publication data
Mazzoli, Marco.
    Credit, investments, and the macroeconomy
Marco Mazzoli.
        p. cm.
    Includes bibliographical references (p.   ).

    ISBN 0-521-58411-6 (hardbound)

    1. Credit.   2. Asset-liability management.   3. Macroeconomics.
I. Title.
HG3701.M348   1998
339–dc21   97-14438
                                                                 CIP

To the memory of my mother

Contents

Preface and acknowledgements

The role of the banking system in the transmission of monetary disturbances is the object of a lively debate. A pattern of causality between credit and real economic activity, significantly different from the one implied by the conventional *IS–LM* framework, has been proposed by the 'credit view', mainly with macroeconomic empirical and theoretical contributions. This book, after analysing some of the main results of the credit view and, more generally, of the economics of financial markets imperfections, investigates the interactions between the real and financial sectors of the economy, with the purpose of looking inside the creditist 'black box' of the (possible) links between credit, financial markets and investments. Some of the issues analysed here (in particular, banks' liquidity preference, industrial firms' oligopsonistic power in the credit market and interactions between firms' investments and financial decisions) have been studied by different branches of economic research with contrasting methodologies and results, or have been almost neglected by the mainstream literature. In some cases, an attempt has been made here to compare and, when possible, find a unifying ground for the implications of several important contributions (in macroeconomics, industrial economics and finance) concerned with the interactions between the real and financial side of the economy.

The analyses contained in this book may interest researchers, postgraduate and advanced undergraduate students in monetary economics, macroeconomics, investment theory and related fields.

My interest and curiosity for the subjects examined in the present study were inspired by the course 'Industrial Structure and the Macroeconomy' taught by Keith Cowling in 1989–90 at the University of Warwick. I am deeply indebted to him and Norman Ireland for their precious suggestions.

I am very grateful to Giovanni Amisano for his valued comments (throughout our stay at Warwick and after) on the empirical parts of this work, David Van Hoose for the very pertinent suggestions he gave me while he was Professor at Johns Hopkins University – Bologna Center, and Pier Luigi Sacco for his patient and constant advice.

The very thorough and detailed comments by Domenico Delli Gatti, Harald Hagemann and Roberto Tamborini on an earlier version of this work are very gratefully acknowledged.

I would also like to thank Jeffrey Bernstein, Giancarlo Bertocco, Carluccio Bianchi, Victoria Chick, David Cobham, Gianluca Femminis, Felix Fitzroy, Umberto Galmarini, Adrian Jimenez Gomez, Colin Mayer, Marcello Messori, Neil Rankin, Alan Roe, Flavio Rovida, Lino Sau, Jeremy Smith and Gerd Weinrich for helpful discussions and comments at different stages of this work. Chapter 5 is partly based on my article 'Free liquidity ratio for commercial banks: an estimate with Italian data', published (in English) in the *Giornale degli Economisti e Annali di Economia*, 50 (July–August 1991), pp. 399–424. I am very grateful to Giovanni Amisano, Wiji Narendranathan and anonymous referees for their helpful comments.

Giovanni Bucchieri and the 'Ufficio Studi' of Mediobanca have kindly provided me with the volumes of data employed in the empirical analysis of chapter 6.

Last but not least, I am very grateful to Patrick McCartan and the anonymous referees at Cambridge University Press for their detailed comments.

Obviously, none of the above is responsible for any mistakes that might be found, nor for the views expressed here.

Marco Mazzoli
Modena, March 1997

1   Introduction

Purpose of the book

Increasing attention has in the last few years been devoted to the 'credit view' approach, which states that banks' assets are as important as banks' liabilities for the transmission of monetary disturbances to the real sector of the economy. Each chapter of this book may be interpreted as an investigation of one particular aspect of the interaction between credit and industry, with specific macroeconomic implications, related to the credit view.

Although the 'creditist' statement *per se* can be consistent with different theoretical approaches and has even been the object of orthodox contributions in the past, the relevance of banks' assets for the transmission of monetary shocks to the real economy relies, in general, on the assumption of imperfect substitution between bank credit and securities as a source of finance for industrial firms. In this sense, the 'creditist' macromodels are usually founded on the results of the literature concerned with the determination of the firm's optimal financial structure,[1] and share many of the initial assumptions of that part of the New-Keynesian literature concerned with the macroeconomic implications of financial markets imperfections.[2]

This work focuses on the following issues, which (in spite of having been almost completely neglected by the mainstream literature of monetary economics) play a very important theoretical and empirical role for the propositions of the credit view with regard to the non-neutrality of credit and the behaviour of the financial sector:

---

[1] The simple assumption that bank credit and other sources of finance are imperfect substitutes is only a more detailed and less general specification of the general statement that the financial structure (interpreted as a choice between internal and external finance) is relevant for the real investment decisions of the firm.

[2] This does not apply to those very few 'creditist' models based on non-Keynesian approaches, such as, for instance, Fuerst (1992); Christiano and Eichenbaum (1992).

(a) macroeconomic relevance of the difference between 'securitized' and 'bank-oriented' financial systems[3]
(b) macroeconomic implications of the (oligopsonistic) market power of industrial firms in the credit market
(c) liquidity preference of banks
(d) interactions and simultaneity between investment and finance decisions of the industrial firms.

The fact that the firm's financial structure affects investment decisions and, as a consequence, real economic activity, has been studied in different contexts (industrial economics, banking and finance, macroeconomics) with different modelling techniques, methodologies and sometimes even with different conclusions. Therefore, incorporating some results of industrial organization and finance into standard models concerned with the macroeconomic implications of banks' behaviour, or with firms' investments is one of the purposes of this study.

Analysing what is frequently taken for exogenous neutral or irrelevant, finding some unifying ground, or putting into context different perspectives is certainly a difficult and, at the same time, stimulating task. The difficulty lies in the fact that choosing which variables are taken as given and which ones are the actual object of an investigation entails some prior assumptions. Several examples can be made of cases where such assumptions do not depend on precise evidence on a hypothesis about the economic process under consideration, but rather on the kind of literature, or discipline, with which one is concerned. For instance, there is no particular reason to assume that the firms' financial structure is given and exogenous for the investment decisions (as is usually assumed in the optimal control investment models), or that the level of investment is given for the choice of the optimal financial structure. Indeed, only very few contributions (and only recently) have regarded the problems of firms' investment and financial structure as simultaneous. Something similar could be said by comparing the industrial economics literature on the 'deep pocket argument' (Telser, 1966; Poitervin, 1989a), and the 'limited liability effect' (Brander and Lewis, 1985; Poitervin, 1989b) with the literature of corporate finance. The former relates the firm's financial decision with strategic market interac-

---

[3] The phenomenon of securitization has been analysed by the literature dealing with the economic analysis of financial institutions (for instance, Rybczynski, 1984; Gardener and Molyneux, 1990; Gardener, 1991). According to these authors, the 'securitized' financial systems, as opposed to the 'bank-oriented' or 'non-securitized' financial systems, are characterized by the quantitative macroeconomic relevance of the funds traded in the security markets, whose magnitude is (unlike the bank-oriented financial systems) significant compared to the intermediated credit.

tions and suggests a precise causal link between financial decisions and market structure, the latter is concerned with the optimization of the firm's financial structure, often without taking into account firms' strategic interactions.

Another feature of this work is the emphasis put on the macroeconomic implications of the phenomenon of 'securitization' (i.e. the gradual process of transition from a bank-oriented toward a 'securitized' financial system). This issue constitutes a sort of premise for this whole study: it is the object of a preliminary empirical analysis (chapter 3) and plays some role even in part III of this book concerned with the interactions between the firm's finance and investment decisions.

Part I of this study (chapters 2 and 3) briefly analyses the main assumptions and contributions of the 'credit view' and introduces the perspective of this work.

After introducing (in chapter 2) Williamson's (1985) contractual framework as a tool to interpret the qualitative difference between bank-oriented and 'securitized' financial systems, the question is raised in chapter 3 of whether the phenomenon of securitization shows any empirically detectable implications for the behaviour of bank credit to industrial firms. In fact, it is in *securitized* financial systems that the issue of substitution between bank credit and recourse to spot financial markets is qualitatively relevant. The empirical investigation of chapter 3 consists of a comparative analysis of the identifiability of credit supply and demand in two different financial systems: a bank-oriented and a securitized one. The analysis refers to two countries whose magnitude is comparable, whose banking system follows the same model (universal banking) and shows a very similar degree of concentration and, finally, where the regulations concerning banking competition are very similar, apart from those aspects strictly connected with the phenomenon of 'securitization', i.e. the ability of banks to undertake long-run contractual relations with their customers. Britain and West Germany before unification satisfy all these requirements and their macro data have been consequently employed.

Part II (chapters 4 and 5), deals with two crucial elements of the interactions between credit and industry: the market power of industrial firms in the credit market and banks' liquidity preference.

Chapter 4 contains a theoretical model where it is shown that, *ceteris paribus*, an increase in industrial firms' oligopsonistic power in the credit market reduces the equilibrium level of investments and affects the transmission mechanism of monetary policy by a direct 'first-impact' effect that tends to reduce the effectiveness of monetary policy and various 'indirect effects' whose sign and intensity depends on the analytical form (i.e. curvature and cross-elasticities) of the various excess demand functions for the various financial assets.[4]

Chapter 5 focuses on the banks' liquidity preference. It contains an econometric analysis of commercial banks' free liquidity ratio for Italy, based on a theoretical framework consistent with the literature on investments under uncertainty and sunk costs. In such a context, the banks' liquid reserves are interpreted as a 'non-investment' decision determined by the banks' choice of collecting additional information, in the presence of uncertainty. The empirical specification (based on assumptions whose validity is actually confined to the Italian institutional context) is related to a frequent objection to the credit view, stating that the response of banks' assets to monetary shocks is caused by disturbances in banks' liabilities (i.e. deposits, which contribute to determining the money stock) transmitted to banks' assets via the balance-sheet constraint of the aggregate banking sector, as suggested by mainstream monetary economics. This statement would not be true to the extent that the level of banks' reserves is the result of an active and deliberate 'liquidity preference' choice, interpreted as a 'non-investment' decision, caused by an increase of the degree of uncertainty of the whole economy.

Analysing the interactions between firms' finance and investments decisions within the framework of investment models (which is done in part III, chapters 6 and 7) can be interpreted as an investigation inside the 'black box' of the macroeconomic link between credit and real macroeconomic activity postulated in many 'creditist' econometric analyses.

Chapter 6 contains an empirical analysis of investments performed on the basis of a very simple theoretical framework which interprets the speed of adjustment of investments as an effect of transaction costs. Most economists share the idea that the neoclassical model with costless and instantaneous adjustment holds when transaction costs are zero and that this makes institutions irrelevant.[5] Since, however, institutions are relevant when transaction costs are positive, it is argued in chapter 6 that in 'non-securitized' financial systems the influence of transaction costs can be particularly relevant for the adjustment mechanism of investments. The econometric estimates of the investment function (containing financial variables, interpreted as an element of heterogeneity among different firms of the same industry) are performed with panel data techniques applied to a sample of Italian chemical firms.

Chapter 7 deals with the problem of interactions between financial and investment decisions within the firm. The problem is analysed with the help

---

[4] This chapter is also related – in spirit rather than methodology – to the literature concerned with the connections between industrial structure and the macroeconomy, such as Cowling (1982); Eichner (1976); Henley (1990).   [5] See, in this regard, Williamson (1985).

of an optimal control model complicated by the assumption of simultaneity between investments and financial decisions. Some of the main assumptions apply, once again, to non-securitized financial systems, and are meant to describe the implications (for the firm's investment problem) of raising financial funds on security markets, interpreted as an institution where a particular mechanism of information spreading takes place. The model might also be interpreted as a qualitative microeconomic description of the investment problem for firms operating in financial systems that experience the transition from non-securitized to securitized financial systems. It is resolved by introducing an algebraically tractable functional link between the profits and the costs of financial capital, which is motivated by results in the literature of finance. It is shown that a real exogenous shock in the marginal profitability of physical capital can affect the level of investments of the firm not only through the usual 'real' channel (i.e. the link between marginal profitability of capital and optimal level of investments), but also through a 'financial' channel, given by a mechanism of information spreading, associated with negotiations in the financial markets. Thus, the different 'real' and 'financial' channels of transmission of real shocks, pointed out in several macroeconomic contributions of the credit view, are analysed within the microeconomic framework of investment theory.

Part III has several connections with the debate on 'credit and the macroeconomy', since it can be interpreted as a 'microeconomic' look inside the 'black box' of the macroeconomic link between banks' assets and real economic activity suggested by the credit view. Interpreting firms' financial structures as an element of heterogeneity within the same industry (as in chapter 6) is consistent with a central statement of the credit view: credit shocks may have heterogeneous effects on firms relying to a different extent on debt. Secondly, the model of chapter 7 introduces a microeconomic analysis of the interaction between real investments and risk premium (such as is perceived by the lender), that accounts, in addition, for the mechanism of information spreading associated with security markets. In this sense, chapter 7 is also strictly linked to the issue of 'securitization', which plays such an important role in this study. Given the complexity of the problem under examination, the model has had to be simplified with the help of a few assumptions, based on contributions in financial economics. This kind of methodological attitude is shared by many economists concerned with economics of financial markets imperfections:

Not every piece of research has to begin at the beginning. We know that there are good reasons, based on problems of adverse selection and moral hazard, that equity markets may not function well. We also have ample empirical evidence that firms make limited use of equity markets, and event studies confirm that when they do raise additional capital through the issue of equities, stock prices are lowered significantly. It thus seems perfectly appropriate for macroeconomic studies to begin with the hypothesis that equity markets do not function efficiently. For some purposes, it may not matter what the precise source of this market failure is. (Stiglitz, 1991, p. 10)

The above quotation raises several methodological points. Therefore it might be useful to introduce a very brief and informal description of some of the main elements of the methodological approach (shared in this work) characterizing the 'New-Keynesian' Macroeconomics. It will only be a very brief discussion, since a detailed methodological analysis is far beyond the scope of this work.[6]

Methodological premises

The reader familiar with the methodological debate within the New-Keynesian macroeconomics will not find anything particularly new in this section, since it discusses a few common objections to the 'New Classical Macroeconomics – Real Business Cycle' methodology. However, dealing with an issue such as the interactions between banks and industrial firms raises the well known (and controversial) problems of relations between micro and macro theory, microfoundation and use (or non-use) of the representative agent.

According to the usual argument of the supporters of the concept of microfoundations based on a representative agent, a macroeconomic theory inconsistent with the implications of the microeconomic behaviour of a (representative) rational individual is not acceptable; on the other hand, according to a common 'Keynesian' objection to this argument, a micro-founded theory that fails to explain relevant empirical phenomena (such as credit rationing or the existence of an optimal financial structure for the firm) is even less acceptable.

Until the mid-1980s, the neoclassical macroeconomic literature regarded Modigliani and Miller's neutrality theorem as an acceptable simplifying hypothesis for macroeconomic modelling. Only heterodox and Post-Keynesian economists regarded the financial structure of the firms as non-neutral, and argued that business fluctuations could be originated by financial market perturbations. However, in finance, even mainstream contributions had regarded the optimal financial structure of the firm as a central issue, long before[7] the relevance of financial structure was incorpo-

---

[6] See, for instance, Stiglitz (1992).
[7] See for example Jensen and Meckling (1976); Leland and Pyle (1977); Ross (1977); Myers (1984); Myers and Majluf (1984).

rated in widely accepted micro-founded macroeconomic models (for instance, Greenwald and Stiglitz, 1988; Bernanke and Gertler, 1989). The different aims of economic and financial analysis did not *per se* justify such different theoretical approaches. Obviously, the discrepancies were to be found in a different evaluation of the relevance of market imperfections, but the doubt that strong priors might have played a role in this regard seems to be legitimate, as Gertler (1988) argues:

The methodological revolution in macroeconomics in the 1970s also helped shift away the attention from financial factors, in a less direct but probably more substantial way. The resulting emphasis on individual optimization posed an obstacle. (Gertler, 1988, p. 565)

Similar objections to the mainstream methodology have been raised, even more explicitly, by Stiglitz (1991), who calls for a greater attention towards the empirical purposes of economics, a concern that had been shared in the past (although in a completely different theoretical context, and without any particular emphasis on microfoundations and optimizing behaviour of the representative agent) by the 'old Keynesians':[8]

Economics is, or is supposed to be, an empirical science: how could economists' views be so divergent? Were these so-called scientists studying the same economy? Were they – or should I say, are we – simply ideologues looking for justifications for our political biases, or, no less worse, technicians, taking the assumptions provided to us by our ideologue brethren, and exploring their consequences, trusting that the models we are analyzing bear some semblance to the world, because we have been told so by others! (Stiglitz, 1991, p. 5)

Economists have had two responses to [such] inexplicable phenomena. One is to suggest that because we cannot explain them, they do not exist. It is as if a biologist, finding it difficult to explain how blood can be pumped to the head of a giraffe, were to assume that it therefore must have a short neck. (Stiglitz, 1991, p. 21)

Stiglitz's strong criticism of the mainstream methodological approach is focused on his objections to the use of 'first principles'. In connection with this point and in support of it, Stiglitz mentions the results of Debreu 1974, Mantel 1974 and Sonnenschein 1972, 1974, showing that *any set of market excess demand functions satisfying Walras' Law can be derived from utility maximizing individuals*, which means, in other words, that the rationality

---

[8] Recently, in another completely different theoretical context, not related to this study, Kurz's 'rational beliefs' approach (Kurz, 1993, 1994a, 1994b, 1994c, 1994d) has provided a new paradigm of individual rationality consistent with Keynes' thought, where the hypothesis of rational expectation is interpreted as a very special case, determined by very strong restrictions. One of the main implications of Kurz's theory is that different rational agents with the same information set can have different beliefs on the dynamic law of motion that generates the observable data.

hypothesis does not put any relevant restriction on the observed behaviour.[9]

Furthermore, Stiglitz argues that the use of representative agents' models seem to contain an intrinsic paradox, since, 'when all individuals are identical there is no need for trade, and hence there are no consequences of the absence of markets' (Stiglitz, 1991, p. 11). In addition, representative agents' models are not suitable for describing problems arising from information asymmetries and coordination failures, unless 'a particular kind of schizophrenia on the part of the representative agent' is assumed (Stiglitz, 1991, p. 11). However, in spite of the wide acceptance of microfoundations and representative agents as rigorous bases for macromodels, a series of assumptions commonly accepted in micro-founded models are accused by Stiglitz of being 'ad hoc'. One of them is cash in advance, which is 'obviously not binding for most transactions' (Stiglitz, 1991, p. 19–20) while, concerning other well known theoretical equilibrium requirements, the objection is even more extreme: 'What faith do we have that any propositions derived in the artificial economy in which individuals meet at most only once and there are no intervening financial institutions have any validity for our economy?' (Stiglitz, 1991, p. 11). Even if the consistency between microeconomic and macroeconomic behaviour is certainly a very relevant issue (and in this sense the New Classical Macroeconomics has provided a very important contribution to the methodological debate), it is important to point out that the problem could be seen in the opposite way: the consistency of microeconomic theory with empirical (macroeconomic) phenomena. In other words, one should not ignore the fact that even the behaviour of observable macroeconomic variables might have strong implications for the economic theory. Furthermore, not every kind of microfoundation has necessarily to rely on the assumption of a representative agent.

The New-Keynesian macroeconomics, while accepting (unlike the Post-Keynesians) the principle of microfoundations, introduces some form of heterogeneity among the different agents and assumes various kinds of market imperfections: in particular, the models concerned with capital markets inefficiencies are based on the assumption of information asym-

---

[9] We might briefly anticipate here that these points made by Stiglitz are relevant for the analysis of chapter 7, which contains some assumptions based on the empirical observations contained in Brioschi *et al.* (1990); Mayer (1989, 1992, 1993a, 1993b), showing that in the Italian financial markets hostile takeovers are extremely rare, not to say virtually absent, while the transactions concerning the control and the majority shares of a company are usually performed through private negotiations among the management of the parties interested in the transaction. In chapter 7 it is assumed that the market for firms' control is not associated with the market for shares.

metry[10] and bankruptcy costs, which may determine (in the models concerned with the connections between firms' net worth and macroeconomic equilibrium, but not in the 'credit view') credit or equity rationing.

The use of Williamson's (1985) contractual framework could help to solve the contradiction between the assumption of individual rationality and 'inexplicable phenomena', like the 'widespread phenomena of individuals holding dominated assets', since, as Stiglitz points out, 'it is hard for any economic theory to explain why . . . cash management accounts, [a financial asset that should *dominate* all of the other liquid assets] . . . did not exist twenty years ago, and it is hard for any economic theory to explain why they are not even more widespread today' (Stiglitz, 1991, p. 21, emphasis added). In Williamson's (1985) contractual framework, the assumption of rationality is not eliminated, but rather substituted by the well known assumption of 'bounded rationality' or 'intended rationality', and the concept of asset specificity is regarded as the endogenous contractual outcome determined by all of the informationally relevant elements (such as timing, frequency of transaction, and many other details) affecting the decision process of individuals.[11]

Confronted with the realities of bounded rationality, the costs of planning, adapting, and monitoring transactions need expressly to be considered. . . . Transactions that are subject to ex post opportunism will benefit if appropriate safeguards can be devised ex ante. (Williamson, 1985, pp. 46–8)

Williamson's (1985) approach, based on the relevance of transaction costs, suggests an interpretation of the behaviour of economic agents in terms of contractual relations: the relevance of transaction costs is implied by those interpretations of the Arrow–Debreu model that define commodities not only by physical, spatial and time characteristics, but also by those elements of environmental uncertainty referred to as the 'state of the world'. In Williamson's view, economies on transaction costs can be implemented by assigning transactions to governance structures chosen among different institutional alternatives: the 'classical market contracting' at one extreme, a centralized hierarchical organization at the other, and mixed

---

[10] Another branch of the New-Keynesian macroeconomics, not concerned with credit and financial markets (and therefore not very relevant for this study) focuses on the macroeconomic implications of other forms of market imperfections, such as adjustment costs, demand constraints, imperfect competition in the goods markets, and (sometimes) non-unit elasticity of price expectations with respect to actual prices. Also this kind of literature yields – like the other New-Keynesian approach based on financial markets imperfections – the general result of non-neutrality of money and possible macroeconomic equilibria with unemployment.

[11] On this point, see also chapter 2, which contains a more detailed description and analysis of all the points just mentioned.

models of firms and market organization in between. In this context, bounded rationality can be a premise for interpreting a few institutional features of the financial systems (such as the relevance of security markets compared to bank credit) and contrasts with the traditional approach, which assumes *a priori* the existence of spot (and not transaction-specific) capital markets, whose definition entails in any case some degree of aggregation.

We could understand, in this sense, why the 'cash management accounts' mentioned by Stiglitz have only recently appeared and still do not have a wide diffusion, if at all only to the extent that they correspond to a specific contractual outcome satisfying precise safeguard needs and determined by means of a decision process with 'bounded rationality', where information, planning and calculations are not costless or timeless.

Williamson's (1985) contractual framework seems to be particularly appropriate to provide an economic justification and interpretation for the development and coexistence of transaction-specific and spot financial markets. Furthermore, it provides a 'microeconomic' justification (consistent with the methodological approach followed in the literature concerned with financial market imperfections) for some relevant features of the financial systems. This framework is discussed more in detail in chapter 2, and is particularly relevant for the empirical analysis of chapter 3, which constitutes an initial premise for the analyses contained in the later chapters. Each of the later chapters 4–7 deals with a specific aspect of the interactions between credit and industry and can be interpreted as an investigation of the link between banks' assets and real economic activity, suggested by the 'creditist' literature.

Finally, a specific role should be recognized for empirical analyses, at least with respect to the problem of consistency between macroeconomic and microeconomic theory, since a micro theory unable to account for observable macro data is as unacceptable as a macro theory violating the evidence of microeconomic (possibly heterogeneous) agents' behaviour: microfoundations of macroeconomics are not necessarily more important than 'macrofoundations of microeconomics'.

Part I

Banks, credit and
the macroeconomy: a puzzle

2 Credit, financial markets and the macroeconomy: different approaches and a proposed perspective

Credit and the macroeconomy

The role of the banking system in the transmission of monetary disturbances is the object of a lively debate. While a certain consensus has been established on the fact that monetary policy affects economic activity, at least in the short run, there is no agreement on how monetary policy affects output, prices and employment.

The traditional 'textbook' analyses of the monetary policy transmission mechanism are based on *IS–LM* models (or on aggregate demand and supply frameworks if one assumes price flexibility). Monetary policy interventions by the central bank induce impulses to the economic activity through changes in interest rate in liquid assets first and, in the long run (because of substitutionality among the different financial assets), interest rates. This 'traditional' approach, denominated 'money view' and based on the conventional Hicks–Modigliani–Patinkin framework,[1] is founded on the assumption of perfect substitution between the different financial assets and neutrality of firms' financial structure. The emphasis is put on the role played by the liabilities of the banking system, directly affected by monetary policy shocks and as a consequence affecting only bank assets.

The 'credit view' or 'lending view', although not necessarily in conflict with the 'money view', is based on the assumption of imperfect substitution between bank credit and securities and, at least implicitly, between internal and external finance. These models are usually based on the assumption of information asymmetries in financial markets and macroeconomic relevance of firms' financial structure.[2] Banks' assets are assumed

---

[1] The *IS-LM* model was invented by Hicks (1937), while Modigliani (1944) and Patinkin (1956) provided very important contributions to its theoretical framework of analysis.

[2] When referring to the lending view, many authors talk about 'rediscovering' credit, since in the past a few economists had already emphasized the macroeconomic role of credit and firms' financial structure – such as, for instance, Fisher (1933) and Gurley and Shaw (1955) (who obviously did not refer to information asymmetries in their analyses); Minsky (1975); Kindleberger (1978); and all of the Post-Keynesians, albeit in a completely different theoretical and methodological context.

to be as relevant as banks' liabilities for the transmsssion of monetary shocks to the real sector of the economy and bank lending is regarded as a 'special asset' that might (in some cases) incorporate monitoring costs and long-run contractual relationships between lenders and borrowers. In such a context, the liquidity preferences and investment decisions of the banking system play a relevant role for the determination of the macroeconomic equilibrium:

> What distinguishes the credit view from conventional neoclassical models is the recognition that households and/or firms do have liabilities, together with the presumption that these liabilities play a role in the determination of nonfinancial economic activity that is at least conceptually on a par with that reserved for money in neoclassical models . . . Private agents therefore have balance sheets, in the nontrivial sense that there must be assets and liabilities, and that any agent's liability must be some other agent's asset. It must also be the case that not all private agents are identical. (B. Friedman and Kuttner, 1993, p. 201)

The credit view has been developed through the contributions by Bernanke (1983, 1990); Bernanke and Blinder (1988, 1992); Bernanke and Campbell (1988, 1990); Bernanke and Gertler (1989, 1990); B. Friedman and Kuttner (1992, 1993); Gertler and Gilchrist (1993); Kashyap *et al.* (1993); and many others, while – independently of these contributions – the models employed for simulations and monetary policy by the central banks in most of the 'non-securitized' financial systems of Continental Europe have for years assumed that banks' credit plays a very relevant macroeconomic role (see for instance Banca d'Italia, 1986, the econometric model of the Bank of Italy). The transmission of monetary policy is a major concern of the 'creditist' models, but it is certainly not the only object of analysis of this kind of literature: particular attention is also dedicated to modelling the effects of changes in banks' capital requirements and capital position (as in Bernanke and Gertler, 1989), shocks in the risk of business debt default (as in Bernanke and Campbell, 1988; Gertler and Gilchrist, 1991; Friedman and Kuttner, 1993) and in the cash flows of non-financial firms (again as in Friedman and Kuttner, 1993). A modification in the perceived risk of loans is specifically mentioned in Bernanke and Blinder (1988) (probably one of the most representative theoretical 'creditist' models) as one of the causes that can potentially modify the macroeconomic equilibrium by allowing for exogenous shocks in the locus of simultaneous equilibria in the goods and credit markets.

When referring to the credit view many authors have in mind the 'credit view of the transmission mechanism of monetary policy', i.e. the idea that owing to reserve requirements on deposits, monetary policy directly influences the availability of bank credit and therefore the borrowing and spending of bank customers. Others (for instance, B. Friedman and Kuttner, 1993) use the broader definition of 'credit view of linkages between financial and non-financial economic activity', including in it part of the literature on 'excess sensitivity', i.e. the mechanism '. . . whereby credit market frictions may serve to amplify the impact of disturbances on borrowers' spending decisions' (Gertler and Gilchrist, 1993, p. 47). However, Friedman and Kuttner's definition of the credit view does not include *all* of the 'excess sensitivity' literature, but only that which is specifically concerned with the role of the banks in the transmission of monetary shocks and perturbations (not necessarily monetary policy shocks). In this sense, Friedman and Kuttner's (1993) contribution suggests a more general interpretation of the 'credit view', not confined to the debate on monetary policy, but presenting a wider theoretical framework that encompasses the interactions between industrial firms and financial intermediaries, as suggested in their Introduction:

Part of our objective here is simply to clarify a discussion that has often been confused by different researchers meaning different things while using similar or even identical terminology. More specifically, this discussion also seeks to distinguish a credit view of how monetary policy affects output from a credit view of financial–nonfinancial linkages more generally. (B. Friedman and Kuttner, 1993, p. 196)

This work adopts Friedman and Kuttner's broader definition of the 'credit view' since (as shown in the following sections of this chapter) many of the assumptions that justify the particular information structure characterizing the new macroeconomics of imperfect financial markets are often employed also to justify the 'specialness' of bank lending and the imperfect substitutability between banks' lending and other financial assets.

The critics of the credit view argue that banks' loans 'specialness' and imperfect substitution between bank lending and negotiable securities (the main theoretical justifications for the existence of the 'lending channel' of monetary policy) tend to reduce their influence on the transmission of financial shocks because of financial innovation and deregulation (Thornton, 1994), while money is a better predictor of aggregate income than credit aggregates (Romer and Romer, 1990; Ramey, 1993).

The evolution of this debate has been mainly determined by empirical analyses, often focused on problems of identification and causality, briefly described on pp. 32–47. In spite of being generally regarded as a branch of the New-Keynesian macroeconomics, the credit view itself could be compatible with non-Keynesian approaches, as suggested by Bernanke (1993) who quotes in this regard the articles by Fuerst (1992) and Christiano and Eichenbaum (1992). However, most creditist theoretical models are founded on assumptions of financial markets imperfections similar to those that characterize the New-Keynesian literature. For this reason, and also because the focus of this work is on 'credit, investments and the macroeconomy', rather than on the credit view in a narrow sense, the second section of this chapter is dedicated to various aspects of the debate on financial market imperfections. The third section is dedicated to credit and the macroeconomy in the Post-Keynesian literature, and briefly describes the main contributions within the New-Keynesian 'creditist' approach and some of the main objections to it. The fourth section is dedicated to a 'new wave' of recent empirical contributions, while the fifth section briefly describes the perspective of this work and illustrates the open issues analysed in the chapters that follow.

Financial market imperfections: a brief overview

Until the end of the 1980s, the neoclassical macroeconomic literature almost unanimously regarded Modigliani and Miller's neutrality theorem as an acceptable simplifying assumption. Only in Post-Keynesian and heterodox contributions had business cycles and recessions been interpreted as the effects of financial markets' perturbations (for example, Kindleberger, 1978; Minsky, 1975, 1982; Taylor and O'Connell, 1985). The mainstream literature of corporate finance, on the other hand, had for years already been discussing the issue of optimal firm's financial structure, and at the end of the 1970s an increasing number of papers started raising objections to the applicability of Modigliani and Miller's theorem, concerned with explaining what was considered the 'empirical puzzle' of the optimal leverage ratio. Most of the early contributions dealing with the 'exceptions to Modigliani and Miller's theorem' were models with asymmetric information based on some kind of 'lemon problem' à la Akerlof.[3]

Stiglitz (1974) shows that the Modigliani–Miller neutrality theorem applies only under very restrictive assumptions: individuals' expectations on future prices and firm value must not be influenced by changes in the firm's financial policy; the borrowing of individual agents has to be regarded as a perfect substitution for firms' borrowing; firm bankruptcy is ruled out and taxation is not taken into account.[4] In macroeconomics, the

[3] In Akerlof's (1970) article, the information asymmetry between a buyer and a seller of a second hand car determines a situation of market inefficiency. This happens because the market price reflects the buyers' perception of the average quality of the product. Therefore bad-quality sellers receive a premium at the expense of good-quality sellers. The effects of this phenomenon can be a distortion in the level of market activity, the exclusion from the market of a certain number of good-quality sellers and, under certain conditions, of all the sellers.

[4] Modigliani and Miller (1963) contains a reformulation of the neutrality theorem that takes taxation into account.

issue of imperfect and asymmetric information is first analysed in its implications for credit rationing, but even in the famous contribution by Stiglitz and Weiss (1981) the issue of financial structure is not taken into account, since investments are assumed to be financed only with debt. However credit rationing is a major and very influential result of the literature on financial markets imperfections. It can be derived from the same sources of market imperfections explaining the existence of banking and financial intermediation. Furthermore, it is one of the most rigorous explanations (to others with equity rationing) of how financial markets imperfections affect the macroeconomy. For these reasons it constitutes the object of the next section, although it is not strictly related to the credit view.

Asymmetric information and credit rationing

The literature on credit rationing has been analysed and surveyed in a large number of articles and books.[5] Therefore, only a few major results will be summarized here. Credit rationing is generally associated – at least in the literature of the last two decades – with asymmetric information, since under asymmetric information the interest rate can be used by financial intermediaries to affect the quality and risk of their portfolio. However, in a number of early contributions credit rationing is generated in models with full information, as in Hodgman (1960); Miller (1962); Freimer and Gordon (1965), where the result of credit rationing is based on the existence of a credit supply curve with a perfectly inelastic or a backward bending portion; or in Jaffee and Modigliani (1969), where it critically depends on the constraint that the bank must require the same interest rate from different borrowers. In the more recent literature, the perfect-information framework is generally considered inadequate to describe the main stylized facts of credit rationing. Nevertheless, even in recent contributions on asymmetric information the discussions on modelling approaches and policy implications are rather controversial: De Meza and Webb (1987) and Hillier and Ibrahimo (1993) point out that the possibility of credit rationing in models with financial market imperfections is not robust to changes in the assumptions concerning the probability distribution of the expected return, while S. Williamson (1987) points out that credit rationing does not necessarily provide a justification for stabilization policies.

The famous contribution by Akerlof (1970) and two seminal papers by Arrow (1963, 1968) show how asymmetric information can cause markets

---

[5] For example, Stiglitz (1987); Blanchard and Fischer (1989); Stiglitz and Weiss (1992); Hillier and Ibrahimo (1993); Mattesini (1993); Ardeni and Messori (1996).

to behave differently from the conventional equilibrium patterns, because of the moral hazard problem. This may happen when one party (called the principal) enters into a contract with another (called the agent) whose actions cannot be perfectly monitored by the principal. The two parties are assumed to have different preferences (so that they can be in conflict) and the actions of the agent affect both parties. The crucial point is that the behaviour of the agent is a function of the terms of the contract, and the problem for the principal is to determine a contract inducing the agent to perform actions (not fully monitored by the principal) desired by the principal. Such a theoretical framework can easily be applied to the credit market: if the interest rate on a loan affects the future behaviour of a borrower, then it might be convenient for the bank to choose an interest rate different from the market-clearing one, to the extent that the interest rate is set partly in order to influence the unobservable behaviour of the borrower and the use made of the loan.

In Stiglitz and Weiss' (1981) adverse selection model the firm's return is a random variable and the concept of mean-preserving spread plays a very important role: it means that the distributions of the project returns differ from one another in terms of their variance only, and have a common mean. In other words, the riskier projects are those with a higher variance: if we define R^* is the common expected return of each project, R_i^s the specific return for the ith project and p_i its probability of success, and assume that the projects either fail and yield zero or succeed in the period immediately after they are set up, the following condition must hold for all the projects:

$$p_i \cdot R_i^s = R^* \text{ for all } i \tag{2.1}$$

The riskier projects will be characterized by a lower p_i.

The banking sector is assumed to be perfectly competitive, both banks and borrowers are risk neutral. The banks do not know the probability of success and the value of the ith borrower's project if successful, but they know the characteristics of the borrowers' population. In the model, this determines a rationing mechanism where the banks are not able to discriminate between high-risk and low-risk borrowers: some borrowers are granted loans of a given size B to finance their projects, while others are denied credit. Defining as ρ the interest rate on banks' loans, the borrower pays $B(1+\rho)$ if her project succeeds, and zero if her project fails. The borrower's profit, on the other hand is zero if she fails, or R_i^s if she succeeds. From the borrowers' point of view, an increase in ρ lowers the expected return of the less risky projects by more than it lowers the expected return from the riskier projects. Even if a risk-neutral bank prefers less risky projects, a risk-neutral borrower would be willing to undertake a loan only if her project were sufficiently risky. An increase in the interest rate would therefore worsen the quality of the loans' portfolio of the bank by discouraging the borrowers with safer investment projects.

In an alternative explanation of credit rationing different from (but similar to) the adverse selection case, Stiglitz and Weiss (1981) assume that the banks choose the interest rate on loans to affect the actions of their borrowers rather than to affect the quality of the pool of borrowers. In this case, too, the model describes a non-monotonic relationship between the interest rate on loans and the banks' expected returns and the results are qualitatively similar: credit rationing may emerge because if the bank raises the interest rate too much, it can induce borrowers to choose riskier projects (rather than pushing out of the market the borrowers with less risky projects, as in the adverse selection case).

The outcome of credit rationing has several implications. First of all, with credit rationing, if the banks can distinguish among several classes of borrowers, some of these classes can be denied credit at any interest rate, while other classes obtain credit. But the most striking implication is probably the failure of the 'law of supply and demand': the equilibrium price does not necessarily equate demand and supply and, as a consequence, the usual comparative static analysis cannot be implemented. Furthermore, as pointed out by Stiglitz (1987) and Hillier and Ibrahimo (1993), the supply and demand functions can be interdependent, the 'law of the single price' breaks down, and there can be an underinvestment equilibrium.[6]

All these results suggest that there can be scope for government intervention to improve upon the allocation of funds determined by the competitive credit market. However, a major difficulty of this kind of literature is the lack of robustness to changes in the assumptions concerning the probability distribution of the expected return: De Meza and Webb (1987) show that if instead of assuming that all the projects have the same mean return one assumes that the projects differ in expected return, the result of credit rationing does not hold any longer and the first-best outcome would be overinvestment instead of underinvestment. Another theoretical element that reduces the relevance of credit rationing is collateral. Bester (1985) presents a model where banks, by adjusting simultaneously the interest rate on loans and collateral requirements, induce a particular kind of self-selection among borrowers: low-risk borrowers are willing to provide higher levels of collateral than more risky borrowers, and this determines an equilibrium without credit rationing. In this regard, Hillier and Ibrahimo (1993) point out that

---

[6] For a detailed analysis of all these results, see Stiglitz (1987) and Hillier and Ibrahimo (1993).

A simple way of understanding Bester's argument is to note that in a world where borrowers are protected by liability and pledge no collateral, . . . they would be willing to take out a loan at almost any interest rate to finance an appropriate gamble at a casino, since they are gambling with the bank's money and not their own they can only win and never really lose in this situation. In such a world, a little collateral may go a long way to discouraging such borrowers, even though . . . raising the interest rate may not.' (Hillier and Ibrahimo, 1993, p. 291)

On the contrary, the result of credit rationing even with collateral is obtained by Stiglitz and Weiss (1981, 1986) by assuming that borrowers are risk averse, and that their degree of risk-aversion depends on their wealth.

The theoretical research on credit rationing is closely related to that on the nature of financial intermediation, since they often share some of the main initial assumptions.

A famous contribution by Townsend (1979) shows how real costs in the process of financial intermediation are the result of a problem of incentives with asymmetric information and costly monitoring by the bank on the reliability of the borrower. Diamond (1984) is an oft-quoted model providing a theoretical justification for the role of financial intermediaries. The bilateral agreement between the two contractors yields a risky debt contract where the lender performs monitoring. A crucial hypothesis of the model is the fact that the size of the investment project and the funds endowments of the various subjects are fixed, so that credit users have to collect funds from several sources. The financial intermediary emerges (in this case endogenously) as the institution that, in order to reduce monitoring costs, optimally transfers the funds from the savers to the final users of credit, and performs all of the traditional roles of the banks and financial institutions, i.e. contracts loans, detects any insolvency, holds a diversified portfolio of financial assets and 'transforms' the maturity and the degree of liquidity of financial assets.

Fama, after describing the role of financial intermediaries in efficient and competitive markets as a simple 'veil' on the economy (in a well known article of 1980), comes to substantially different conclusions in a later famous article (1985), where he points out that the interest rate paid by banks' borrowers is higher than the one paid on bonds because, for some categories of borrowers, bank credit is not a perfect substitute for bonds. This phenomenon is again motivated by the economies of scale performed by banks in collecting and processing information. In this context, banks' intermediation is no longer a simple 'veil' on real activity, but it constitutes, under rather general assumptions, the most efficient way to minimize – or at least to reduce – the cost and risk deriving from information asymmetries.

The contributions on the nature of financial intermediation raise an important question: what are the macroeconomic implications of securitization? This question is the object of the empirical analysis contained in chapter 3.

From Modigliani–Miller to the economics of financial markets' imperfections: the contribution of finance studies in the 1970s and early 1980s

The New-Keynesian macroeconomics and, more generally, most of the present macroeconomic literature that postulates a causal link between finance and investments on the basis of financial markets imperfections, has been influenced by several significant contributions of corporate finance (between the end of the 1970s and the early 1980s) dealing with the issue of the optimal firm's financial structure. These influences consist of several modelling techniques applied to the formalization of incentive problems, and, more generally, paying particular attention to the interactions between finance and investment decisions with asymmetric information.

In Myers (1984) a clear distinction is drawn between the 'static tradeoff' and the 'pecking-order' approach. In the former it is assumed that the firm's decision maker establishes a target in terms of debt ratio and, consequently, the firm's financial structure tends to adjust to that target, while the latter assumes an implicit hierarchy of preferences in which the internal funds are preferred to the external ones, and debt is preferred to share issues. In the 'static tradeoff' approach a special emphasis is put on the adjustment costs, taxation and 'financial distress costs', which are assumed to play a relevant role in the adjustment process, while in the 'pecking order' it is often stressed that the empirically observable debt ratio is strongly affected by the need for external finance, cumulated over a certain period of time. Furthermore, it is pointed out that the debt ratio varies significantly among different industries owing to differences in risk and technical characteristics of production processes. It must be said, however, that the survey by Myers (1984) refers to a literature that analyses the issue of an optimal firm's financial structure within a perspective of management science: unlike the mainstream economic literature of that time, the non-neutrality of financial structure in Myers' (1984) analysis is an accepted empirical fact. Modigliani and Miller's mainstream theories (what Myers at the outset of his paper calls 'our theories')

don't seem to explain actual financing behaviour and it seems presumptuous to advise firms on optimal capital structure when we are so far from explaining actual decisions. I have done more than my share of writing on optimal capital structure, so I take this opportunity to make amends, and try to push research in some new directions. (Myers, 1984, p. 575)

On different grounds, formal justifications for the relevance of the firm's financial structure consistent with the methodological approach of mainstream economic literature had already been provided by the celebrated (and oft-quoted) contribution by Jensen and Meckling (1976), where the firm's financial structure and optimal level of debt are determined as a solution of an agency cost problem, and by Leland and Pyle's (1977) model. In Leland and Pyle (1977) the firm's internal decision makers, unlike outsiders, know the exact value of the firm and the quality of its investments. They hold a relevant portion of ownership, allowing them to take any financial decision. They can issue a quality signal given by their share ownership in the future return on investments. With asymmetric information, 'good-quality' firms incur a cost owing to the fact that outside investors cannot distinguish the quality of the securities without a signal. Firms therefore issue a signal that has to be costly in order to prevent low-quality firms from issuing misleading signals. Since the signal is the insiders' share ownership of the returns on investments, the cost of the signal is a limitation on the insiders' portfolio diversification. In the model, the debt issued by the firm is assumed to be non-risky: Leland and Pyle show (under rather general conditions) that the ownership share of the firm's investments held by insiders and the value of the firm are positively correlated. Since in the model another correlation exists between the ownership share held by the insiders and the quantity of debt, an indirect link is established between the firm's value and the quantity of debt employed to finance its activity. Such a causal link contradicts Modigliani and Miller's neutrality theorem. A result similar to the one of Leland and Pyle is obtained by Heinkel (1982) in a model that also provides a theoretical justification for the empirical phenomenon that sometimes sees high-quality firms taking advantage of distortions in the valuations of their shares on the stock markets, and small firms taking advantages of distortions in the valuation of their negotiable debts.

More generally, the 'lemon problem' on which these kinds of models are based lies in the difference between the 'true' value of the firm's investments and the market perception of it: even in the well known model by Myers and Majluf (1984) with asymmetric information, the managers operating on behalf of the existing shareholders maximize the value of the existing shares of the firm, and prefer to give up an investment with positive net present value rather that undertaking it by issuing undervalued shares. It is important to point out how the assumptions concerning the decision timing radically influence the final results. For instance, in more recent times (i.e. after the period considered in the analysis of the present section), Narayanan (1988) obtains results similar to those of Myers and Majluf in a model where debt acts as a barrier to entry for low-quality firms,[7] while in an article by Heinkel and Zechner (1990) it is shown how firms can choose investment projects with a negative net present value in a model with asymmetric information in financial markets where shares may happen to be overvalued to an extent that more than compensates shareholders for undertaking investments with a negative net present value. Narayanan's (1988) model relies on the fact that the financial structure is decided by the managers before the quality of the investment projects is made known, Heinkel and Zechner's (1990) results rely on the fact that the share price does not adjust instantaneously to the value consistent with the actual return on firm's investments, and that the overvaluation of firms' shares is sufficiently persistent.

Significantly different results can be obtained by modifying the timing of the investments decision process. Dotan and Ravid's (1985) model, for example, analyses the interactions between the optimal level of investments and debt financing. The amount of physical capital constitutes a constraint on the firm's production capacity, the debt undertaken by the firm is risky (the possibility of bankruptcy is not ruled out in the model), the price that the firm (price taker) faces on the goods market is uncertain and is described by a random variable. The model removes an implicit assumption contained in some famous models of the late 1970s (such as Jensen and Meckling, 1976 and Brennan and Schwartz, 1978), namely the independence between production and financial structure decisions. Indeed, one of the most crucial assumptions by Dotan and Ravid is the fact that firm's cash flow depends on the decision variables under the control of the firm itself, the stock of debt and the investments level. The optimal level of investments turns out to be a decreasing function of the debt level (which in its turn implies an inverse relation between financial leverage and optimal firm's expansion). Dotan and Ravid also show that the optimal level of investments is different according to whether the firm entirely finances its investments with own capital or by choosing an appropriate leverage. In other words, the simultaneous optimization of investments and debt stock leads to a higher level of borrowing than the one obtainable in the case where debt has been optimized, given the optimal level of investments in a firm initially financed only through shares.

Dotan and Ravid further point out that their results differ from a previous well known contribution by Hite (1979), where an increase in the financial leverage leads to an increase in the optimal stock of capital. Hite's model differs from Dotan and Ravid's for the presence of taxation, for the absence of risk in the firm's borrowing and, above all, for the absence of any

---

[7] In this way Narayanan indirectly resumes Telser's (1966) 'deep pocket argument', also employed – in industrial economics – by Brander and Lewis (1985) and Poitervin (1989a) and (1990) to model the strategic effect of firm's debt and financial structure.

causal link between the firm's cash flow and its decisions concerning the level of debt. However, the implications of Dotan and Ravid's model go well beyond the object of financial economics analysis: in their model the relevance of the firm's financial structure for the investment decision is a consequence of assuming a causal link among cash flow, debt and investments. From there, the step toward postulating the macroeconomic relevance of the firms' financial structure does not seem too long.

Unlike the contributions in industrial economics that explain the relevance of the firm's financial structure by analysing the strategic effect of debt ('deep pocket argument' in Telser, 1966; Poitervin, 1989a, 1990; 'limited liability effect' in Brander and Lewis, 1985; Poitervin, 1989b) Dotan and Ravid's model does not need to assume any form of imperfect competition in the goods markets. The main differences between this last model and its contemporary Post-Keynesian and heterodox contributions (which also postulate the relevance of firms' financial structure and a precise link between internally generated cash flow and investments) are methodological, since Dotan and Ravid's (1985) study is still a microeconomic model with optimizing 'neoclassical' agents acting in a perfectly competitive environment.

It might be incidentally interesting to point out that the existence of a hierarchy among the various sources of finance, and in particular the preference for internally generated cash flow *vis à vis* external finance, is also consistent with the 'managerial capitalism' theories. According to this approach, managers would tend to reduce, as far as possible, the use of external finance, since this would lead to some form of market constraint on their discretional choices. In a sense, the relevance of internally generated cash flow for the investment decisions has been regarded as a by-product of the so-called 'managerial revolution',[8] i.e. the historical process that has determined the separation between ownership and control in large corporations.

The most famous empirical contribution on the relevance of the internally generated cash flow for the firm's investment decisions is probably the one by Fazzari *et al.* (1988) which shows (with micro data) that internally generated cash flow is the most significant explanatory variable for firms' investments. Another relevant finding of this article is the significant difference existing in the behaviour of firms of different size (a common issue even in recent econometric analyses on the transmission mechanism of monetary policy, as will be pointed out on pp. 45 and 47 below), since small firms are more dependent on the internally generated cash flow.

Empirical evidence on the connection existing between firms' invest-

---

[8] For a discussion on this point, see also Myers (1984).

ments and financial structure has also been provided by Peterson and Benesh (1983), while empirical studies on the 'static tradeoff' have been made by Bradley *et al.* (1984) and, in more recent times, by Fischer *et al.* (1989), among others. The empirical specifications contained in these last two articles sometimes present a few difficulties, unlike Fazzari *et al.* (1988), whose specification in terms of internally generated cash flow seems to show good econometric performances. Rather than an optimal debt ratio for the firm, Fischer *et al.* (1989) consider an interval of variation for it, which somehow weakens the relevance of the predictions, while Bradley *et al.* (1984) obtain low coefficients of determination in their estimates and misspecification problems in their cross-section analysis, possibly determined, as they themselves suggest, by the omission of some relevant explanatory variable. Bradley *et al.* do find, however, an inverse relationship between the leverage ratio of the firm and the intensity in R&D and advertising expenditure. Furthermore, the average value for the leverage ratio varies very significantly in different industries (going for instance from 9.1 per cent in the cosmetics sector to 58.3 per cent in the airlines sector, for instance), owing to the intrinsic characteristics of the different production processes, availability of collateral, and, possibly, different industrial structures.

It is very important to point out that two of the relevant regressors employed by Bradley *et al.* (1984) to explain the leverage ratio – R&D and advertising expenditures – are typically regarded by the industrial economics literature as strategic variables that can contribute to determine or modify the barriers to entry. Like the literature on the strategic use of financial structure (the above-mentioned works on the 'deep pocket argument' and the 'limited liability effect'), this last result suggests that a study on the interactions between real investments, cash flow and financial structure should not completely ignore the implications of the industrial economics literature. Another important issue raised by the literature of finance (in particular Dotan and Ravid, 1985) is the relevance of the assumptions on timing in investment and financial decisions: the qualitative behaviour of investments may change significantly if one assumes that investments and optimal financial structure are determined simultaneously, even if this may dramatically increase the complexity of the models. These last two points constitute a specific concern of the whole work.

A first look at this very brief survey of the 1970s and early 1980s literature on firms' financial structure suggests that at the time a latent contrast seemed to exist between mainstream economics and finance on the (non) neutrality of firms' financial structure, or, more precisely, on how acceptable the restrictive assumptions of Modigliani and Miller's neutrality theorem were. Such a contrast can only partly be explained by the different purposes of the two disciplines, while there is very little doubt about the fact that the 1970s and early 1980s financial economics literature on the firm's optimal financial structure could have carried very relevant macroeconomic implications, and that the simplifying assumptions concerning the financial sector contained in the Hicksian *IS–LM* model strongly influenced the results of the debate between Keynesians and Monetarists in the 1970s and early 1980s, as suggested by Gertler (1988).

Money, credit and financial markets in the Post-Keynesian and New-Keynesian approaches

In the 'textbook' Keynesian framework divulged by the 'neoclassical synthesis' money supply is assumed to be exogenous, while money demand is described by a behavioural equation. The money sector is described in a simplified way, by considering two financial assets only: money and 'securities', where the latter include any possible non-money asset, aggregated in a unique market, that can be neglected in a general equilibrium context, as a result of Walras' law. In this framework, bank credit cannot have any relevant role, and the Modigliani–Miller theorem is assumed to apply, so that firms' financial structure is irrelevant. By equating money demand and supply, one obtains the equilibrium interest rate.

The assumption of money supply exogeneity has been strongly criticized by Kaldor (1982), who holds it responsible for having exposed the whole Keynesian macroeconomics to the destructive criticism of Milton Friedman and the Monetarist School. The exogeneity of money supply has been rejected not only by the Post-Keynesian tradition but also by other more recent Keynesian approaches. The whole issue is connected to the theoretical role attributed to the banking system in determining the equilibrium values of the money and credit aggregates. Both the Post-Keynesians and the New-Keynesians argue that changes in money supply determine real effects on the economic activity and aggregate income. Even the idea that the business cycle can be generated by financial shocks is, broadly speaking, common to both theoretical approaches.[9] More controversial (at least within the New-Keynesian approach) is the discussion on the transmission mechanism of monetary policy and on the macroeconomic relevance of bank credit.

[9] Many Post-Keynesians tend to use the expression 'financial instability' in their macroeconomic models where business fluctuations are generated endogenously in the financial markets (as in Minsky, 1982; Taylor and O'Connel, 1985; Delli Gatti and Gallegati, 1989; Delli Gatti *et al.*, 1990); while the New-Keynesians tend to formalize the perturbations in the financial markets with stochastic shocks in prices or mark ups (Greenwald and Stiglitz, 1988, 1989, 1990b, 1993a; Bernanke and Gertler, 1989; Gertler, 1992; Delli Gatti and Gallegati, 1995). However, an unanimously accepted terminology cannot always be found.

The idea that the macroeconomic fluctuations can be generated by financial shocks has not always been regarded as heterodox. Fisher (1933) points out that a high level of firms' debt characterized the period immediately prior to the financial crash of 1929: this caused the insolvency and bankruptcy of many industrial firms and, as a consequence, the failure of many banks and financial intermediaries. Apart from this direct propagation channel, another indirect mechanism can be detected: the dramatic reduction in the price level associated with the first shock significantly increased the real value of the debt of all bank borrowers who, in their turn, further reduced their real expenditure, thus amplifying the recession. While the second propagation mechanism (recession generated by a reduction in expenditure of net borrowers) has for years been one of the major topics of macroeconomic literature, the first one (recessive effects deriving from an increase in the real value of the debt, and the consequent influence on the behaviour of the banking sector) has received much less attention, if one excludes the heterodox approaches.

Money, credit and financial markets in the Post-Keynesian literature

In Keynes' *General Theory* (1936) the financial system does not play a central role, but financial considerations could be included in what Keynes defines the 'state of confidence' which, as Minsky (1975) points out, refers to both the agents' opinions on the future return on real investments and the lenders' opinions on the borrowers' riskiness. Therefore, a reduction in the agents' optimism could have been determined both by a reduction in the expected profitability of future investments and by a more pessimistic attitude of the banks towards the reliability of their actual and potential customers. The interactions between banks and industrial firms, on the other hand, have always been a special concern of Post-Keynesian literature. In Kaldor (1982), for instance, the endogeneity of money supply is a direct consequence of the fact that the stock of money is determined by the negotiations and interactions between banks and industrial firms: under tight money conditions, the economy would end up creating other forms of liquid assets that could be used for transactions, or, using Arestis' words (1988), 'the most important characteristic in this respect is that money is credit-driven'.

With this statement the Post-Keynesians do not simply postulate the relevance of financial intermediaries in determining credit supply but, more precisely, reverse the causation of the traditional money multiplier. According to Arestis (1988), the monetary authorities tend to have an accommodating attitude, by providing the banking system with the required liquid reserves, applying, if necessary, a 'penal' discount rate.

When the central bank applies a penal rate, the commercial banks are assumed to be able to transfer the increased cost of borrowing to their customers. In this situation, the central bank would not refuse to adopt an accommodating attitude in order to avoid the risk of a solvency crisis. Arestis (1988) also identifies three main characteristics of the Post-Keynesian theory of money, credit and finance:

The first is the *existence of uncertainty* in that the future is unknowable and unpredictable and consequently economic agents' expectations can be frustrated easily. The second is the existence of *irreversible time* where production takes time and economic agents enter into commitments well before outcomes can be predicted . . . The third, which is very much related to the second characteristic, is that economic agents commit themselves to contracts which are denominated in money, so that money and contracts are intimately and inevitably related. (Arestis, 1988, p. 42, emphasis in the original)

Another feature, as Davidson (1982) points out, is the particular importance that must be attributed to monetary institutions, since the Post-Keynesian analysis postulates that no general model can be applied to all historical and institutional contexts.

While both the Post-Keynesian monetary theory and most 'creditist' models postulate the endogeneity of money supply and stress the role of uncertainty and contractual relations, it is interesting to point out the different emphasis attributed to banks' behaviour. In Post-Keynesian economics credit is driven by the production process, and banks tend to accommodate the demand for loans from entrepreneurs. The statistical correlations that have been historically detected between M1 and the price level are interpreted as effects of the accommodating behaviour of the central bank (and of the commercial banks) supplying the liquid reserves to the same entrepreneurs that are in the position of contributing to determine the price level (since in most Post-Keynesian contributions the firms are also assumed to be price setters). The emphasis is put on the production process, facing an 'accommodating' banking sector.

Most New-Keynesian 'creditist' economists would not agree (or at least not completely) with the Post-Keynesian claim regarding the accommodating behaviour of the central bank and the banking sector, because in their opinion the banking firm should be regarded and modelled as an active economic agent whose subjective valuations on the riskiness of the whole economy determine its willingness to lend and, as a consequence, the availability of credit for the production process. The central bankers' behaviour is described as rather complex in B. Friedman (1993) and Bernanke and Mishkin (1992). The latter points out that the behaviour of the central bankers is often characterized by a 'crisis' mentality, by the use of targets as signals in order to affect individuals' expectations, while the multiplicity of targets leads to tensions in the monetary policy process. Bernanke and Mishkin admit, however, that central bankers never adhere to 'strict iron-clad rules' for monetary policy, since they are always hostage to new developments in the economy.

It is also interesting to point out that the objection raised by Thornton (1994) (and other neoclassical economists supporting the rational expectations hypothesis) against the relevance of the credit channel for the transmission of monetary policy is very similar to the Post-Keynesian idea that under tight money the economy would tend to create other liquid assets employed for transactions: according to Thornton (1994), financial innovation and the existence of certificates of deposits (not subject to reserve requirements) would enable banks to nullify monetary policy decisions and to satisfy the demand for credit coming from the industrial sector. Obviously, by assuming accommodating behaviour on the part of the central bank, the Post-Keynesian point of view is opposite to the one supported by Thornton (1994), and reaches the result of endogeneity of money supply.

Endogeneity of money supply is an assumption shared both by the New-Keynesian 'creditist' models and by the Post-Keynesians. The most striking difference is methodological: the former do not reject the neoclassical methodological approach concerning the optimizing behaviour of the agents, while the latter are notorious for their criticism of the drawbacks of the neoclassical idea of 'rationality' and 'optimizing behaviour' and many other features of neoclassical methodology. On the other hand, many New-Keynesian contributions share with the Post-Keynesians the idea that aggregate income fluctuations may be originated in the financial markets, although they tend to follow different modelling approaches.

Within a formalized model, Taylor and O'Connell (1985) develop the analysis by Minsky (1982) on financial crises although, as they themselves observe, it is not possible to constrain all of the historical and institutional analysis contained in Minsky's works within the algebra of a model. The generating mechanism of the financial crisis begins in the model with a reduction in the expected profits which reduces the value of the firms and causes a contraction in aggregate wealth which, in its turn, induces the public to increase their demand for liquid assets, in particular money. This causes the interest rate to increase and, therefore, the expected profits to further decrease, thus beginning a deflation associated with firms' debt crisis. This mechanism is founded on two basic assumptions. First of all, nominal wealth is determined, at a macroeconomic level, by the value of financial assets which react to the 'state of confidence of the economy' (described in the model by a variable here defined as ρ, reflecting the difference between the expected future return on physical capital and the present profit rate). Secondly, there is a high degree of substitutability between money and firms' liabilities. Taylor and O'Connell emphasize the fact that these assumptions are connected to the fact that the value of the firm may significantly diverge from the accounting value of physical capital and that there is no coordination between households' and firms' financial assets choices. In fact, if we define N, the net worth of the firms, as the difference between the value of capital stock and the value of shares, the balance sheet of the firms can be written in differential form as follows:

$$P_k I + \dot{P}_k K = P_e \dot{E} + \dot{P}_e E + \dot{N} \tag{2.2}$$

where P_k is the price of the capital stock, P_e the share price, I the investments, E the number of shares, K the capital stock and the dot above the variables indicates time differentiation. The variation of the wealth through the time is given by the following:

$$\dot{W} = \dot{B} + \dot{P}_e E + P_e \dot{E} + \dot{M} = \dot{P}_e E + s \, \pi \, PK \tag{2.3}$$

where W is the wealth, M the money stock, B the stock of public bonds, s the propensity to save out of profits, π the rate of profits and P the price level. One of the main features of the model is the difference existing between the behaviour of the general price level, determined by a mechanism of mark up on real wages, and the price of capital goods, defined as follows:

$$P_k = (\pi + \rho) \, P/i_S \tag{2.4}$$

where i_S is the current short-run interest rate and ρ reflects the difference between the anticipated return to holding capital and the current profit rate π. In the words of Taylor and O'Connell, 'The variable ρ carries a heavy burden in the story that follows. It represents expected high or low profits which in turn depend on the overall state of confidence' (Taylor and O'Connell, 1985, p. 873).

The demand for investments (defined by Taylor and O'Connell as 'orthodox' because it is similar to Tobin's 'q') is given by the following:

$$\text{Investment demand} = PI = (g_0 + h(\pi + \rho - i_S)] PK \tag{2.5}$$

where g_0 is a constant reflecting the autonomous growth of the capital stock and h a coefficient describing the 'response' of the firm to the expected difference between profits and financial costs. The different behaviour of P_k and P is at the basis of the potential financial crises. The crucial importance attributed to the expected future profits, which reflect the 'general state of confidence', recalls the much-discussed issue of expectations in Keynes' thought, and, in particular, how they influence the working of the monetary sector.[10]

Other macroeconomic models showing analogies with the one by Taylor and O'Connell (1985), and where financial markets perturbation are regarded as possible causes for business cycle and recessions (as in Minsky, 1975, 1982, 1986; Kindleberger, 1978), are the ones by Delli Gatti and Gallegati (1989) and Delli Gatti et al. (1990). In Delli Gatti et al. (1990) the investments are influenced, on the one hand, by the different behaviour of the share price and the general price level, and on the other by the internally generated cash flow and by the firm's decision to retain profits.[11] The elasticity of investments with respect to the internally generated cash flow is described by a parameter that tends to assume higher values in the expansionary phases and contracts in recession phases. The variability of such a parameter (an assumption also contained in Delli Gatti et al. (1990) and its cyclical behaviour tends to amplify the business cycle. Delli Gatti et al. (1990) associate the value of the representative unit of the existing capital stock with the share price and the value of the machinery representative of the flow of newly produced investment goods to the output price. The model is completed by an aggregate consumption function à la Kaldor which contains an explicit distinction between the propensity to consume out of labour income and out of capital income. This distinction is particularly relevant because it creates a connection with the assumption that firms' profits retention plays a relevant role in determining the level of investments. In this way, the heterodox assumption of relevance of income distribution for the determination of aggregate income (and therefore for the determination of the business cycle) is explicitly and formally connected to the idea that the internally generated cash flow matters for the firm's investments.

The Post-Keynesian models based on financial instability à la Minsky present some macroeconomic implications similar to those of the 'excess sensitiveness' and 'financial propagation' of the business cycle (Greenwald and Stiglitz, 1988; Bernanke and Gertler, 1989), although the former see financial instability as an endogenous phenomenon and the latter as the effect of stochastic shocks. An interesting connection between the two approaches has been provided in a recent contribution by Delli Gatti and Gallegati (1995), that has employed a modified version of Greenwald and

---

[10] This point has originated a lively debate (especially within the heterodox approach denominated 'of monetary circuit theories', but also among the Post-Keynesians) on the role played by the banking sector in the *Treatise on Money* (1930) and the *General Theory* (1936) and the different emphasis that the Keynes' two masterpieces dedicate to the role of finance. On this specific point see Graziani (1984); Lavoie (1984a, 1984b); Messori (1988).

[11] This assumption is also motivated by the authors on the basis of the Fazzari et al. (1988) results.

Stiglitz's (1988) model to build up a general framework containing – as special cases – 'accommodating lending policy' and 'exogenous credit supply' (i.e. control of the monetary aggregates by the central bank through base money or through the required reserve ratio, respectively). This is, in fact, also a central issue in the debate between the money view and the credit view, which brings us to the subject of the next section, where the credit view will be analysed in its relations with the other contemporaneous New-Keynesian approaches.

The credit view and the New-Keynesian macroeconomics

The 'prologue' to the modern credit view was Bernanke's (1983) empirical analysis, pointing out that the financial distress in 1929 amplified the effects of the Great Depression, whose intensity and persistence could not have been explained by money market forces alone. In Bernanke's (1983) paper it is shown that in the period 1930–3 almost half of the existing American banks failed, and the remaining suffered very relevant losses, while the stock market crisis of 'Black Friday' (which was the initial event of the crash) created an enormous increase in the debt burden of the firms. According to Bernanke, the banks' distress had an effect on real activity by suppressing the financial flows for some categories of firms that did not have direct access to spot financial markets and had to rely on financial intermediaries. In addition, the drastic increase in the debt of industrial companies reduced their ability to obtain finance from intermediaries, who would base their evaluations of the riskiness of customers on indicators of their financial structure. According to Bernanke, and unlike what was argued by Friedman and Schwartz (1963a, 1963b, 1982), the main role in the mechanism of the propagation of the 1929 crisis would not have been played by perturbations in the banks' liabilities (i.e. in money), but rather in the banks' assets – and, in particular, by the elimination (or by the drastic reduction) of the channels through which finance was injected into the real economy. As evidence in support of his thesis, Bernanke shows that the liabilities of the failed banks and the spread between the interest rate on risky and riskless securities significantly increased the explanatory power of the equations determining the level of output. Bernanke (1983) obviously assumes that the 'perceived' riskiness of firms borrowing from the banking system depends on their financial structure. In this way, because of information asymmetries in the credit market, firms' financial structure is not neutral and plays a relevant macroeconomic role.

The main feature of the credit view is the 'specialness' of bank credit in the transmission of monetary policy and financial shocks, although a certain attention towards the role of financial intermediaries has occasionally been paid in the past by mainstream macromodels, too.

In the 1960s, for example, the 'new view' models (Tobin and Brainard, 1963; Tobin, 1969), by weakening the hypothesis of perfect substitutability between money and other financial assets, describe the behaviour of a financial sector where the credit market can play a specific role in the transmission mechanism of monetary policy. Hörngren (1985) presents a modified version of Tobin and Brainard's (1963) model where, even in the presence of non-regulated financial intermediaries and with Certificates of Deposits, modifications in the required reserves coefficient may affect the supply of credit and its interest rate, just as argued by the credit view.[12] In his model Hörngren (1985) also introduces the assumption of 'active liability management', based on the hypothesis that banks' loans are the effect of long-run relationships between lenders and borrowers, and are therefore different from securities negotiated in the spot markets. Unlike the models of the credit view, this assumption does not yield models where bank credit and securities are explicitly formalized as imperfect substitutes, but it only determines a functional link (or even a 'fixed spread', as in Hörngren, 1985), between the interest rate on banks' loans and the interest rate on deposits.

Obviously, the credit view puts a different emphasis on financial markets imperfections and rejects the Modigliani–Miller theorem, by assuming non-neutrality of firms' financial structure, but some similarities with the modelling techniques employed in the 'new view' can be found in the use of aggregate balance-sheet relations and in the formalization of supply functions for some relevant financial assets which allows for imperfect substitutability among different assets. With some additional assumptions that are meant to specify the relevance of the 'credit channel', the 'skeleton' of the 'new view' models could be employed to analyse the macroeconomic implications of imperfect competition in credit markets. This, in particular, will be done in chapter 4.

Other models, where (within a conventional approach) the existence of a credit channel beside the money channel of transmission of monetary policy is not completely ruled out, have been introduced by Modigliani and Papademos (1980, 1987): the flavour, however, is still very different from that of the credit view, since the conventional neoclassical framework, without any specific assumption on financial markets imperfections, does not provide sufficient foundations to account for the 'specialness' of bank credit to the economy.[13]

---

[12] At that time, according to United States regulations, even certificates of deposits were subject to reserve requirements.   [13] In this regard, see also Bertocco (1987, 1989).

The particular branch of the New-Keynesian macroeconomics concerned with the propagation of financial shocks to the real sectors has been denominated the 'excess sensitivity', 'financial propagation' or 'financial accelerator' literature (Greenwald and Stiglitz, 1988, 1990b, 1993a; Bernanke and Gertler, 1989, 1990; Calomiris and Hubbard, 1990; Gertler, 1992). The main feature of these models, unlike the creditist models, is that they are based on some assumption of credit or equity rationing. The basic idea of this literature is that economic disturbances (generally modelled as stochastic shocks) may affect the net worth of the borrowers and cause, as a consequence, a countercyclical change in the risk premium included in the interest rate on borrowing. A similar mechanism had been earlier described by Minsky (1975, 1982, 1986), with a few relevant differences: the first one is that Minsky's *financial instability* is endogenous (and not associated with stochastic variables); the second is that Minsky makes an explicit distinction between the way risk affects the lender and the borrower ('lender' and 'borrower' risk in Minsky terminology). A mechanism vaguely similar to the 'borrower' risk is introduced in the various models by Greenwald and Stiglitz with the formalization of bankruptcy costs for risk-averse entrepreneurs.

One of the most frequently quoted models of this kind of literature is Greenwald and Stiglitz (1988), the first of a long series of macroeconomic models characterized by the assumption of equity rationing. Firms are assumed to employ only labour as a production input, while output is assumed to be an homogeneous good and the labour market is assumed to be described by a reservation wages mechanism: below a critical real wage level $\underline{w}$, the workers are not willing to supply any quantity of labour, while they are willing to supply whatever quantity of labour is required up to a fixed limit n, where the salary is above the reservation level.[14] The firm's borrowing (in nominal terms) is equal to the difference between the (nominal) labour cost required to produce the optimal output level and the nominal value of the equity base:

$$B_t^i = w_t P_t \xi(q_t^i) - A_t^i \tag{2.6}$$

where B_t^i is the nominal borrowing of firm i in period t, $w_t P_t$ is the nominal wage in period t, A_t^i is the ith firm's nominal equity in period t, and $\xi(q_t^i)$ is the labour required to produce q_t^i units of output. The firm goes bankrupt when the cash flow is lower than the debt previously accumulated and increased by a contractually agreed (and exogenous) interest rate. The real

---

[14] Greenwald and Stiglitz point out that 'having aggregate labour supply be a continuously increasing function of wages would considerably increase the complexity of the analysis without altering its fundamental conclusions' (Greenwald and Stiglitz, 1988, p. 111).

revenue, which contributes to determine the cash flow, is given by output times the relative price of the individual firm, which in the model can differ from the general price level due to stochastic shocks, even though the firms are assumed to produce an homogeneous good. The model contains a crucial assumption: the prices faced by the (price taker) firms contain a stochastic disturbance. The managers are assumed to be risk averse, and consequently the firm maximizes a profit function that contains the 'bankruptcy costs' of the managers (which increases linearly with the level of production and is affected by the probability distribution of the firm's price), subject to a constraint describing the maximum output consistent with the expected state of solvency of the firm. In other words, the production of the firm is associated with a level of borrowing that, given the probability distribution of the price, has to be consistent with the expected solvency of the firm. On the basis of these assumptions Greenwald and Stiglitz obtain a 'microeconomic' firm's supply which is also a function of the net worth. With a few standard aggregation assumptions an aggregate supply with the same characteristics is obtained:

$$q_t = \Sigma g_t^i(w_t, r_t^l, a_t, F) \equiv g_t(w_t, r_t^l, a_t, F) \tag{2.7}$$

where g_t^i is the individual supply of firm i at time t, g_t is the aggregate supply, r_t^l is the rate of return required by lenders in period t (real interest rate), a_t is the equity base, or net worth at time t, and F is the probability distribution of the firm's relative prices. The model is closed with a 'permanent income' consumption function and with an equilibrium condition on the money market. The goods market-clearing condition puts the consumption level into relation with the lagged output. A few algebraic manipulations yield a difference equation where the real equity base at time $t+1$ is a function of its value at time t, as well as the real interest rate, wage and output, still at time t.

The model presents some analogies with the neoclassical models with money neutrality: with rational expectations, only unanticipated disturbances, both in money supply and in the behaviour of the individual agents, can generate real effects. However, other forms of monetary interventions affecting lenders' information sets may generate real effects. The presence of the aggregate net worth in the aggregate supply amplifies macroeconomic fluctuations. Some heterodox (at least at that time) elements, like the macroeconomic relevance of firms' net worth and financial structure, are introduced in a micro-founded model reproducing money neutrality as a special case (under the assumptions of perfect foresight and perfectly anticipated monetary policy). But the most interesting feature of the model is that information asymmetries in financial markets are associated with business fluctuations, even though it must be said that the rationale for the hypothesis of asymmetric information is the intrinsic diversity among the different investment projects of the various firms: since Greenwald and Stiglitz (1988) postulate perfect competition on the (homogeneous) goods market, the discriminatory element among 'good' and 'bad' investments lies fully and only in the stochastic behaviour of the relative prices faced by each individual firm. Greenwald and Stiglitz (1993a), unlike their 1988 paper which includes only labour and working capital as output, introduce physical capital investments by an investment function which depends on the net worth, as well as the usual relevant real variables, and obtain a model reproducing in more detail than the 1988 paper a mechanism of the business cycle.

A relevant modification to Greenwald and Stiglitz's framework is introduced in Delli Gatti and Gallegati (1995), where, unlike Greenwald and Stiglitz (1988), the real interest rate is not assumed to be given and constant. Delli Gatti and Gallegati argue that Greenwald and Stiglitz's price shock is in practice analogous to Lucas' 'price surprise', and therefore the fact that monetary policy can only be affected through price shocks is equivalent to saying that changes in monetary policy are effective only if not anticipated, as in Lucas' framework. In the Delli Gatti and Gallegati model it is shown that under a regime of accommodating lending policy, even with perfect foresight, monetary policy is effective since the interest rate is both a target of monetary policy and an argument of the long-run aggregate supply. On the other hand, under a regime of exogenous credit supply the central bank controls monetary aggregates through base money and the required reserve ratio, while the interest rate is endogenous:

A change of high powered money is neutral if anticipated but monetary policy can influence real output through the required reserve ratio. In fact, if the central bank pushes down the required reserve ratio given the stock of high powered money, the credit multiplier . . . increases more than the money multiplier . . ., the real credit supply increases and firms expand production. (Delli Gatti and Gallegati, 1995, p. 16)

In this case, even issues with a structural flavour like 'money vs. credit transmission' depend on how accommodating the supply of credit is, a point also considered in the early analyses within the 'credit view' approach: Bernanke and Blinder (1988) in the 'empirical evidence' section of their paper focus on the higher degree of stability (statistically speaking) of the money demand in 1974–9 and credit demand in 1979–85, two periods characterized, among other things, by two very different monetary policy regimes. This point also suggests that a certain degree of interaction between 'institutional' factors and short-run analysis should be taken into account, in theoretical models, especially within an approach like the credit view, which is meant, at least in B. Friedman's (1993) interpretation, to provide a theory of the interactions between financial markets and real output.

Bernanke and Blinder (1988) is, in its striking simplicity, probably the most representative theoretical model of the credit view. It is a modification of the *IS–LM* framework and contains all the elements that allow for the theoretical definition of imperfect substitution among credit on the one hand, and bonds and securities on the other. Like any other 'credit view' model, it explicitly introduces the balance-sheet constraint of the banks, which plays a very important macroeconomic role:

$$B^b + FR + L^s = D(1-q) \qquad (2.8)$$

In this equation, B^b is the quantity of bonds held by the banks, FR the free reserves (assumed to be a negative function of i the interest rate on bonds), L^s the credit supplied by firms, D the deposits, and q the reserve requirements. The deposits are determined by equating the demand for deposits $D(i,y)$ with the supply of deposits determined by the liquid reserves through the money multiplier:

$$D(\overset{-+}{i,}\overset{+}{y})=m(\overset{+}{i})R \qquad (2.9)$$

where D are the demand deposits, y the aggregate income, $m(i)$ the money multiplier, and R the liquid reserves. Equation (2.9) also implicitly defines the money market equilibrium, i.e. the *LM* locus, which, in Bernanke and Blinder's (1988) model does not differ from the conventional *IS–LM* framework. Bernanke and Blinder further assume that the portion of banks' assets invested as credit to the industrial firms depends positively on the interest rate on loans and negatively on the interest rate on bonds, and is determined by the following relation:

$$L^s = \mu(\rho,i)D(1-q) \qquad (2.10)$$

where μ is the portion of financial resources that banks invest in loans and ρ the interest rate on loans. The demand for bank credit is:

$$L^d = L(\rho,i,y) \qquad (2.11)$$

Using (2.10) and (2.11), Bernanke and Blinder solve the equilibrium condition on the market for loans with respect to the interest rate on loans ρ, so that ρ is expressed as a function of the liquid reserves R, of the income y, and the interest rate on bonds i. The resulting equation is

$$\rho = \phi(i,y,R) \qquad (2.12)$$

(2.12) is then substituted into the equilibrium locus of the goods market, the *IS* curve, $y = Y(i,\rho)$, yielding the following 'modified *IS* curve':

$$y = Y(i, \, \phi(i,y,R)) \tag{2.13}$$

(2.13) contains the disturbances and the macroeconomic fluctuations determined by the attitude of the banks in their lending decisions. For example, a variation in the degree of riskiness attributed by the banks to the firms' investments determines a shift in the 'modified *IS*', which is defined by Bernanke and Blinder's '*CC* curve', i.e. the locus of simultaneous equilibrium points on the goods and credit market.

The *CC* curve is negatively sloped like the *IS* curve of the *IS–LM* model. It reacts like the *IS* curve to all the shocks affecting the market for goods, but, unlike the *IS* locus, is shifted by monetary policy shocks (i.e. by a modification in *R*) or by any credit market shocks (i.e. not only monetary policy shocks) that affect $L^s(\cdot)$, $L^d(\cdot)$ or $\mu(\cdot)$.

The *CC* curve degenerates to an *IS* curve if one of the following conditions applies:

$$\partial L^d(\cdot)\partial\rho \to -\infty \text{ (loans and bonds perfect substitutes to borrowers)} \tag{2.14}$$

$$\partial\mu(\cdot)\partial\rho \to \infty \text{ (loans and bonds perfect substitutes to lenders)} \tag{2.15}$$

$$\partial Y(\cdot)\partial\rho = 0 \text{ (aggregate demand for goods insensitive to loans interest rate)} \tag{2.16}$$

The 'credit-only view' case applies when money and bonds are perfect substitutes, i.e. when the *LM* curve is horizontal.

Bernanke and Blinder focus their attention on the 'issues that elude the *IS–LM* model'. They point out, for instance, that a decrease in the perceived riskness of loans (i.e. a shift in $\mu(\cdot)$) causes the locus *CC* to shift outwards along a fixed *LM* curve, ρ to fall, i and y to increase. The opposite would happen after an upward shift in the credit demand function L^d. In such a context, both a policy trying to stabilize money and another one trying to stabilize credit would be (at least qualitatively) effective if they had to counterbalance an expansionary *IS* shock. But on the contrary,

Suppose that demand for money increases . . ., which sends a contractionary impulse to GNP. Since this shock raises *M* [money stock], a monetarist central bank would contract reserves in an effort to stabilize money, which would destabilize GNP. This is, of course, the familiar Achilles heel of monetarism. Notice, however, that this same shock would make credit contract. So a central bank trying to stabilize credit would expand reserves. In this case a credit-based policy is superior to a money-based policy.

The opposite is true, however, when there are credit-demand shocks . . . If money-demand shocks are more important than credit-demand shocks, then a policy of targeting credit is probably better that a policy of targeting money. (Bernanke and Blinder, 1988, p. 438)

Bernanke and Blinder's (1988) model is obviously not meant to provide a detailed description of the financial sector, but simply to show what are the theoretical implications for the *IS–LM* framework of the assumption of imperfect substitability between credit and securities. One creditist theoretical model that contains a formalized analysis of the various financial assets and operators to a higher degree of detail is that of B. Friedman and Kuttner (1993). A very interesting feature here is that the model contains what the authors call the 'non-price' cost of borrowing, defined as 'other than the observed interest rate . . . costs of obtaining external funds' (B. Friedman and Kuttner, 1993, pp. 212–13). In the case of bank loans these non-price costs could originate fees, such as the requirement to purchase unrelated services, underwriting or trust operations, earned by banks as lenders.

The non-financial firms are described by their balance-sheet constraint:

$$PE^i + B^i = L^i + P^i + A^i \tag{2.17}$$

where the superscript i indicates the individual firm to whom the balance sheet refers, PE represents the stock of physical capital, B its holdings of Treasury bills, L its borrowing from banks, P its commercial paper outstanding and A its net worth. Each individual firm equates its source of funds with investments. By assuming that aggregation among different firms is possible, an aggregate financing constraint for all the non-financial firms can be defined as follows:

$$I + \Delta B^F = NR + \Delta L^F + \Delta P^F \tag{2.18}$$

where the superscript F means aggregate non-financial firms, I are the aggregate investments, and NR the net revenues for operations not paid out in interest or dividends. The financial choices of the non-financial firms are meant to cover the financial gap $I - NR$, and are formalized according to the principles of risk-averse portfolio selection, by means of the following system, where the non-price cost elements are assumed to be zero in the bill market:

$$\Delta L^F = f_1(\overset{+}{I - NR}, \overset{-}{\rho_L}, \overset{-}{\theta_L}, \overset{+}{r_P}, \overset{+}{\theta_P}, \overset{+}{r_B})$$

$$\Delta P^F = f_2(\overset{+}{I - NR}, \overset{+}{\rho_L}, \overset{+}{\theta_L}, \overset{-}{r_P}, \overset{-}{\theta_P}, \overset{+}{r_B}) \tag{2.19}$$

$$\Delta B^F = f_3(\overset{-}{I - NR}, \overset{-}{\rho_L}, \overset{-}{\theta_L}, \overset{-}{r_P}, \overset{-}{\theta_P}, \overset{+}{r_B})$$

The expected signs are shown above the corresponding variables, r_B the interest rate on treasury bills, ρ_L the interest rate on loans, r_P the interest rate on commercial paper; the θ_i represent the corresponding non-price cost elements which do not apply to the bill market. Given the balance-sheet constraint (2.18), the system (2.19) contains only two independent relations:

The inclusion here of θ_L and θ_P – and, in particular, the nonparallel treatment of these two nonprice cost elements from the perspective of the lender – strengthen this model's ability to explain observed relationships between price–quantity interactions in the credit markets and real economic activity . . . From the perspective of nonfinancial firms, the two non-price costs of borrowing are parallel. Greater θ_L depresses ΔL^F just as would higher (ρ_L), while $_P$ depresses ΔP^F . . . The nonparallel treatment lies in the effect of these nonprice costs on lenders. (B. Friedman and Kuttner, 1993, p. 218)

Again, this modelling technique closely recalls Minsky's (1975) distinction between lender and borrower risk. From a formal point of view, a relevant factor of asymmetry lies in the fact that the non-price cost element for the commercial papers does not depend on its price, but rather on its outstanding level and its variation:

$$\theta_L = \theta_L(\overset{+}{\rho_L},\overset{+}{L},\overset{+}{\Delta L}) \qquad\qquad (2.20)$$

$$\theta_P = \theta_P(\overset{+}{P},\overset{+}{\Delta P}) \qquad\qquad (2.21)$$

The other classes of agents included in the model are banks and households. The individual households is described by two equalities, the balance sheet of the ith investor, and another constraint equating total sources with total uses of funds. The individual bank is also characterized by a balance-sheet constraint, while both the aggregate banking and households sectors are assumed to behave according to the standard portfolio allocation theory. The model is simplified by assuming that commercial papers and certificates of deposits are perfect substitutes, and by a 'no arbitrage' condition, which allows us to say that the interest rate on commercial paper can also represent the interest rate on the certificates of deposits.

The scale of the system, given the reserve and capital requirements, is determined both by the reserves supplied by the central bank and by the capital that banks have accumulated from past earnings.

The model is closed by appropriate market-clearing conditions and by an investment equation which provides the link between the real and financial sectors, and is based on the typical 'credit view' assumption that internally generated funds are less costly than external funds due to asymmetric information and financial market imperfections. The investment equation is formalized as follows:

$$I = I(\overset{+}{NR},r_I\overset{+}{-}\underset{-}{r},\underset{-}{\theta},\sigma^2) \qquad\qquad (2.22)$$

where r_I is the rate of return on investments, $\underline{r}$ is the composite interest cost of additional funds (which depends on r_P, ρ_L, r_B), $\underline{\theta}$ the composite non-price cost of external funds (which, in its turn depends on θ_L and θ_P), and σ^2 the risk associated with the return on investments.

B. Friedman and Kuttner (1993) also provide some empirical results consistent with the implications of their theoretical model and a wide empirical creditist literature. First they show that monetary policy shocks are associated with changes in the spread between loans and commercial papers. This happens because when the industrial firms do not receive bank loans, they look for other sources of finance. In this way, both the quantity and the interest rate on commercial paper tends to increase. Secondly, they point out that increases in interest rate spreads can be determined by variations both in the non-price costs of borrowing and in the lending risk. As mentioned earlier, this formalization recalls Minsky's (1975) lender's and borrower's risk and, as the authors point out, with appropriate lags in the investment function could explain the empirical results found by Kashyap *et al.* (1993) where a modification in the mix between loans and commercial paper (with an increase in the relative amount of commercial paper) anticipates a decline in output. The Friedman–Kuttner model also explains the real effects of bank capital shocks, default risk shocks and cash flow shocks. Furthermore, the article contains some estimates consistent with the creditist approach. Some results are analogous to those of Kashyap *et al.* (1993) where monetary shocks affect the mix of the different financial sources of the firm. In other estimates, difference structural equations for the bank loans undertaken by financial corporations, commercial paper issued by non-financial firms, commercial and industrial loans, commercial paper, and negotiable certificates of deposits behave consistently with the credit view and yield satisfactory results.

Friedman and Kuttner's (1993) model could probably be considered a sort of 'generalization' of the credit view, since non-price elements as well as uncertainty and asymmetry are introduced not just in the banks' behaviour but in the actions of many categories of agents. This interesting point goes beyond the specific issue of the role of the banking system and raises the very wide question of whether non-price factors take part in market dynamics.

After the first wave of empirical analyses meant to detect causal links between credit availability (as well as other financial variables such as the net worth of banks and industrial firms) and aggregate income, the 'creditist' econometric analyses first turned to the investigation of how and why interest rate spreads react to financial shocks (Bernanke, 1990; Bernanke and Blinder, 1992), and then more recently to the different effects of credit shocks on different-sized firms (Gertler and Gilchrist, 1991, 1993; Angeloni *et al.*, 1995), and to how institutional features, regulation (Buttiglione and Ferri, 1994; Marotta, 1995) and loan interest rate stickiness (Cottarelli and

Kourelis, 1994; Cottarelli *et al.*, 1995) affect the credit channel or, more simply, the behaviour of bank credit. Research on these last points (often based on micro data and panel data techniques) seems to be giving promising results, although it is so far only empirical and has not yet been organized within a general theoretical framework.

The empirical analyses focused on the behaviour of interest rate spreads are actually attempts to show that the correlation between aggregate output and credit is not a spurious correlation, caused by the fact that credit demand is determined by the aggregate output or by the fact that money supply affects credit only to the extent that it affects deposits, as suggested by the conventional 'money view'.

Bernanke (1990) shows that the spread between the commercial paper rate and the Treasury bill rate has a greater predictive power than the variables commonly employed in (previous) VAR analyses (as in Sims, 1980) to forecast macroeconomic variables such as industrial production, unemployment and inflation rates. According to Bernanke, such a predictive power does not depend on modifications in the expected risk, as commonly argued by the previous literature, but on the fact that the spread between commercial paper and Treasury bill rates is a good indicator of monetary policy regime, even though its predictive power could be reduced by phenomena of financial innovation.

Bernanke and Blinder (1992) criticize the interpretation of the empirical results contained in King (1986) and Sims (1980). The former, by following the 'unrestricted VAR' methodology find that bank deposits seem to be better predictors for the aggregate output than bank assets, thus supporting the 'money view' as opposed to the 'credit view'. The latter interprets, as evidence against monetary policy effectiveness, the fact that some interest rates seem to dominate money as a predictor for aggregate output when added to a VAR containing money, income and prices. With respect to King's (1986) article, Bernanke and Blinder observe that 'it is extremely risky to make structural inferences from unrestricted vector autoregressions which after all are only reduced forms' (Bernanke and Blinder, 1992, p. 901). On the other hand they point out that Sims' (1980) results could be interpreted as evidence for the greater predictive power of interest rates, rather than evidence of policy ineffectiveness.

By using Granger causality tests, Bernanke and Blinder (1992) show that the interest rates on Federal Reserve funds are better predictors than M1 and M2 for all of the relevant macroeconomic variables. This provides evidence in favour of the effectiveness of monetary policy, and against the 'neutrality' assumptions of the real business cycle literature, since the interest rates on Federal Reserve funds are under direct control of the monetary authority. Bernanke and Blinder then estimate a reaction function for the monetary authority – where the interest rate on federal funds appears as a policy instrument – obtaining plausible results, and they show, with both monthly and quarterly data, that demand shocks do not seem to have significant effect on the federal funds rate. These last results clearly show that the Federal funds rate has been manipulated for monetary policy purposes. Bernanke and Blinder's (1992) results are rather powerful. First of all they show, in their 'Granger causality' tests, that monetary policy does induce real effects on the economy. Secondly, the transmission of monetary policy seems to take place through both banks' assets and banks' liabilities. Thus one could claim, as mentioned earlier, that the credit view and the money view are not mutually exclusive. Bank loans seem to react quicker to variations in the Federal funds interest rate, while they are found to react with a certain time lag to modifications in the money supply, showing a certain degree of hysteresis due to the time length of bank contracts.

A frequent objection to the credit view is the 'financial innovation argument', which goes as follows: since the process of financial innovation generates new and more sophisticated financial assets and contracts, it becomes harder and harder to postulate that there is a particular asset (bank loans) which can be considered 'special' and non-substitutable. Furthermore, since (at least in the United States) banks can issue certificates of deposits and other assets not subject to the reserve requirement, it becomes increasingly difficult for the monetary authority to control banks' credit.

This objection (illustrated and formalized in detail by Thornton, 1994) has been seriously taken into account by most 'creditist' studies, but finds a limit in the fact that banking firms are found to perform relevant economies of scale in collecting and processing information. On this premise, the rationale for the 'specialness' of bank credit lies in the information asymmetry that always exists between lender and borrower, and can be reduced by bank monitoring. The transaction contract that emerges from bank monitoring relies on a long-run relationship between lender and borrower (a 'customer market', in Okun's, 1981, terminology or a 'special-purpose' as opposed to 'general-purpose' technology contract, in Williamson's, 1985, terminology), and yields an asset that is qualitatively different from (and therefore an imperfect substitute for) a bond or any security. This is not only due to the fact that it may incorporate monitoring costs,[15] but also to the fact that it is generated in a context of incomplete markets with a long-standing implicit contract, as opposed to a 'one-shot' transaction. This point is consistent with Mayer's (1993a) and (1993b) empirical observations on the fact that bank credit is, unlike securities, a

---

[15] 'Safeguards against opportunism', in Williamson's (1985) terminology.

countercyclical source of finance for industrial firms. In another sense, it is also consistent with the theoretical model by Anderson (1994) and the empirical analyses by Pagano *et al.* (1994), which point out that borrowing from banks and issuing securities are complementary rather than alternative choices for industrial firms, since the effect of information spreading determined by security price fluctuations reduces the monitoring costs for the banks and, as a consequence, the cost of bank borrowing.

Furthermore, in an historical perspective, the 'financial innovation argument' fails to explain why the process of 'securitization' can only be considered fully achieved in the US and British financial systems. In other words, if financial innovation is an irreversible process, it is not quite clear why all of the non-English speaking industrialized countries have financial systems where the security markets are hardly quantitatively relevant compared to the intermediated credit. These points will be taken into consideration again in chapter 4, dealing with the macroeconomic (empirical) effects of the phenomenon of securitization.

Other objections to the credit view have been addressed by some empirical papers (King, 1986; Romer and Romer, 1990; Ramey, 1993) which argue that monetary aggregates have typically been better forecasters of economic activity than credit variables. Therefore, according to these papers, the credit channel is less relevant and effective than the money channel. Ramey (1993) considers a trend-corrected measure of M2 velocity that performs very good results in terms of aggregate output forecasting. Even though some credit aggregates seem to be good forecasters, they lose most of their predictive power when the trend-corrected measure of M2 velocity is added into the regressions. Ramey therefore concludes that the credit channel is scarcely relevant and can be ignored without any major loss of information. Bernanke (1993) on the other hand, argues that Ramey's (1993) results are uninformative on the specific point of credit channel effectiveness:

Suppose that only the credit channel is operative – that is, imagine that firms do not respond to policy-induced changes in short term interest rates, so that the money channel is closed down. Even under these extreme circumstances, with no role for the conventional channel to affect output, we would still expect a tightening of monetary policy (open market sales) to reduce money supply . . . We would expect the change in the money supply to occur earlier than the change in loans . . . In this scenario the change in the money supply would be a better predictor . . . even though, by hypothesis, the actual effect of policy is being transmitted through loans only. (Bernanke 1993, p. 30)

If the macroeconometric analyses do not always allow us to draw clear-cut conclusions, more promising results for the credit view seem to emerge from a new wave of microeconometric analyses which focus on the differences between small and large firms in their access to the financial markets and in their relations with banks.

Recent approaches

The fact that small and large firms are differently exposed to monetary policy shocks was originally introduced by Gertler and Gilchrist (1991). Following a VAR methodology and using as monetary policy indicators the innovations in the Federal Reserve funds rate and the dummies especially introduced by Romer and Romer (1989) to 'catch' the periods of tight money, Gertler and Gilchrist (1991) find that the sales of small firms react much more significantly to monetary policy changes. Furthermore, corresponding to these modifications, loans to small firms tend to contract and loans to large firms to expand. Gertler and Gilchrist admit that their results might derive from an intra-industry effect. In other words, it might be possible that small firms tend to be more concentrated in sectors that are more exposed to the business cycle and interest rate modifications. Another possible explanation is the fact that small firms might be 'more volatile' because they are less capital-intensive. In any case, Gertler and Gilchrist's (1991) paper indirectly raises the issue of interactions between business cycle, firms' financial structure and market structure.

Evidence in favour of the credit view (at least in the theoretical formulation by B. Friedman and Kuttner, 1993) is provided by Kashyap *et al.* (1993) who find that monetary policy affects the composition of firms' borrowing, causing an expansion of commercial paper with respect to bank loans. A similar result is found by Gertler and Gilchrist (1993), who also find further evidence consistent with the results of their (1991) paper.

In a panel of Italian firms, Angeloni *et al.* (1995) surprisingly find that the impact of monetary policy seems to be stronger in large companies than in smaller ones. This result may be partly due to the very peculiar market structure of the Italian banking sector where small banks, often operating only locally with relatively strong market power in rural areas, keep long-run contractual relations with small non-financial companies, and large banks tend to keep long-run contractual relations with large corporations.[16] Apart from these peculiar results, Angeloni *et al* (1995) obtain evidence consistent with the credit view: the interbank market is weakly exogenous to the bond market, the interbank and bond market are weakly exogenous to the loan and deposit markets and, comparably to the results

---

[16] These long-run contractual relations can be simply explained by the need for the banks to diversify their portfolio: since large non-financial firms tend to undertake large loans, for a small bank a long-run contractual relation with a big company would imply a loss of diversification.

by Buttiglione and Ferri (1994), the spread between bank loan and long-term Government bonds is influenced by the fact that lending rates tend to overshoot bond market rates.

Cottarelli and Kourelis (1994) find that the degree of stickiness of bank rates varies significantly from country to country, especially in the short run, but does not seem to be affected by the market structure in the banking sector. Market structure, on the other hand, is found to affect the elasticity of demand for bank loans which, in its turn, affects the adjustment costs of lending rates. However, a very interesting result is that 'the existence of markets for instruments issued by enterprises (for example commercial papers) did not appear to affect loan rate stickiness' (Cottarelli and Kourelis, 1994, p. 618). In this case, the 'financial innovation argument' against the credit view does not completely correspond to the empirical evidence. On the one hand, the introduction of negotiable certificate of deposits and the absence of constraints on international capital movements and bank competition seems to reduce loan rate stickiness, on the other hand, a relatively high degree of loan rates stickiness seems to be persistent.

A very important role in the development of the credit view has been played by empirical analyses, often dealing with two main problems. The first is an identification problem, determined by money endogeneity: if money stock is endogenous, as argued in most contributions in the credit view, the relative predictive power of of credit vs. money might be difficult to find. The second is a problem of identification between credit demand and supply. In other words, changes in the observable credit stock might reflect either changes in demand or in supply. Furthermore, the correlation between aggregate output and credit might be a 'spurious' correlation, due to the conventional 'money channels'. For instance, an increase in the money supply could generate two simultaneous effects. The first is a reduction in the interest rate, followed by an increase in real output, which would determine, in its turn, an increase in the demand for credit. The second is an increase in the deposits (through the money multiplier), associated to the banks' assets (i.e. liquid reserves, bonds and credit supply) through the aggregate balance constraint of the banking sector: according to the conventional 'money view', in this case, the increase in credit supply would be carried by the increase in the aggregate output (causing an increase in the demand for bank credit) and by the increase in deposits (causing an increase in the level of all the banks' assets).

These last points suggest that the behaviour of the free liquid reserves of commercial banks might be crucial in understanding whether and to what extent banks' assets are merely determined by inertia or by an active role of the banking sector. Obviously, the degree of 'securitization', i.e. the degree of macroeconomic relevance of the security markets compared to the intermediated credit, is qualitatively important to understand the degree of substitutability between bank credit and other sources of finance. This implies, for instance, that in the countries characterized by a 'non-securitized' financial system (i.e. where the magnitude of the security markets is very small compared to that of the intermediated credit) even changes in the market structure in the banking sector might carry macroeconomic implications.

Another issue raised in the literature surveyed in this chapter (in particular in Dotan and Ravid, 1985 and in other contributions in financial economics) is the relevance of timing in investment and financial decisions. In chapter 7 the investment decision of the firm will be analysed in a context of intertemporal optimization, assuming simultaneity between investment and financial decisions in the presence of various forms of financial market imperfections. A specific concern of this particular analysis is to investigate how the process of information spreading that takes place in security markets may affect the cost of capital and the investment decision of the firm. It is not a macroeconomic problem, but it is closely related to the issue of securitization and it is a major element of the interactions between industrial firms and financial markets: in this regard, it is strictly related to the literature dealing with financial perturbations.

All these points will be discussed in the next section, which describes the theoretical framework of analysis adopted, and constitutes the object of analysis of the rest of this work.

Open issues and theoretical perspective of the book

The survey of the previous sections has shown that most empirical studies of the credit view tend to support the following general statements:

(a) The transmission mechanism of monetary policy (and more generally of monetary disturbances) determines its effects through both banks' assets and banks' liabilities. In particular, a reduction in banks' loans, after a monetary restriction, plays a very important role in reducing the expenditure of those agents that mainly rely on bank credit as an external source of finance.

(b) Not all categories of borrowers have access to security markets and to other sources of external finance alternative to bank credit. This implies that monetary shocks may have different effects on different categories of agents.

The creditist literature has provided detailed and sophisticated empirical analyses on the link between aggregate credit and real economic activity, but not much has been done to investigate inside that macroeconomic 'black box'. In other words, a certain theoretical gap exists in the credit view concerning the interpretation of the (microeconomic) interactions between lenders and (heterogeneous) borrowers.

These points are strictly connected with the analyses contained in the rest of the book, whose premises are briefly described in the next two sections.

The phenomenon of securitization in the light of Williamson's (1985) contractual relations framework

A central question in the debate on the transmission mechanism of monetary policy is: 'how special is bank credit?' As discussed in the previous sections, the issue of substitutability between bank credit and securities is indeed very important for the credit view. Therefore, an economic analysis of the main institutional features of financial markets can reveal many relevant points for the debate on the transmission of monetary policy and contribute to evaluating how general the theoretical statements of the 'money view' and 'credit view' are.

Chapter 3 contains an empirical study that can be considered preliminary (and therefore strictly connected) to point (a) above: it is argued that the macroeconomic relevance of security markets (i.e. the degree of securitization of a given financial system) plays a very important role in assessing the relevance of the credit channel, and the whole analysis is dedicated to investigating whether the phenomenon of 'securitization' is empirically detectable at a macroeconomic level. Since the phenomenon of 'securitization' is strictly connected to the substitutability between bank credit and securities, the analysis of chapter 3 may be associated with a discussion on the conditions under which the *CC* curve of Bernanke and Blinder's (1988) model reduces to the *IS* curve.

The focus of chapter 3 is on bank credit to industry and it is argued that if credit aggregates behave differently according to whether a financial system is securitized or non-securitized, such differences should be explicitly taken into account when looking at all the relevant information for policy making purposes.

The empirical evidence[17] shows that the most relevant source of finance is profit retention, while stock and bond markets are relevant sources of financial funds for the industrial firms only in the 'securitized' financial systems (i.e. mainly the United States, the United Kingdom, and Canada). On the other hand, in Continental Europe external finance is predominantly provided by the banking system.

A distinction between the countries whose financial sectors are 'intermediary-oriented' and the ones whose financial sectors are 'securitized' is

---

[17] For a discussion, see Mayer (1993a).

made, among others, by Rybczynski (1984) and Gardener (1991). While Japan is often quoted as a typical example of a non-securitized financial system, the distinction between securitized and non-securitized financial systems might be useful for quite a few European countries. Gardener (1991), following Rybczynski's classification, argues that the United Kingdom is, at the moment, in the phase of 'securitization', France and Germany are approaching it, while Italy is only entering an intermediate stage of gradual development of financial markets. According to Gardener, the reason for such an evolution could lie in the increasing efficiency of markets and in their increasing capacity for risk bearing. Similar analyses have been made by Frankel and Montgomery (1991) and Mayer (1993a). The latter also points out that in the German 'non-securitized' financial sector (unlike in the British 'securitized' one) hostile takeovers are a very rare phenomenon. This fact, due to a highly concentrated ownership structure, might suggest that in non-securitized financial sectors the connection between the market for shares and the market for control could be less direct and less straightforward.

Outside Europe, the most significant example of a 'securitized' financial sector is given by the United States, while Japan is an oft-quoted example of a financial system strongly oriented towards intermediaries. The impressive economic growth of Japan and Germany in the last few decades shows that no value judgement should be associated with the concept of 'securitization'. In the 'intermediary-oriented' financial systems, a direct control on bank credit by the government authorities is, theoretically speaking, feasible (although not necessarily advisable), and constitutes an historically relevant experience. In the next section it is argued that Williamson's (1985) contractual relations framework can be adopted in order to interpret the existence of securitized and non-securitized financial systems. Chapter 3 contains some empirical evidence confirming such implications. In particular, it will be argued that the phenomenon of securitization can make the demand for bank credit by industrial firms more unstable than the supply. Empirical evidence in favour of this last point will be provided by an analysis based on British and German data. The purpose of the empirical analysis is not to provide updated estimates of some empirical specifications, but rather to perform a comparative analysis of the financial systems of two countries in a period where the respective sizes of the economies, the regulatory systems, and the industrial structures could allow some meaningful comparison. In this sense the sample period is relevant to the extent that it identifies two well defined (and comparable) institutional contexts.

Williamson's (1985) approach, based on the relevance of transaction costs, suggests an interpretation of the behaviour of economic agents in terms of contractual relations. Williamson's general framework of analysis could also be applied to bank intermediation and security markets. It might not be the only possible interpretation, but since most institutional analyses of securitization (such as Rybczynski, 1984 and Gardener, 1990) describe the development of security markets in Continental Europe as a phenomenon that takes place only gradually, an approach based on the hypothesis of 'bounded rationality' – stating that collecting and processing information is time-consuming and costly – seems to be more appropriate to describe the emergence and evolution of the choice between 'asset specific' and 'general-purpose' contracts that characterize the difference between intermediation and spot markets.

According to Williamson (1985), economies on transaction costs can be implemented by assigning transactions to governance structures chosen among different institutional alternatives: the 'classical market contracting' at one extreme, a 'centralized hierarchical organization' at the other, and mixed models of firm and market organization in between. What determines the different institutional alternatives is the outcome of the actions of the agents, whose behaviour is interpreted in terms of 'bounded rationality': in fact, in a context of unbounded rationality, contracts would determine a world of planning. On the other hand, in a world with transaction costs:

the organizational imperative that emerges . . . is this: *organize transactions so as to economize on bounded rationality while simultaneously safeguarding them against the hazards of opportunism.* Such a statement supports a different and larger conception of the economic problem than does the imperative 'Maximize profits'! (Williamson, 1985, p. 32, emphasis in the original)

Applying Williamson's (1985) theoretical contracting framework to the bank credit market, and making a few terminological adjustments, instead of the 'supply for a commodity', we would have the 'supply for financial funds'; instead of the 'general-purpose technology', a 'spot market for financial funds', and instead of Williamson's 'transaction-specific asset', the credit supplied by the bank to the specific firm.[18]

Referring to figure 2.1, if one defines k as a measure of transaction-specific sunk cost for collecting information about borrowers' riskiness (corresponding to Williamson's 'transaction-specific asset'), financial funds may be supplied on a bonds market, or intermediated and supplied by banks. Banks can be thought of as agencies specialized in performing

---

[18] Such a definition shows some similarity with Okun's (1981) distinction between 'auction markets' and 'customer markets'. According to Okun, in the latter, the kind of contract ties together particular sellers and particular buyers (in our case, particular financial intermediaries and particular firms), creating a sort of long-run relationship where the quantities (in our case, the financial flows) or the prices (in our case, the interest rates) might be fixed in the short run.

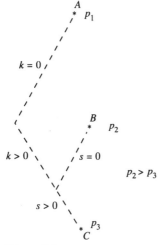

Figure 2.1

economies of scale in collecting information. In Williamson's terminology, the first case corresponds to the general-purpose technology and the second one to the special-purpose technology. Since parties have an interest in creating safeguards to protect investments in transactions, s can be defined as the *magnitude* of those safeguards which could be assimilated to the collaterals in banks' loans.

Following Williamson (1985) again, one can assume that suppliers are risk neutral, willing to supply under either kind of transaction, and accept any safeguard condition provided that expected breakeven results can be obtained. In the absence of transaction-specific sunk costs ($k=0$), node A in figure 2.1 is reached; this corresponds to a breakeven price (interest rate) p_1. Node B is reached in the presence of transaction-specific sunk costs ($k>0$) without safeguards (in our case, without collateral, i.e. $s=0$). In the contract corresponding to node C we have transaction-specific sunk costs in the presence of safeguard ($k>0$, $s>0$).

k, s and p are determined simultaneously by a contract, and obviously influence each other. Transactions performed under each of those regimes can take place at the same time. In particular, in the real world, we see banks supplying credit with or without collateral (obviously at different breakeven levels of interest rates) when they lend different amounts of money to different categories of borrowers and, above all, we see the coexistence of bonds markets and intermediated credit.

We can further imagine that, since in node A transactions take place without asset specificity, such a situation may be reached when the state of nature is such that the number of relatively low-risk agents is high enough to trigger a supply of financial funds under a general-purpose contract. This may happen if the governance institution is able to prevent forms of moral hazard and opportunistic behaviour that would undermine the feasibility of *general purpose* contracts. In other words, the existence, efficiency, size and macroeconomic relevance of stock markets might depend on the effectiveness of governance structure and, of course, on all the other features influencing the number of relatively low-risk borrowers and agents, which might have to do with the degree of economic development. Securitized financial systems could be thought of as institutional contexts where the magnitude of financial flows negotiated under the kind of contracts associated with node A is macroeconomically relevant compared to those associated with nodes B and C.

We can think of nodes B and C as different 'hierarchical' contractual forms of banks loans. Williamson's observation that 'transactions located at node B . . . are apt to be unstable contractually . . . [and] . . . may revert to node A . . . or be relocated to node C ' (Williamson, 1985, p. 34), could be interpreted as a description of phenomena relating to credit rationing (i.e. unwillingness to supply credit to those agents unable to provide collateral) or other situations where the supply of bank credit to industries is affected by the willingness of banks to lend, and by their subjective valuation of the riskiness of lenders.

An empirical analysis of the macroeconomic relevance of securitization can be based on the idea that only in a securitized financial system is substitutability between bank credit and security quantitatively relevant to the point of allowing us to estimate, in a monoequational context, a supply of bank credit to industry, as shown in chapter 3.

Interactions between investments and credit sector

Chapters 4 and 5 can be interpreted as investigations of the interactions between banks and industrial firms within a 'creditist' perspective. In addition to the typical 'creditist' analyses, particular attention is dedicated in chapter 4 in particular to the effects of industrial structure on the interactions between banks and industrial firms.

After pointing out that in 'non-securitized' or 'bank-oriented' financial systems the transmission of monetary disturbances depends almost entirely on the interactions between banks and borrowers, in Chapter 4 it is shown that, *ceteris paribus*, an increase in industrial firms' oligopsonistic power in the credit market reduces the equilibrium level of investments and affects the transmission mechanism of monetary policy with a direct 'first-impact' effect that tends to reduce the effectiveness of monetary policy and various 'indirect effects' whose sign and intensity depends on the analytical form (i.e. curvature and cross-elasticities) of the various excess demand functions for the various financial assets with effects whose sign and intensity depend on some analytic assumptions (such as the magnitude of the curvatures and cross-elasticities) of the demands and supplies of financial assets. The problem is analysed within a portfolio model *à la* Tobin and Brainard (1963) and not within a creditist macromodel, in order to stress the fact that the relevance of oligopsony in the credit market cannot be confined to the credit view.

With respect to a representative creditist model (like for instance Bernanke and Blinder, 1988), the model of chapter 4 reaches a lesser level of generalization: it contains more financial assets, but instead of the 'macroeconomic' (2.12) and (2.13), describing the equilibrium in the goods market, it contains an equation describing firms' demand for loans as the result of the aggregation of the optimal investment levels of individual firms operating in an oligopsonistic credit market. Therefore the analysis of chapter 5 can be associated with a frequent objection to the 'credit view', stating that the response of banks' assets to monetary shocks is simply caused by disturbances in banks' liabilities transmitted to banks' assets via the balance-sheet constraint of the aggregate banking sector (which can be better seen by looking at (2.8) on p. 37). This statement would not be true to the extent that the level of banks' liquidity preference (i.e. FR in (2.8)) is the result of an active and deliberate choice of 'non-investing' financial resources, caused by the degree of uncertainty of the whole economy. In order to investigate this point, chapter 5 contains an econometric analysis of the commercial banks' free liquidity ratio for Italy (a non-securitized financial system for the period under consideration), based on a theoretical framework consistent with the literature on investments with uncertainty and sunk costs. In this sense, the banks' liquidity preference can be reduced to a common theoretical framework, commonly applied to industrial firms.

'Inside-the-firm' interactions between finance and investments.

In part III, the interactions between the real and the financial side of the economy are observed inside the firm, either by regarding the firm's financial structure as an element of heterogeneity (as in chapter 6) or by assuming simultaneity between finance and investment decisions.

Chapter 6 contains an empirical analysis of investments performed on the basis of a very simple theoretical framework which interprets the speed of adjustment of investments as an effect of transaction costs. The econometric estimates of the investment function (containing financial variables, interpreted as an element of heterogeneity among different firms of the same industry) are performed with panel data techniques applied to a sample of Italian chemical firms.

In chapter 7 the problem of connection between finance and investment decisions is formalized with the help of an optimal control model complicated by the assumption of simultaneity between investments and financial decisions. Some of the main assumptions apply, once again, to non-securitized financial systems, and are meant to describe the implications (for the firm's investment problem) of raising financial funds on security markets, interpreted not simply as a place where the trade of financial funds take place, but also as an institution where a particular mechanism of information spreading takes place. The model is resolved by introducing an algebraically tractable functional link between the profits and the costs of financial capital, which entails some loss of generality although it is motivated on the basis of results in the literature of finance. It is shown that a real exogenous shock in the marginal profitability of physical capital can affect the level of investments of the firm not only through the usual 'real' channel (i.e. the link between marginal profitability of capital and optimal level of investments), but also through a 'financial' channel, given by the fact that information on the profitability of the firm spreads in the financial markets and affects the (firm-specific) cost of financial capital. In this sense, the distinction between 'real' and 'financial' channels of transmission of real shocks, pointed out in several macroeconomic contributions of the credit view are analysed in the microeconomic context of an optimal control investment model.

Part III has several connections with the rest of this study. First of all, interpreting firms' financial structures as an element of heterogeneity within the same industry is consistent with the creditist idea that credit shocks may have heterogeneous effects on firms relying to different extent on debt. Secondly, the model of chapter 7 is meant to introduce a rationale for 'heterogeneity' among different firms without introducing the assumption of credit rationing, that accounts, in addition, for the mechanism of information spreading associated to the phenomenon of securitization.

Putting into context different perspectives and the results of different research fields (often based on different modelling techniques) is certainly a difficult and, at the same time, stimulating objective. The difficulty lies in the fact that choosing which variables should be taken as given and which ones should be considered endogenous with respect to a theoretical analysis entails some prior assumptions. However, the whole modern credit view has been developed after theoretical and empirical analyses often motivated by the difficulties of conventional theoretical approaches to explain some very relevant empirical phenomena: this is, for instance, the case for Bernanke's (1983) study, where it is pointed out that the conventional money view cannot completely explain the magnitude of the 1929–33 Great Depression. Bernanke's study attempts to take in – at least in spirit –

Stiglitz's concern for not 'taking the assumptions provided to us by our ideologue brethren, and exploring their consequences, trusting that the models we are analysing bear some semblance to the world, because we have been told so by others!'

3 Securitization and the empirics of bank credit

Securitization and the macroeconomy

In chapter 2 it was suggested that Williamson's (1985) contractual framework is a valuable tool to interpret the phenomenon of securitization. One of the premises of the 'credit view' is the idea that bank credit and security markets are not perfect substitutes. Furthermore, for a large number of small and medium-sized industrial firms bank loans are almost the only external source of finance. However this idea has not only been expressed in the 'creditist' literature. If, as Fama (1985) suggests, bank credit is a non-substitutable source of finance for the firms penalized on bond and share markets by phenomena of asymmetric information and agency costs, then in a 'securitized' financial system banks would conceivably face two different kinds of customers: firms not penalized on capital markets, for which the different sources of funds are substitutable, and firms penalized on capital markets. Firms of the first type (usually big corporations with a 'strong' reputation), due to the high substitutability among the different sources of funds, would probably express a more unstable demand for bank credit than firms of the second. Therefore, since big and well reputed firms express a relevant share of the aggregate economic activity, in a 'securitized' financial system the demand for bank credit to the industries should be, *ceteris paribus*, more unstable than in 'non-securitized' systems. This means that a situation where the demand for bank credit to the industries is more unstable than the supply is more likely to be found in a securitized financial system than in a non-securitized one.

Fama's (1985) results are consistent with the financial economics literature which describes the dividend decision by the firm's controlling group as a problem of signalling (Leland and Pyle, 1977): in the presence of information asymmetry, if the dividend policy can be used as a 'signal' (of the quality of the firm's investment) in order to reduce the transaction costs, smaller firms (with lower market power and lower profit flow) might not be able to send the 'signal' that would enable them to reduce the transaction costs. For this reason, they may be more dependent on the supply of credit by agencies specialized in monitoring, and in economies of scale in collecting information (i.e. banks).

For the same reason, in securitized financial systems, where the spot market for financial funds is empirically relevant, substitution between bank credit and securities is likely to be an empirical phenomenon too. Then, to the extent that bank credit to large corporations represents a substantial portion of the total bank credit to industry, the demand for bank credit expressed by 'strong' firms would contribute to determining an empirically observable stock level of bank credit to industry consistent with the behaviour of a supply rather than a demand function. In fact, if the demand function for bank credit is more unstable than the supply (due to the high substitutability between bonds, shares and bank credit for industrial firms) then, looking at the observable values of bank credit a supply function could be identified (and estimated with a monoequational model), rather than the usual demand function. This contrasts with the approach followed by most empirical works, which tend to estimate a demand function with the assumption of partial adjustment. On the other hand, in a non-securitized financial sector there is no reason to expect the demand for bank credit to industry to be more unstable than the supply. Therefore, a demand function for bank credit to industry could be identified in this last case. All these points deserve an intuitive explanation.

Let us consider a supply of bank credit (in our case, to the industrial sector) similar to the one employed in the theoretical part of Bernanke and Blinder's (1988) paper, i.e. :

$$L^s = \mu(\overset{+}{\rho_L}, \overset{-}{r_B}) \cdot D(1-q) \tag{3.1}$$

where L^s = banks' credit supply
D = banks' deposits
q = banks' required reserves coefficient
ρ_L = interest rate on banks' loans
r_B = interest rate on bonds
Let us assume that the following function

$$D = D(\overset{+}{Y}, \overset{+}{P}, \overset{-}{r_D}) \tag{3.2}$$

describes the deposits issued by banks.

In this function (where Y is defined as the GDP, P the price level, and r_D the interest rate on banks' deposits), the deposits supplied by the banks are assumed to depend positively on the aggregate income and on the price level, and negatively on their cost, i.e. the interest rate r_D. Let us further assume that a stable functional link exists between the two liquid assets

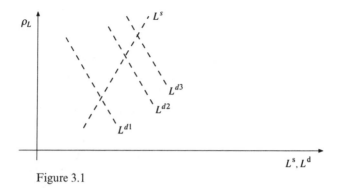

Figure 3.1

traded on spot markets: bank deposits and bonds. Let us define this functional link as follows:

$$r_D = r_D(\overset{+}{r_B})$$ (3.3)

the behaviour of such a functional link may be determined by the term structure of the interest rate. The above-mentioned case, where the demand for bank credit is more unstable than the supply, may be intuitively described with the help of figure 3.1 (assuming, only for the sake of this figure, that competition between different banks determines a fixed spread between ρ_L and r_D, so that ρ_L may be expressed as a function of r_D, and, figure 3.1 may be drawn, for simplicity, with one interest rate only):

L^s=supply of bank credit to the industrial firms
L^d=demand for bank credit by the industrial firms

Figure 3.1 shows (although in a somewhat simplistic way) that if, in a monoequational context, the demand function is more unstable than the supply, the simple observation of the stock values of the bank credit to industry would identify a supply rather than a demand function. In fact, when the credit demand shifts from L^{d1} to L^{d2} and L^{d3}, the three observable equilibrium stocks of credit lie in the same supply function, which is then identified.

The results of Fama (1985) imply that in a 'securitized' financial system, the bank credit to industry is highly substitutable by recourse to the 'spot' market. Therefore, the demand for bank credit by industrial firms might shift when the business cycle affects the transaction and monitoring costs by making the spot market comparatively less or more convenient. Substitutability between bank credit and non-intermediated credit is possible both in a securitized and in a non-securitized financial sector. It is a relevant phenomenon in a macroeconomic perspective to the extent that large corporations express an empirically relevant demand for financial funds. It is logical to assume, for example, that refinancing short-term bank debt with long-term bonds as interest rates decline could lead to fluctuations in the amount of credit demanded from banks. More generally, any disturbance affecting asymmetrically or unequally the interest rate on bank lending and the interest rate on bonds, and inducing the industrial firms to switch from bank credit to securities (or vice-versa) could be empirically relevant in a securitized financial sector, while it cannot be empirically relevant in a non-securitized financial sector since, by definition, a non-securitized financial system is characterized by the scarce empirical relevance of the spot markets for financial funds. It must be stressed that observable data correspond to actual transactions of bank credit to industry. In other words, they are, *per se* both demand and supply values, and it is the relatively larger instability of one of the two functions that allows for the identification of the other.

An empirical analysis for the United Kingdom and Germany

The British and German banking systems

To perform a comparative analysis of the behaviour of bank credit to industry in two different kinds of financial systems, the United Kingdom and Germany have been examined, during the period between the 1974 oil shock and German unification. Such a choice is due to the fact that the magnitude of the two economies is comparable and, as Frankel and Montgomery (1991) point out, many legal issues and structural features (such as the degree of concentration in the banking sector) are very similar, in spite of the two countries having very different financial systems. Thus, by comparing the behaviour of bank credit in the two countries, it might be possible to 'isolate' (at least to some extent) the effects of the two different financial systems.

In Frankel and Montgomery (1991), a comparison of several different legal issues between Germany, the United Kingdom, the United States and Japan shows that:

regulation of British and German banks follows a universal bank model, under which banks are permitted to engage in a wide range of financial activities, including all insurance and securities activities. The main difference between the British and the German versions of the universal bank is that British banks usually conduct their securities business through subsidiaries, while German banks conduct their business directly. (Frankel and Montgomery, 1991, p. 273)

The regulation issues analysed by Frankel and Montgomery are: the principal regulators of commercial banks, geographic and regulatory banking restrictions, the scope of permissible activities (such as securities, insurance and industrial investments), capital requirements, deposit protection schemes and reserve requirements. No relevant differences have been found, in this regard, between the British and the German banking systems, while some relevant differences are pointed out in a few institutional features which are, incidentally, at the core of attention in most studies on securitization, namely customer relationships and bankruptcy procedures. Concerning customer relationships, in Germany (like Japan), banks are able to establish 'very close ties' with industrial firms, whilst this happens only very rarely in the United Kingdom and in the United States. Concerning bankruptcy procedures, while the British (and American) law heavily penalizes banks that have close relationships with customers, and imposes greater losses on banks than on other creditors, not only are banks less penalized in Germany than in Britain, in case of customers' distress, but they

often take responsibility for organizing creditor coalitions for financially troubled firms. A bank's behaviour in such a workout may be disciplined by its interest in establishing and maintaining a reputation as a structurer and arranger of successful firms' finance. (Frankel and Montgomery, 1991, p. 288)

For this reason, informal bankruptcy arrangements in Germany are more frequent than informal ones, and this may help to explain why the number of corporate bankruptcies has greatly increased in the United Kingdom (and in the United States), while it does not show any clear upward trend for Germany (and Japan). Frankel and Montgomery (1991) also report some empirical data concerning the trend of real assets of the largest banks (dramatically increasing for Germany, more stable for Britain, between 1970 and 1989), and the comparison between funds raised through securities and bank loans. The data reported in Frankel and Montgomery (1991) clearly show that by comparing all the quinquennia between 1965 and 1989 in the United Kingdom, any increase in aggregate bank loans is associated with a decrease in funds raised through securities, and vice-versa. Such a phenomenon (which, curiously, has not been pointed out by Frankel and Montgomery) only affects the United Kingdom and the United States (i.e. the two securitized financial systems), and seems to be consistent with the fact that (as previously argued in this book) the securitized financial systems are characterized by higher instability than non-securitized financial systems in the demand for bank credit to industry. This might also be consistent with Mayer's (1993a) observation of the fact that bank credit is the most relevant 'anti-cyclical' source of financial funds for the industrial firms.

Concerning the degree of concentration in the banking sector, the data

Table 3.1 *Degree of market concentration and size of the banking systems for Germany and the United Kingdom, 1988*

(a) Concentration, market share (%)

	Total assets		Deposits	
	5 banks	3 banks	5 banks	3 banks
Germany	31.2	21.2	30.5	19.1
United Kingdom	32.6	26.5	30.3	21.6

(b) Size of the banking sector

	Number of banks	Assets (billion $)
Germany	4465	1465.0
United Kingdom	661	1337.8

Source: Gardener (1991)

reported by Frankel and Montgomery show that the concentration of bank assets in the five largest banks is very similar between the United Kingdom and Germany, while the German banking system seems to be slightly more concentrated if one looks at the 10 largest banks. Data on the degree of concentration in the banking sector are also reported by Gardener (1991), on the basis of OECD data, and data from *The Banker* (concerning the concentration ratios).

According to the concentration ratios calculated with three or five banks, the British banking system seems to be only slightly more concentrated than the German one. On the other hand, if one calculates the ratio between the size of the banking sector (measured by the assets in billion dollars) and the number of banks operating in the market, it can be seen that the average size of banks is larger in the United Kingdom than in Germany.

The British and the German banking sectors seem, then, to differ in all features connected with the phenomenon of securitization (such as customer relations, bankruptcies procedures and substitutability between bank credit and securities), while they do not show any relevant difference concerning regulatory issues and market structure. In addition, both economies are in a stage of advanced industrialization, their magnitude is comparable (at least until German unification), and they are highly integrated, which could lead us to assume that they are partly subject to the same sources of disturbances at a macro level. For these reasons, a comparative analysis of the behaviour of bank credit to industry should be able to provide information on the institutional differences of the two financial systems by isolating, at least to some extent, their macroeconomic implications.

Concerning Germany, bank credit is modelled following the standard approach (namely a demand function containing an interest rate representative of the cost of borrowing, and another interest rate containing information on the money market conditions); because the German financial system is non-securitized, substitutability between securities and bank credit is not empirically relevant. On the other hand, a supply function of bank credit to industry (analogous to the one contained in the theoretical part of the paper by Bernanke and Blinder, 1988) has been estimated for the United Kingdom. This because in the securitized British financial system substitutability between bank credit and securities is expected to be empirically relevant. The empirical specification derived from such a function contains an interest rate representative for bank assets and another for banks' liabilities. If these two interest rates have similar coefficients, they may capture (if considered jointly) the information for the interest rate spread between banks' liabilities and banks' assets, which could be interpreted either as a mark up pricing mechanism, or (if one does not assume imperfect competition in the banking sector) as a proxy for the margin of intermediation necessary in order to cover the administrative costs of the bank.

A counterfactual experiment has been made by also attempting to estimate for Germany a supply function of bank credit to industries analogous to the one estimated for the United Kingdom. As expected, the estimates are unsatisfactory concerning the diagnostic tests, the significance of the regressors – and their sign. Therefore, a supply function of bank credit to industries has given – in the simplified monoequational context presented here – satisfactory results (in terms of statistical properties, significance of the parameters and sign of the regressors) only in the case of the United Kingdom, a country characterized by a 'securitized' financial system.

The analytical form of supply for bank credit to industry is log linear like the following:

$$C_t = a_0 + a_1 \cdot \ln(Y_t) + a_2 \cdot \ln(P_t) + a_3 \cdot r_L - a_4 \cdot r_D \qquad (3.4)$$

This equation may be obtained by substituting (3.2) and (3.3) into (3.1), and approximating the resulting equation with a Cobb–Douglas exponential in the interest rates. A more complex dynamic structure of (3.4) will be obtained by following the general-to-specific approach. In this case, (3.4) will be considered in the more general form

$$C_t = b_0 + b_1(L)\ln(Y_t) + b_2(L)\ln(P_t) + b_3(L)r_L - b_4(L)r_D \qquad (3.4')$$

where $b_1(L)$, $b_2(L)$, $b_3(L)$, $b_4(L)$ are lag polynomials on which a series of zero restrictions have been tested according to the 'general-to-specific' methodology, as explained in the next section.

Econometric methodology: general-to-specific and partial adjustment

The purpose of the following analysis is to show how the behaviour of bank credit to industrial firms is affected by such an institutional feature as the relevance of the stock market. To do so, the behaviour of some relevant credit aggregates for Germany and the United Kingdom will be compared and contrasted. The specifications of the different equations have been obtained following the 'general-to-specific' (Hendry, 1985, Harvey, 1989) methodology, starting from a general unrestricted specification containing four lags. Simulation studies have shown that this seems to be an appropriate dynamic structure to start with in order to capture the dynamic properties of the models, while several studies in the 1980s (for example Hendry, 1988; Muscatelli, 1988) have shown that feedback mechanisms (such as one at the basis of the general-to-specific approach) yield better econometric performances than the 'forward-looking' ones (for instance, Cuthbertson, 1985).

The final 'restricted' specification is obtained by imposing zero restrictions in the 'general unrestricted model' and by testing them with variable deletion tests. For the sake of simplicity, only the final 'restricted' specifications have been included in tables 3A.5–3A.12 in the appendix (p. 71). The appendix also contains the list of the variables and a few technical details. All the estimates have been implemented with 'Microfit', version 3.0. In the tests, the 95 per cent level of confidence has been used unless otherwise specified.

The partial adjustment mechanism is very commonly employed in many macroeconomic empirical specifications. As is well known, it can be also consistent with an optimizing behaviour of economic agents facing at the same time a cost of adjustment and a cost of being 'out of equilibrium'.

In the estimates unadjusted data have been employed, because, as Wallis (1974) points out, the use of seasonally adjusted data could induce distortions in the estimates, apart from the very particular case where the same filter applies for the dependent variable and the regressors. The general-to-specific methodology could not be applied to estimates of the bank credit to manufacturing sector for Germany, since the presence of a structural break in 1980Q3–1980Q4 (detected in preliminary analyses) would not allow us to run meaningful (i.e. with sufficiently high degrees of freedom) variable deletion tests. In that specific case (and in that case only) a specification with a lagged dependent variable has been assumed *a priori*, as in Bernanke and Blinder (1988). The presence of structural breaks does not conflict, however, with the conclusions of the present analysis.

The Hausman test of exogeneity has been implemented in the final specifications of estimated functions, in order to detect simultaneity between income and the dependent variable considered. In the cases where the null hypothesis has been rejected at the 95 per cent level of confidence, the final estimates have been performed with the method of Instrumental Variables, while in all the other cases they have been performed with the method of Ordinary Least Squares. In tables 3A.5–3A.12 in the appendix only the final 'restricted' specification has been reported.

Empirical Results

In what follows, the main results of the estimates for each country and the relative economic implications are briefly illustrated and commented on. The comments and the tables in the appendix contain the estimates, the diagnostic tests and further technical details.

Some preliminary Granger causality tests have been run both for Germany (tables 3A.1 and 3A.2) and for the United Kingdom (tables 3A.3 and 3A.4). For Germany, unlike bank credit to the manufacturing sector, $M1$ is a significant regressor in the forecast equation for GNP (table 3A.1). In table 3A.2 it is shown that while bank credit to the manufacturing sector is significant in the forecasting equation for $M1$, $M1$ is not significant in the forecasting equation for the bank credit to the manufacturing sector. Although these preliminary tests are not particularly informative *per se*, and have to be considered together with the rest of the empirical analysis, we may still observe that the results of tables 3A.1 and 3A.2 can be consistent with the systematic use of $M1$ as an instrument of monetary policy and with the fact that bank credit to the manufacturing sector is correlated with industrial production. Therefore, it might not be very surprising to observe that a monetary policy instrument ($M1$) reacts to an indicator of the business cycle (industrial production, strictly correlated to the bank credit to the manufacturing sector) generating, in this way, a context of money supply endogeneity.

Similar results have been obtained for the United Kingdom, where $M1$ (table 3A.3) seems to be less significant than in Germany in the forecasting equation for GDP (although the sample period chosen for United Kingdom for these preliminary Granger causality tests ends in 1988Q4, when $M1$ was abandoned as an official target of monetary policy) and more significant in the forecasting equation for the bank credit to the manufacturing sector (table 3A.4). It might be relevant to observe in this regard the fact that $M1$ was about to be abandoned as an official monetary policy target.

The United Kingdom

In the case of the United Kingdom, three credit aggregates have been considered: bank credit to industry, bank credit to sectors other than industry, and total bank credit, given by the sum between bank credit to industry and bank credit to the other sectors. For the last two aggregates, a demand function similar to the one introduced in the empirical part of Bernanke and Blinder (1988) has been estimated; the interest rates employed also are analogous to the ones used by Bernanke and Blinder: the interest rate on short-run Treasury bills ($TRBR$) and the interest rate on bank overdrafts (ROV). The bank credit to other sectors than industry ($LCROIN$) is a very wide credit aggregate affected by the behaviour of several different categories of agents: therefore it is reasonable to expect that the function employed to describe and estimate the behaviour of such aggregates might turn out to be more unstable than the function employed to describe the behaviour of bank credit to industry, which is referred to a much more narrowly defined category of borrowers. In the case of bank credit to industry ($LCRIN$), for the reasons mentioned earlier, a supply function for bank credit to industry has been estimated instead of a demand function. The estimates for the three credit aggregates have been performed for the sample period 1975Q2–1991Q4 and, concerning $LCRIN$ and $LCROIN$, also for 1975Q2–1988Q4, in order to run a predictive failure test for the years immediately after the Bank of England abandoned $M1$ as an intermediated target monetary policy.

The specification for $LCRIN$ contains the interest rate on seven-day notice deposit accounts with London clearing banks (here defined $RLCB$, which can be regarded as a leading interest rate on banks' deposits market), and the interest rate on banks' overdrafts (ROV). The former is an indicator of the interest rates on banks' liabilities, the latter is obviously an interest rate on banks' assets. The spread between these two interest rates could represent a proxy for the 'gross margin of intermediation' existing in the banking system. If we accept such an interpretation, in an hypothetical estimation of the supply function of bank credit to industry, the coefficient referred to as $RLCB$ should be negative, while the one referred to as ROV should be positive and, if one regards the difference '$ROV-RLCB$' as a proxy for the banks' margin of profit, or for the margin of intermediation, they should have very close absolute values. We could imagine, as a first approximation, a partial adjustment mechanism of the kind:

$$S_t - S_{t-1} = \beta(S^*_t - S_{t-1})$$

with $S^*_t = S(ROV_t, RLCB_t, P_t, Y_t)$
where the asterisk indicates 'desired value', S_t is the supply of bank credit

to industrial firms at time t, P_t the level of prices, and Y_t the real output. The lagged dependent variable mechanism could be justified with the same kind of arguments which justify a partial adjustment mechanism for a financial asset demand function.

Preliminary analyses have shown that, even if the data employed are not seasonally adjusted, seasonal dummies were not significant in any credit aggregate 'general' unrestricted specification. Therefore seasonal dummies were not included in the general unrestricted models employed for the 'general-to-specific' analysis.

By applying the general-to-specific methodology, it has been found that both the specifications for the three credit aggregates support a dynamic structure with a lagged dependent variable.

The estimates for *LCRIN* and *LCROIN* have been implemented both with IV (instrumental variables, tables 3A.5 and 3A.6 respectively) and with OLS (ordinary least squares), although in the OLS estimates both for *LCRIN* (table 3A.7) and for *LCROIN* (table 3A.8) the null hypothesis of exogeneity of *LRYUK* with respect to the various dependent variables was not rejected, at the 95 per cent level of confidence. Concerning *LCRTO*, the null hypothesis of exogeneity of *LRYUK* with respect to the various dependent variables was rejected, at the 95 per cent level of confidence, therefore the only estimates shown for this credit aggregate are the ones with IV (table 3A.9).

All the estimates of the supply of bank credit to industry (table 3A.5 for 1975Q2–1991Q4 with IV, table 3A.7 for the same sample period with OLS, table 3A.10 for 1975Q2–1988Q4 with OLS in order to run a predictive failure and Chow test) yield satisfactory results both in terms of diagnostic tests, and joint and individual significance of the regressors. The values of the coefficients for the OLS and IV estimates are very close.

The estimates for the total bank credit (*LCRTO*, table 3A.9) are satisfactory in terms of diagnostic tests and joint and individual significance of the regressors.

Concerning the bank credit to other sectors than industry (*LCROIN*), in the sample period 1975Q2–1991Q4 both the IV and the OLS estimates fail the residuals normality test. The GDP is not highly significant, especially for the IV estimates over the sample period 1975Q2–1991Q4. The estimates for the sample period 1975Q2–1988Q4 (table 3A.11) fails the predictive failure and the Chow test.

These results suggest that bank credit to other sectors than industry seems to be very sensitive to changes in monetary policy targeting, and its specification does not seem to be very stable. The results are quite different and much more satisfactory concerning the bank credit to industry (*LCRIN*), both in terms of stability and statistical significance of the estimates. For the reason illustrated on p. 58, $LCRIN$ has been estimated as a supply function. All the diagnostic tests yield satisfactory results, and for the predictive failure and Chow test. The IV equation for $LCRIN$ for the sample period 1975Q2–1991Q2 is reported below:

$$LCRIN = 0.91097 + 0.51374\ LCRIN_{-1} + 0.031864\ ROV$$
$$-0.028554\ RLCB + 0.62970\ LNIP + 0.16719\ LRYUK$$

$$R^2 = 0.99792$$

The results reported in tables 3A.5–3A.12 in the appendix suggest that the 'supply function' for bank credit to industry is much more stable than the 'demand function' for bank credit to sectors other than industry. One of the possible reasons for such a result is the fact that the bank credit to industry refers to a category of borrowers which is much more homogeneous, and bank credit to sectors other than industry, apart from being a highly heterogeneous aggregate, might be affected by a larger set of disturbances.

Germany

If one had to explain the concept of structural break, the best example would probably be that of Germany in 1989–90. Since testing for structural stability on the post-unification data would yield too obvious results, the regressions have been run on the sample period 1975Q1–1989Q3 (i.e. until the announcement of the opening of the East German frontiers, which could rationally be interpreted as the first step of unification), while the last quarter of 1989 and the first one of 1990 have been employed to run a meaningful predictive failure test, since the formal process of unification took place gradually after the elections of 1990.

The bank credit to the manufacturing sector has been estimated as a demand function with partial adjustment, since in this case the points raised by Fama (1985) and the empirical evidence for substitutability between security and bank credit do not apply, given that the German financial system (at least for the period considered in the sampling period) is not 'securitized'. A set of interest rates analogous to those employed by Bernanke and Blinder (1988) has been used (the interest rate on three-month bank loans and the interest rate on German Treasury bills). Preliminary analyses on the behaviour of the (log of) bank credit to the manufacturing sector ($LCRMA$) have shown a structural break (in 1980Q3–1980Q4), probably determined jointly by the effects of the implementation of the European Monetary System (EMS) and by the recession which took place that year. In this case $LCRMA$ has been interpreted as a demand function, because it has been argued that in a non-securitized financial sector there is not high substitutability between bank credit and securities or bonds. As a consequence, in a monoequational framework one can follow the predominant approach in the existing empirical literature, and estimate a demand function for bank credit which, in this context, is properly identifiable.

Because of the structural break and the high instability of the demand for bank credit by the manufacturing sector ($LCRMA$), the general-to-specific methodology could not be applied in this specific case since the degree of freedom would have been too low to run meaningful variable deletion tests. Therefore, a specification with a lagged dependent variable has been assumed *a priori*, adopting in this case a specification extremely common in many empirical contributions on the demand for credit.

The estimates of the demand for bank credit to the manufacturing sector are shown in table 3A.12 in the appendix. The results are satisfactory for all the diagnostic tests excepting the Functional Form test.

The implicit deflator of GNP has not been included since preliminary analyses have shown that it is not statistically significant either before or after the structural break. The IV equation for $LCRMA$ (for the sample period 1980Q4–1989Q3) are reported below:

$$LCRMA = 2.0754 + 1.4692 \, LRGGNP - 0.011491 \, R3ML$$
$$+ 0.025318 \, GTRBR + 0.16554 \, LCRMA_{-1} + 0.0864 \, S1$$
$$+ 0.063588 \, S2 + 0.035790 \, S3$$

$$R^2 = 0.95211$$

In order to run a 'counterfactual' experiment, the estimation of a supply function for banks credit to the manufacturing sector analogous to the one estimated for the United Kingdom (following different specifications and methodologies) has been attempted without any economically sensible result.

A possible interpretation of the empirical results shown in this analysis is that, in a monoequational context, a supply function for bank credit to industries may be identified only for a country where the demand for bank credit to industries is more unstable than the supply. This is more likely to happen in a 'securitized' financial system, where the substitutability between recourse to bank credit and the securities market can be a relevant macroeconomic phenomenon, potentially able to increase the instability of the demand for bank credit expressed by large corporations.

Concluding comments

In the previous sections it has been argued that institutional factors, such as the relevance of stock markets compared to intermediated credit, may carry important (and empirically detectable) implications for the qualitative behaviour of credit aggregates. For this purpose, an empirical investigation of the behaviour of the bank credit to industry and other credit aggregates has been performed for Germany and the United Kingdom.

While the widely defined credit aggregates are generally characterized by an unstable behaviour for the British 'securitized' financial system, in the case of a well identified category of credit users, industrial firms, a stable supply function has been estimated in a monoequational framework. This fact has been interpreted as an effect of the role of endogenous contractual response, which becomes empirically relevant and detectable in the context of a securitized financial system, because of the relevance of the 'spot' financial markets and because of the substitutability (at least for large firms) between bank credit and securities.

The simplifying assumption of the traditional *IS–LM* model, which envisages a distinction only between money and generic 'bonds', and implicitly aggregates any form of credit (i.e. bank credit and securities) in a unique financial sector, might be incorrect to the extent that it ignores the role of 'asset specificity' and the endogenous contractual response that characterizes the behaviour of the financial sector. The role of endogenous contractual response becomes empirically relevant in the context of securitized financial systems, because of the substitutability between bank credit and securities.

The institutional factors taken into account in this analysis are those associated with the distinction between 'securitized' financial systems, like the British one, and 'intermediary-oriented' financial systems, like the German. Such a distinction is significant if we consider that some classes of enterprises, facing agency costs in financial markets due to informational asymmetry phenomena, are heavily dependent on bank credit. In such a context, banks could face two kinds of customers (in the industrial sector): 'strong' enterprises which can easily substitute bank credit by issuing assets on the capital markets, and firms penalized by access costs in financial markets. The demand for bank credit expressed by the 'strong' firms could be more unstable than the supply, due to the high substitutability between direct emission of financial market assets and recourse to the bank credit. The fact that the demand for bank credit expressed by large firms is highly relevant in a macroeconomic context contributes to creating the conditions which allow for the estimation (within a monoequational model) of a supply function of bank credit, rather than a demand function. Such a situation seems to apply in the 'securitized' financial sectors, in our case in the United Kingdom, where a supply function of bank credit to industry has been estimated. On the other hand, for the total bank credit (where it is not possible to picture a particular class of agents having homogeneous characteristics), a demand function has been estimated according to the approach most commonly followed in empirical works, and similar to what was done by Bernanke and Blinder (1988).

The empirical literature often implicitly assumes that the stock of credit is 'demand determined'. In fact, in such an interpretation it is implicitly assumed that the banking sector plays a passive role in macroeconomic allocation of credit, such as in the *IS–LM* model. In other words the relevant behavioural relation would be a demand function, and the existing stock would differ from the one desired by agents only because of adjustment costs, lags in correcting expectations, or modifications in the equilibrium levels of the relevant variables. Such a specification derives often from the application to credit demand of the specifications commonly employed to describe money demand, and implicitly assumes that the supply of banks' credit adjusts to the shocks and modifications originating on the (credit) demand side of the market.

By drawing a few conclusions in the spirit of Poole, one could argue that in a securitized financial system, if monetary policy must rely on the most stable behavioural relation then, to the extent that a policy target may be represented by the volume of activity of the industrial sector, some proper intermediate target could be chosen among the variables appearing in the supply function of bank credit to the industrial sector. A monetary policy based on a strict control of money aggregates may be less effective in a securitized sector where substitutability between different sources of financial funds and endogenous contractual response could determine other forms of liquidity.

A further implication of the results is that it might be misleading to assume (as in the *IS–LM* model) that any kind of financial asset can be aggregated into one (albeit broadly defined) category, regardless of the intrinsic differences in the various types of contracts, and assuming no asset specificity. Finally, the results seem to testify to the relevance of long run and contractuals links in determining the behaviour of financial assets.

Appendix

The variables employed in the regressions are:
$CONST$=intercept term
$S1, S2, S3$=seasonal dummies for the first, second and third terms respectively

United Kingdom

$CRIN$=bank credit to industry
$CROIN$=bank credit to sectors other than industry
$CRTO=CRIN+CROIN$
IP=implicit price deflator of GDP
$LCRIN=\log(CRIN)$
$LCROIN=\log(CROIN)$
$LCRTO=\log(CRTO)$
$LNIP=\log(IP)$
$LNM1=\log(M1)$
$LRYUK=\log(YUK/IP)$
$RLCB$=interest rate on seven-day notice deposit account with London clearing banks
ROV=interest rate on bank overdraft
$TRBR$=interest rate on Treasury bills
YUK=UK GDP at market prices
$UHAUS$=residuals for the Hausman-test of exogeneity of $LRYUK$.

Germany

$CRMA$=bank credit to the manufacturing sector
$GTRBR$=German Treasury bill rate
$HAUSRG$=residuals for the Hausman-test for exogeneity for $LRGGNP$ in the equation for $LCRMA$

$GGNP$=GNP at current prices
$IPGNP$=implicit price deflator of the GNP
$LIPGNP$=log($IPGNP$)
$LNM1$=log of $M1$
$LCRMA$=log($CRMA$)
$LRGGNP$=log($GGNP/IPGNP$)
$R3ML$=interest rate on three-month bank loans.

Source of data: DATASTREAM SERVICES at the University of Warwick, on the basis of seasonally unadjusted OECD data.

Diagnostic Tests

The diagnostic test performed in tables 3A.1–3A.12 are those provided by the package Microfit 3.0. In particular, the main references are the following:

The diagnostic test for *serial correlation* is the one suggested by Godfrey (1978a, 1978b).

The diagnostic test for the *functional form* is Ramsey's RESET-test (Ramsey, 1969, 1970).

The diagnostic test for the *normality of regression residuals* is the Jarque–Bera-test (Jarque and Bera, 1980; Bera and Jarque, 1981).

The tables with estimates and diagnostic tests are on pp. 78–84.

The diagnostic test for *heteroscedasticity* is based on the auxiliary regression

$$e^2_t = \text{const} + \beta \bar{y}_t$$

where e_t are the residuals of the regression and $\bar{y}_t$ the fitted values of the dependent variable. The auxiliary regression gives the LM- and F-test for the null hypothesis H_0: $\beta=0$.

The diagnostic test for *predictive failure* is the one suggested by Salkever (1976) and Dufour (1980).

Granger causality tests

Germany

Table 3A.1

Significance levels of monetary and credit indicators for forecasting real German GNP
Sample period: 1975Q1–1989Q3

Forecasted variable is $LRGGNP$; $LRGGNPP$ is regressed on 4 lags of itself, a constant, 4 lags of $LNM1$, 4 lags of $LCRMA$, 4 lags of $GTRBR$, 4 lags of $R3ML$, 4 lags of $LIPGNP$
Ordinary Least Squares Estimation
Sample period: 1975Q1–1989Q3

Joint test of zero restrictions on the coefficients of 4 lags of $R3ML$:

Lagrange Multiplier-Statistic	$CHI\text{-}SQ(4) = 2.9034$ [0.574]
Likelihood Ratio-Statistic	$CHI\text{-}SQ(4) = 2.9773$ [0.562]
F-Statistic	$F(4,34) = 0.43994$[0.779]

Joint test of zero restrictions on the coefficient of 4 lags of $GTRBR$:

Lagrange Multiplier-Statistic	$CHI\text{-}SQ(4) = 3.5882$ [0.465]
Likelihood Ratio-Statistic	$CHI\text{-}SQ(4) = 3.7020$ [0.448]
F-Statistic	$F(4,34) = 0.55042$[0.700]

Joint test of zero restrictions on the coefficient of 4 lags of $LCRMA$:

Lagrange Multiplier-Statistic	$CHI\text{-}SQ(4) = 2.1199$ [0.714]
Likelihood Ratio-Statistic	$CHI\text{-}SQ(4) = 2.1589$ [0.707]
F-Statistic	$F(4,34) = 0.31679$[0.865]

Joint test of zero restrictions on the coefficient of 4 lags of $LNM1$:

Lagrange Multiplier-Statistic	$CHI\text{-}SQ(4) = 22.3414$ [0.000]
Likelihood Ratio-Statistic	$CHI\text{-}SQ(4) = 28.0776$ [0.000]
F-Statistic	$F(4,34) = 5.1803$ [0.002]

Table 3A.2

Significance levels of Bank credit to manufacturing sector for forecasting stock of *M1*
Sample period: 1975Q1–1989Q3

Forecasted variable is *LNM1*; *LNM1* is regressed on 4 lags of itself, a constant, 4 lags of *LRGGNP*, 4 lags of *LCRMA*, 4 lags of *GTRBR*, 4 lags of *R3ML*, 4 lags of *LIPGNP*
Ordinary Least Squares Estimation
Sample period: 1975Q1–1989Q3

Joint test of zero restrictions on the coefficient of 4 lags of *LCRMA*:

Lagrange Multiplier-Statistic	$CHI\text{-}SQ(4)=14.2000[0.007]$
Likelihood Ratio-Statistic	$CHI\text{-}SQ(4)=16.2445[0.003]$
F-Statistic	$F(4,38)=\ 3.0112[0.030]$

Significance levels of *M1* for forecasting the Bank credit to the manufacturing sector

---

Forecasted variable is *LCRMA*; *LCRMA* is regressed on 4 lags of itself, a constant, 4 lags of *LRGGNP*, 4 lags of *LNM1*, 4 lags of *GTRBR*, 4 lags of *R3ML*, 4 lags of *LIPGNP*
Ordinary Least Squares Estimation
Sample period: 1975Q1–1989Q3

Joint test of zero restrictions on the coefficient of 4 lags of *LNM1*:

Lagrange Multiplier-Statistic	$CHI\text{-}SQ(4)=7.4101[0.116]$
Likelihood Ratio-Statistic	$CHI\text{-}SQ(4)=7.9184[0.095]$
F-Statistic	$F(4,38)=1.3645[0.264]$

United Kingdom

Table 3A.3

Significance levels of monetary and credit indicators for forecasting real UK GDP
Sample period: 1975Q2–1988Q4

Forecasted variable is *LRYUK*; *LRYUK* is regressed on 4 lags of itself, a constant,
4 lags of *LNM1*, 4 lags of *LCRIN*, 4 lags of *TRBR*, 4 lags of *ROV*, 4 lags of *LNIP*
Ordinary Least Squares Estimation
Sample period: 1975Q2–1988Q4

Joint test of zero restrictions on the coefficients of 4 lags of *TRBR*:

Lagrange Multiplier-Statistic	$CHI\text{-}SQ(4) = 7.3389[0.119]$
Likelihood Ratio-Statistic	$CHI\text{-}SQ(4) = 7.8770[0.096]$
F-Statistic	$F(4,30) = 1.1549[0.350]$

Joint test of zero restrictions on the coefficients of 4 lags of *ROV*:

Lagrange Multiplier-Statistic	$CHI\text{-}SQ(4) = 7.2994[0.121]$
Likelihood Ratio-Statistic	$CHI\text{-}SQ(4) = 7.8314[0.098]$
F-Statistic	$F(4,30) = 1.1477[0.353]$

Joint test of zero restrictions on the coefficients of 4 lags of *LCRIN*:

Lagrange Multiplier-Statistic	$CHI\text{-}SQ(4) = 8.5174[0.074]$
Likelihood Ratio-Statistic	$CHI\text{-}SQ(4) = 9.2540[0.055]$
F-Statistic	$F(4,30) = 1.3743[0.266]$

Joint test of zero restrictions on the coefficients of 4 lags of *LNM1*:

Lagrange Multiplier-Statistic	$CHI\text{-}SQ(4) = 11.2362[0.024]$
Likelihood Ratio-Statistic	$CHI\text{-}SQ(4) = 12.5689[0.014]$
F-Statistic	$F(4,30) = 1.9256[0.132]$

Table 3A.4

Significance levels of bank credit to industry for forecasting the stock of M1
Sample period: 1975Q2–1988Q4

Forecasted variable is $LNM1$; $LNM1$ is regressed on 4 lags of itself, a constant, 4 lags of $LRYUK$; 4 lags of $LCRIN$, 4 lags of $TRBR$, 4 lags of ROV, 4 lags of $LNIP$ Ordinary Least Squares Estimation Sample period: 1975Q2–1988Q4	
Joint test of zero restrictions on the coefficient of 4 lags of $LCRIN$:	
Lagrange Multiplier-Statistic	$CHI\text{-}SQ(4)=13.2995[0.010]$
Likelihood Ratio-Statistic	$CHI\text{-}SQ(4)=15.2251[0.004]$
F-Statistic	$F(4, 30)= 2.3920[0.073]$

Significance levels of $M1$ for forecasting the Bank credit to industry

Forecasted variable is $LCRIN$; $LCRIN$ is regressed on 4 lags of itself, a constant, 4 lags of $LRYUK$, 4 lags of $LNM1$, 4 lags of $TRBR$, 4 lags of ROV, 4 lags of $LNIP$ Ordinary Least Squares Estimation Sample period: 1975Q2–1988Q4	
Joint test of zero restrictions on the coefficient of 4 lags of $LNM1$:	
Lagrange Multiplier-Statistic	$CHI\text{-}SQ(4)=15.7640[0.003]$
Likelihood Ratio-Statistic	$CHI\text{-}SQ(4)=18.5756[0.001]$
F-Statistic	$F(4,30)= 3.0133[0.033]$

A note on the Hausman-test

The Hausman exogeneity test is composed of two phases: in the first phase the variable subject to exogeneity test must be regressed on a set of instruments. The residuals of this regression must be included, in a second phase, in the original regression containing the variable subject to the exogeneity test. If the coefficient referred to the residuals does not seem to be significant (according to the t-statistics), then the variable subject to test can be considered exogeneous with respect to the independent variable.

The variable $UHAUS$ corresponds to the residuals of the auxiliary regression of $LRYUK$ on a constant term, $LCRTO(-1)$ (for the United Kingdom), $LNIP(-1)$, $TRBR(-1)$ and $ROV(-1)$. It has been employed to run the Hausman-test of exogeneity of $LRYUK$ in the equations of the different credit aggregates considered for the United Kingdom and in the demand for money. The estimates for $LCRIN$ (table 3A.5) and $LCROIN$ (table 3A.6) have been implemented with IV, although in the estimates with OLS both for $LCRIN$ (table 3A.7) and for $LCROIN$ (table 3A.8) the null hypothesis of exogeneity of $LRYUK$ with respect to the various dependent variables was not rejected, at the 95 per cent level of confidence. Concerning *LCRTO*, the null hypothesis of exogeneity of *LRYUK* with respect to the various dependent variables was rejected, at the 95 per cent level of confidence, therefore the only estimates shown in the tables in the appendix are the ones with IV (table 3A.9).

For Germany, the equation for *LCRMA* has been estimated with IV only (table 3A.12) because in the Hausman-test of exogeneity of *LRGGNP* the null hypothesis of exogeneity of *LRGGNP* with respect of *LCRMA* has been rejected, at the 95 per cent level of confidence.

United Kingdom

Table 3A.5

Instrumental variable estimation

Dependent variable is *LCRIN*
List of instruments:
CONST   *LCRIN*(−2)   *ROV*(−1)   *RLCB*(−1)   *LNIP*(−1)   *LRYUK*(−1)
65 observations used for estimation 1975Q2–1991Q2

Regressor	Coefficient	Std. err.	T-ratio[prob]
CONST	0.91097	1.2250	0.74368[0.460]
LCRIN(−1)	0.51374	0.072708	7.0659 [0.000]
ROV	0.031864	0.0078062	4.0819 [0.000]
RLCB	−0.028554	0.0080649	−3.5405 [0.001]
LNIP	0.62970	0.12043	5.2285 [0.000]
LRYUK	0.16719	0.18808	0.88894[0.378]

R-squared	0.99792	*F*-Statistic $F(5, 59)$	5666.8[0.000]
R-bar-squared	0.99775	SE of regression	0.028261
Residual sum of squares	0.047124	Mean of dependent variable	10.2549
SD of dependent variable	0.59526	Value of IV minimand	0.0000
DW-Statistic	1.7661	Sargan's	NONE

Diagnostic tests

Test statistics	*LM* version	*F* version
A:Serial Correlation	*CHI-SQ*(4)=3.7365 [0.443]	Not applicable
B:Functional Form	*CHI-SQ*(1)=0.0047300[0.945]	Not applicable
C:Normality	*CHI-SQ*(2)=0.32609 [0.850]	Not applicable
D:Heteroscedasticity	*CHI-SQ*(1)=0.33578 [0.562]	Not applicable

A:Lagrange multiplier-test of residual serial correlation
B:Ramsey's RESET-test using the square of the fitted values
C:Based on a test of skewness and kurtosis of residuals
D:Based on the regression of squared residuals on squared fitted values

Table 3A.6

Instrumental variable estimation

Dependent variable is *LCROIN*
List of instruments:
CONST   LRYUK(−1)   *TRBR*(−1)   *ROV*(−1)   *LNIP*(−1)   *LCROIN*(−2)
67 observations used for estimation from 1975Q2 to 1991Q4

Regressor	Coefficient	Std. err.	T-ratio[prob]
CONST	−0.83194	1.2162	−0.68405[0.497]
LRYUK	0.15191	0.22228	0.68341[0.497]
TRBR	0.037268	0.014076	2.6476 [0.010]
ROV	−0.035671	0.013018	−2.7401 [0.008]
LNIP	0.12054	0.034311	3.5132 [0.001]
LCROIN(−1)	0.94234	0.028255	33.3512 [0.000]

R-squared	0.99918	*F*-Statistic *F*(5, 61	14791.6[0.000]
R-bar-squared	0.99911	SE of regression	0.029947
Residual sum of squares	0.054705	Mean of dependent variable	11.2562
SD of dependent variable	1.0029	Value of IV minimand	0.0000
DW-Statistic	1.6080	Sargan's	NONE

Diagnostic tests

Test statistics	*LM* version	*F* version
A:Serial Correlation	*CHI-SQ*(4)=8.3088 [0.081]	Not applicable
B:Functional Form	*CHI-SQ*(1)=1.2909 [0.256]	Not applicable
C:Normality	*CHI-SQ*(2)=8.6777 [0.013]	Not applicable
D:Heteroscedasticity	*CHI-SQ*(1)=0.96793[0.325]	Not applicable

A:Lagrange multiplier-test of residual serial correlation
B:Ramsey's RESET-test using the square of the fitted values
C:Based on a test of skewness and kurtosis of residuals
D:Based on the regression of squared residuals on squared fitted values

Table 3A.7

Ordinary Least Squares estimation

Dependent variable is *LCRIN*
65 observations used for estimation from 1975Q2–1991Q2

Regressor	Coefficient	Std. err.	T-ratio[prob]
CONST	0.79068	0.50182	1.5756[0.120]
LRYUK	0.19881	0.082961	2.3964[0.020]
LNIP	0.64950	0.067195	9.6660[0.000]
ROV	0.032855	0.0043631	7.5303[0.000]
RLCB	−0.028242	0.0040932	−6.8997[0.000]
LCRIN(-1)	0.49464	0.048295	10.2420[0.000]

R-squared	0.99796	F-Statistic $F(5, 59)$	5786.0[0.000]
R-bar-squared	0.99779	SE of regression	0.027969
Residual sum of squares	0.046155	Mean of dependent variable	10.2549
SD of dependent variable	0.59526	Maximum of log-likelihood	143.3988
DW-Statistic	1.7666	Durbin's h-Statistic	1.0213[0.307]

Diagnostic tests

Test statistics	*LM* version	*F* version
A:Serial Correlation	$CHI\text{-}SQ(4)=4.4276[0.351]$	$F(4, 55)=1.0051[0.413]$
B:Functional Form	$CHI\text{-}SQ(1)=2.3694[0.124]$	$F(1, 58)=2.1942[0.144]$
C:Normality	$CHI\text{-}SQ(2)=0.34882[0.840]$	Not applicable
D:Heteroscedasticity	$CHI\text{-}SQ(1)=0.047012[0.828]$	$F(1, 63)=0.045599[0.832]$

A:Lagrange multiplier-test of residual serial correlation
B:Ramsey's RESET-test using the square of the fitted values
C:Based on a test of skewness and kurtosis of residuals
D:Based on the regression of squared residuals on squared fitted values

Notes:
Hausman exogeneity test
Test for *LRYUK* (log of the real UK GDP) in the equation of *LCRIN* (log of
bank credit to UK industry):
Dependent variable is *LCRIN*
67 observations used for estimation from 1975Q2 to 1991Q2
T-ratio for *UHAUS* −0.93370
The null hypothesis of exogeneity of *LRYUK* with respect to *LCRIN* is not
rejected at the 95 per cent level of confidence
In any case the equation for *LCRIN* has been estimated with IV as well, as shown
in table 3A.8.

Table 3A.8

Ordinary Least Squares estimation

Dependent variable is *LCROIN*
67 observations used for estimation from 1975Q2 to 1991Q4

Regressor	Coefficient	Std. err.	T-ratio[prob]
CONST	−0.71216	0.48714	−1.4619[0.149]
LRYUK	0.12476	0.089084	1.4004[0.166]
TRBR	0.012572	0.0060654	2.0728[0.042]
ROV	−0.011654	0.0057443	−2.0289[0.047]
LNIP	0.10470	0.029404	3.5607[0.001]
LCROIN(-1)	0.95169	0.015402	61.7914[0.000]

R-squared	0.99936	*F*-Statistic *F*(5, 61)	19077.9[0.000]
R-bar-squared	0.99931	SE of regression	0.026371
Residual sum of squares	0.042422	Mean of dependent variable	11.2562
SD of dependent variable	1.0029	Maximum of log-likelihood	151.6514
DW-Statistic	1.4756	Durbin's *h*-Statistic	2.1635[0.031]

Diagnostic tests

Test statistics	*LM* version	*F* version
A:Serial Correlation	*CHI-SQ*(4)= 4.8465[0.303]	$F(4, 57)$=1.1112[0.360]
B:Functional Form	*CHI-SQ*(1)= 5.3024[0.021]	$F(1, 60)$=5.1566[0.027]
C:Normality	*CHI-SQ*(2)=29.5368[0.000]	Not applicable
D:Heteroscedasticity	*CHI-SQ*(1)= 1.0968[0.295]	$F(1, 65)$=1.0818[0.302]

A:Lagrange multiplier-test of residual serial correlation
B:Ramsey's RESET-test using the square of the fitted values
C:Based on a test of skewness and kurtosis of residuals
D:Based on the regression of squared residuals on squared fitted values

Notes:
Hausman exogeneity test
Test for *LRYUK* (log of the real UK GDP) in the equation of *LCROIN* (log of bank credit to UK sectors other than industry):
Dependent variable is *LCROIN*
67 observations used for estimation from 1975Q2 to 1991Q2
T-ratio for *UHAUS* −1.1935.
The null hypothesis of exogeneity of *LRYUK* with respect to *LCROIN* is not rejected at the 95 per cent level of confidence
In any case the equation for *LCROIN* has been estimated with IV as well, as shown in table 3A.9

Table 3A.9

Instrumental variable estimation

Dependent variable is LCRTO			

List of instruments:
CONST   LCRTO(−2)   ROV(−1)   TRBR(−1)   LNIP(−1)   LRYUK(−1)
67 observations used for estimation from 1975Q2 to 1991Q4

Regressor	Coefficient	Std. err.	T-Ratio[Prob]
CONST	−2.0808	1.1444	−1.8182[0.074]
LCRTO(−1)	0.89730	0.032254	27.8196[0.000]
ROV	−0.028443	0.013603	−2.0909[0.041]
TRBR	0.030492	0.014708	2.0731[0.042]
LNIP	0.13561	0.037605	3.6061[0.001]
LRYUK	0.40326	0.21640	1.8635[0.067]

R-squared	0.99887	F-Statistic F(5, 61)	10804.5[0.000]
R-bar-squared	0.99878	SE of regression	0.031267
Residual sum of squares	0.059636	Mean of dependent variable	11.5937
SD of dependent variable	0.89506	Value of IV minimand	0.0000
DW-Statistic	1.6072	Sargan's	NONE

Diagnostic tests

Test statistics	LM version	F version
A:Serial Correlation	CHI-SQ(4)=3.0776[0.545]	Not applicable
B:Functional Form	CHI-SQ(1)=2.0112[0.156]	Not applicable
C:Normality	CHI-SQ(2)=1.0142[0.602]	Not applicable
D:Heteroscedasticity	CHI-SQ(1)=0.0060655[0.938]	Not applicable

A:Lagrange multiplier-test of residual serial correlation
B:Ramsey's RESET-test using the square of the fitted values
C:Based on a test of skewness and kurtosis of residuals
D:Based on the regression of squared residuals on squared fitted values

Table 3A.10

Ordinary least squares estimation

Dependent variable is *LCRIN*
55 observations used for estimation from 1975Q2 to 1988Q4

Regressor	Coefficient	Std. err.	T-ratio[prob]
CONST	0.80853	0.52561	1.5383[0.130]
LRYUK	0.23453	0.092817	2.5268[0.015]
LNIP	0.69678	0.072310	9.6360[0.000]
ROV	0.028274	0.0063952	4.4212[0.000]
RLCB	−0.024785	0.0055098	−4.4983[0.000]
LCRIN(-1)	0.45151	0.054591	8.2708[0.000]

R-squared	0.99697	F-Statistic $F(5, 49)$	3220.9[0.000]
R-bar-squared	0.99666	SE of regression	0.027950
Residual sum of squares	0.038279	Mean of dependent variable	10.0879
SD of dependent variable	0.48341	Maximum of log-likelihood	121.8885
DW-Statistic	1.7188	Durbin's h-Statistic	1.1405[0.254]

Diagnostic ests

Test statistics	LM version	F version
A:Serial Correlation	$CHI\text{-}SQ(4)=4.2798[0.369]$	$F(4, 45)=0.94928[0.445]$
B:Functional Form	$CHI\text{-}SQ(1)=1.4592[0.227]$	$F(1, 48)=1.3082[0.258]$
C:Normality	$CHI\text{-}SQ(2)=0.26491[0.876]$	Not applicable
D:Heteroscedasticity	$CHI\text{-}SQ(1)=0.018527[0.892]$	$F(1, 53)=0.017859[0.894]$
E:Predictive Failure	$CHI\text{-}SQ(10)=10.0813[0.433]$	$F(10, 49)=1.0081[0.450]$
F:Chow-test	$CHI\text{-}SQ(6)=5.1444[0.525]$	$F(6, 53)=0.85740[0.532]$

A:Lagrange multiplier-test of residual serial correlation
B:Ramsey's RESET-test using the square of the fitted values
C:Based on a test of skewness and kurtosis of residuals
D:Based on the regression of squared residuals on squared fitted values
E:A Test of adequacy of predictions (Chow's second test)
F:Test of stability of the regression coefficients

Table 3A.11

Ordinary least squares estimation

Dependent variable is *LCROIN*
55 observations used for estimation from 1975Q2 to 1988Q4

Regressor	Coefficient	Std. err.	*T*-ratio[prob]
CONST	−0.24058	0.48144	−0.49971[0.620]
LRYUK	0.030167	0.090003	0.33518[0.739]
TRBR	0.0093062	0.0060473	1.5389[0.130]
ROV	−0.0080704	0.0059709	−1.3516[0.183]
LNIP	0.091203	0.032716	2.7877[0.008]
LCROIN(-1)	0.97143	0.019598	49.56900[0.000]

R-squared	0.99921	*F*-Statistic *F*(5, 4)	12339.0[0.000]
R-bar-squared	0.99913	SE of regression	0.023823
Residual sum of squares	0.027809	Mean of dependent variable	10.9378
SD of dependent variable	0.80556	Maximum of Log-likelihood	130.6756
DW-statistic	1.5695	Durbin's *h*-Statistic	1.6137[0.107]

Diagnostic tests

Test statistics	*LM* version	*F* version
A:Serial Correlation	*CHI-SQ*(4)=2.7165[0.606]	*F*(4, 45)=0.58453[0.675]
B:Functional Form	*CHI-SQ*(1)=0.62058[0.431]	*F*(1, 48)=0.54778[0.463]
C:Normality	*CHI-SQ*(2)=3.1669[0.205]	Not applicable
D:Heteroscedasticity	*CHI-SQ*(1)=0.15508[0.694]	*F*(1, 53)=0.14987[0.700]
E:Predictive Failure	*CHI-SQ*(12)=25.7471[0.012]	*F*(12, 49)=2.1456[0.031]
F:Chow-test	*CHI-SQ*(6)=12.9889[0.043]	*F*(6, 55)=2.1648[0.060]

A:Lagrange multiplier-test of residual serial correlation
B:Ramsey's RESET-test using the square of the fitted values
C:Based on a test of skewness and kurtosis of residuals
D:Based on the regression of squared residuals on squared fitted values
E:Test of adequacy of predictions (Chow's second test)
F:Test of stability of the regression coefficients

Germany

Table 3A.12

Instrumental variable estimation

Dependent variable is *LCRMA*
List of instruments:
| *CONST* | *LRGGNP*(−1) | *R3ML*(−1) | *GTRBR*(−1) | *LCRMA*(−2) |
| *S1* | *S2* | *S3* | | |

36 observations used for estimation from 1980Q4 to 1989Q3

Regressor	Coefficient	Std. err.	*T*-ratio[prob]
CONST	2.0754	0.42284	4.9083[0.000]
LRGGNP	1.4692	0.24238	6.0615[0.000]
R3ML	−0.011491	0.0062548	−1.8371[0.077]
GTRBR	0.025318	0.010378	2.4395[0.021]
LCRMA(−1)	0.16554	0.14324	1.1557[0.258]
S1	0.086400	0.024644	3.5059[0.002]
S2	0.063588	0.017967	3.5392[0.001]
S3	0.035790	0.016013	2.2351[0.034]

R-squared	0.95211	*F*-Statistic $F(7, 28)$	79.5211[0.000]
R-bar-squared	0.94013	SE of regression	0.021845
Residual sum of squares	0.013362	Mean of dependent variable	5.2647
SD of dependent variable	0.089284	Value of IV minimand	0.0000
DW-Statistic	1.6555	Sargan's	NONE

Diagnostic tests

Test statistics	*LM* version	*F* version
A:Serial Correlation	*CHI-SQ*(4)= 5.8909[0.207]	Not applicable
B:Functional Form	*CHI-SQ*(1)=11.8081[0.001]	Not applicable
C:Normality	*CHI-SQ*(2)= 0.10794[0.947]	Not applicable
D:Heteroscedasticity	*CHI-SQ*(1)= 0.68453[0.408]	Not applicable

A:Lagrange multiplier-test of residual serial correlation
B:Ramsey's RESET-test using the square of the fitted values
C:Based on a test of skewness and kurtosis of residuals
D:Based on the regression of squared residuals on squared fitted values

Part II

Interactions between credit and industry: firms' market power and banks' liquidity preference

4 Investments and monetary policy with oligopsony in the market for credit

Introduction

After analysing (in chapter 3) the macroeconomic implications of securitization, we focus now our attention on the interactions between banks and industrial firms, and begin by analysing an almost completely neglected issue: the macroeconomic effects of industrial firms' oligopsonistic power in the credit market.

Of course, the macroeconomic implications of imperfect competition in the goods market have been studied not only by the heteorodox literature, but also in New-Keynesian models with a more conventional description of the monetary sector (such as Blanchard and Kiyotaki, 1987; Starz, 1989), in connection with the debate on non-neutrality of monetary policy. However, imperfect competition in the credit market has not received the same attention: while a few (rare) theoretical contributions have analysed the macroeconomic implications of bank market structure on the deposit market or on the 'supply side' of credit by focusing on the behaviour of monopolistic or oligopolistic bankers[1] (and in any case without explicitly formalizing any interaction between the real and the financial sectors of the economy), the issue of market concentration on the 'demand side' of the credit market has been practically ignored.[2] This is rather surprising if one thinks that in bank-oriented financial systems the industrial firms' (or banks') market power in the credit sector might have a direct effect on the equilibrium credit supply and interest rates and, as a consequence, in the real sector.

It is even more surprising that the heterodox literature concerned with the connections between industrial structure and the macroeconomy (such as Cowling, 1982 or Henley, 1990) and the theories of the monetary circuit

---

[1] See, for instance, Van Hoose (1983, 1985).
[2] Bank market structure, has actually been the object of a few recent empirical analyses (Conti, 1991; Cottarelli et al., 1995; Cottarelli and Konrelis, 1994) but still only limited to the 'supply side of credit' and without a proper complete theoretical model.

have completely neglected this issue, since changes in the market structure of the credit sector could potentially affect not only the macroeconomic equilibrium but also the transmission mechanism of monetary policy.

In order to clarify this point and introduce the object of analysis of the present chapter, let us introduce a very simplified example of oligopsony in the credit market. Its purpose is only to stress the relevance of the issues discussed in this chapter by showing the 'first-impact' effect of an exogenous change in the oligopsonistic power of industrial firms.

Let us assume that in the market there are N equal enterprises producing a unique homogeneous good and using a production process whose characteristics may be described by a standard Cobb–Douglas production function

$$y = g(k) = Bk^{\alpha}; \text{ with } 0 < \alpha < 1 \qquad (4.1)$$

where y is output and k the capital (at constant prices) employed by the single representative enterprise. Let us assume that the enterprises are owned by n firms, each of the same dimension, so that N/n is the number of enterprises per firm. Again, we will assume that N, the number of enterprises, is fixed, while n, the number of firms, can vary. In this way, by letting n vary, the scale of the economy will not be affected. Only the degree of concentration, or in other words the number of enterprises per firm N/n, will be affected. Let us also assume that the life of physical capital is one period only, so that k is both the capital stock of each enterprise and the investment of each enterprise, and that the firms finance their investment only with borrowed money. We have then

$$K = Nk \qquad (4.2)$$

where the aggregate stock of capital also corresponds to the aggregate level of investments.

Let us assume that the reduced form of the monetary sector of the economy may be described by the following constant elasticity credit supply function:

$$S(r,\theta) = A \, r_L^{\beta} \theta \qquad (4.3)$$

where A is a constant, r_L the interest rate on loans granted to the enterprises, β the interest rate elasticity of the supply function of loans, and θ a generic parameter describing the monetary policy such that the higher θ, the more expansive the monetary policy.[3]

---

[3] A Cobb–Douglas (in general linearized by taking logs) is often employed in empirical works for the equations describing the behaviour of financial assets. The analytical form of the credit supply function employed here is similar to the one employed by Van Hoose (1985) for the inverse deposit asset demand function. In particular, Van Hoose defines

Let us now analyse the behaviour of the firms. Let us assume that the credit market can be described by an oligopsony à la Cournot, while the industrial firms operate on perfectly competitive goods markets. The problem of the representative firm can be described as follows:

$$\max \ \pi = \frac{N}{n} \cdot [g(k) - r_L k] \tag{4.4}$$

$$\text{s.t.} \ \frac{N}{n} k + K' = S(r_L, \theta) \tag{4.5}$$

where π are the profits, and K' the capital of all the other firms. The constraint of the optimization problem of the firm can be rewritten as:

$$k = [S(r_L, \theta) - K']n/N \tag{4.5'}$$

Assuming that the second-order conditions are satisfied, the following first-order conditions can be obtained:

$$\partial \pi / \partial r_L = \frac{N}{n} \left([\partial g(k)/\partial k - r_L] \frac{\partial S(\cdot)}{\partial r_L} \cdot \frac{n}{N} - k \right) = 0 \tag{4.6}$$

hence

$$\frac{\partial g(k)}{\partial k} = r_L + \frac{kN/n}{\partial S(\cdot)/\partial r_L} \tag{4.7}$$

since in equilibrium we have $S(r_L \theta,) = Nk$, then we can write

$$\alpha B k^{\alpha-1} = r_L \left(1 + \frac{1}{n\beta} \right)$$

hence, solving for k:

$$k = \left(\frac{1}{B\alpha} (1 + 1/n\beta) r_L \right)^{1/(\alpha-1)} \tag{4.8}$$

from $S(r, \theta) = A \ r_L^{\ \beta} \theta = Nk$
we get $r_L = (Nk/A\theta)^{1/\beta}$
substituting for r_L in (4.8):

$$k = \left(\frac{1}{B\alpha} (1 + 1/n\beta)(Nk/A\theta)^{1/\beta} \right)^{1/(\alpha-1)}$$

$r_{Dt} = \beta r_{st}^{\alpha} D_t^{\varepsilon}$ with $\varepsilon, \ \alpha, \ \beta > 0$

where r_{Dt} is the interest rate on deposits, ε is the deposit demand elasticity, $-\alpha/\varepsilon$ is the elasticity of the demand for deposits with respect to the security rate, r_{st} is the interest rate on the securities held by banks, and β measures the absolute size of the market.

which, solving for k, determines:

$$k=\left(\frac{1}{B\alpha}(1+1/n\beta)(N/A)^{1/\beta}\right)^{\beta/[\beta(\alpha-1)-1]}\cdot\theta^{1/[1-\beta(\alpha-1)]} \qquad (4.9)$$

In this very simplified framework, the effect of the monetary policy on investments of industrial firms will be given by:

$$dK/d\theta=d(Nk)/d\theta$$

In order to verify whether variations in the degree of concentration in the industrial sector exert any influence on the effectiveness of monetary policy, we have to see how $dK/d\theta$ varies when n varies. We therefore have to calculate the derivative of $dK/d\theta$ with respect to n. Since N, the number of enterprises, is fixed, and the firms are identical, we can equivalently look at the multiplier

$$\frac{d(dk/d\theta)}{dn}$$

We can then calculate

$$dk/d\theta=\frac{1}{1-\beta(\alpha-1)}\left(\frac{1}{B\alpha}(1+1/n\beta)(N/A)^{1/\beta}\right)^{\beta/[\beta(\alpha-1)-1]}\cdot\theta^{\beta(\alpha-1)/[1-\beta(\alpha-1)]} \qquad (4.10)$$

$$\frac{d(dk/d\theta)}{dn}=\frac{-\beta}{[\beta(\alpha-1)-1]^2}\left(\frac{1}{B\alpha}[1+1/(n\beta)](N/A)^{1/\beta}\right)^{[\beta(2-\alpha)+1]/[\beta(\alpha-1)]}$$

$$\cdot(1/B\alpha)(N/A)^{1/\beta}[-1/(n^2\beta)]\theta^{\beta(\alpha-1)/[1-\beta(\alpha-1)]} \qquad (4.11)$$

From (4.5) and (4.6) it is easy to verify that

$$dk/d\theta>0 \text{ and } d(dk/d\theta)/dn>0$$

The first inequality simply shows that an expansionary monetary policy (described by an increase in the value of θ) increases the level of investments of the industrial firms. The second inequality shows that the multiplier of the monetary policy is an increasing function of n. This means, in other words, that an increase in the degree of competition in the industrial sector will increase (in this simplified framework) the effectiveness of monetary policy.

This is due to the fact that an exogenous increase in the degree of competition in the industrial sector (in other words a reduction in the oligopsonistic power of firms in the credit market), by reducing the difference existing between marginal productivity of capital and interest rate implies, *ceteris paribus*, an increase in the optimal level of investments of the industrial firms. Such an expansionary effect also causes an increase in the absolute value of the monetary policy multiplier.

Of course, with a more elaborated model containing several assets and a more detailed description of the banking sector, the results will be not so clear-cut, as shown in the rest of this chapter, where the banks' behaviour is modelled by introducing a few assumptions consistent with the rest of this work.

In the orthodox literature, the role of banks is still a controversial theoretical issue: as discussed in chapter 2, it has been explained as a response to financial markets' imperfections and incompleteness (Diamond, 1984), which means that financial intermediaries would be unnecessary and irrelevant in a complete market system *à la* Arrow–Debreu.

This study is actually meant to isolate the effects of market concentration without explicitly considering other forms of market imperfection, although it is well known and accepted that information asymmetry is a key feature in understanding the credit market. For this purpose, the model contains an assumption of exogenous change in the industrial structure. This might seem to contrast with the approach followed by most contemporary contributions in industrial economics, which tend to regard market structure as an endogenous variable, resulting from the strategic interaction of rival firms. Nevertheless, the purpose of this work is not to analyse how market structure is affected by the strategic behaviour of the industrial firms, but to see whether, and how, a change in the market structure (no matter how such a change occurs, therefore even an exogenous change) can affect the macroeconomy, within a theoretical framework of partial equilibrium.

Since the matter under investigation here is very specific (the oligopsonistic power of industrial firms on the credit market), some simplifying assumptions are made in order to 'isolate' the interaction between banks and industrial firms from other forms of interactions involving the goods market. In particular, while assuming oligopsony on the market for bank credit, the goods market is assumed to be perfectly competitive.

Such an assumption, apart from dramatically simplifying the structure of the model, might describe those institutional contexts, relatively frequent in Continental Europe, where large industrial firms are exposed to international competition in the goods market while enjoying some market power on the internal market for credit. This situation can also be determined by the pro-competitive effects caused, in many institutional contexts, by financial deregulation. In the model of the next section, an increase in the degree of competition (a reduction in the degree of concentration) of the industrial sector on the credit market has an expansionary effect, increasing the optimal level of investments of the industrial firms. The effects of modifications in the market structure on the transmission mechanism of monetary policy can be decomposed into a 'direct' or 'first-impact' effect, and various 'indirect effects'. The latter are given by modifications in the equilibrium level of investments, determined by changes in the equilibrium levels of the relevant interest rates, caused, in their turn, by the original exogenous change in the industrial structure. It is shown that the 'direct' and the 'indirect effects' might have opposite signs. In particular, while the 'direct effect' of an increase in the degree of competition in the industrial sector determines an increase in the effectiveness of monetary policy, the 'indirect effects' are more complex and affected by the cross-elasticities of the various demand and supply functions.

In the next section the assumption of oligopsony in the market for credit is introduced in a portfolio allocation model *à la* Tobin and Brainard (1963). It is a very popular and rather conventional 'partial' model, where the interdependencies with non-financial variables are disregarded. Furthermore, it must be interpreted as a short run equilibrium model because some dynamic phenomena such as asset accumulation and the feedbacks from non-financial developments are ignored. Consistently with the concern of the present study for the macroeconomic consequences of the differences between securitized and bank-oriented financial systems, the conventional model *à la* Tobin and Brainard includes a modelling assumption which takes into account the intrinsic difference between assets traded in spot markets (for instance Government bonds) and assets associated with a long-run contractual relationship between lender and borrower (i.e. banks' loans): 'active liability management'. This assumption starts from the consideration that premature termination of loans may upset established customer relations. If dissatisfied customers decide to take their business somewhere else, this causes future loss of deposits. Therefore, it may be profitable for the banks to accommodate the need for 'liquid' assets by increasing (when necessary) the supply of deposits. All this determines a functional link (in some authors, even a fixed spread) between the interest rate on banks' loans and the interest rate on deposits.

'Active liability management', discussed in detail by Wood (1974), has been introduced by Hörngren (1985) in a standard portfolio model, where it is associated with Okun's (1981) distinction between auction and customer markets, where the latter are characterized by long-term commitments between banks and their customers. Since it describes a situation where banks are concerned with keeping their long-run relationships with customers, it seems to be appropriate for a model of oligopsony in the credit market.

Oligopsony in a market for credit model *à la* Tobin and Brainard

In this model the credit market behaves according to a standard portfolio model *à la* Tobin and Brainard (1963).

The agents operating in the model are industrial firms, banks, monetary authorities and households, and all variables are expressed in real terms. The industrial sector is constituted, as in the preliminary model on p. 88, by symmetric enterprises, producing the same homogeneous good, with a strong market power with respect to the banking system. The physical capital lasts for one period only, and corresponds to the level of investments. All industrial enterprise investments are financed by loans obtained from banks. Following the literature on banks' behaviour, it is assumed, concerning the demand and supply for financial assets, that the partial derivatives with respect to their own interest rates are greater, in absolute values, than the cross-derivatives.

The industrial sector

The characteristics and behaviour of the industrial sector are analogous to the ones of the simplified introductory model on p. 88. Therefore equations (4.1), (4.2), (4.4), (4.5), (4.5'), (4.6) and (4.7) and the assumptions associated with them are assumed to hold. Obviously, the function $S(\cdot)$ appearing in these equations is very different here, since it is the result of a more complex model, as shown below. Let us start now from (4.7), rewritten as follows:

$$\partial g(k)/\partial k - r_L - \frac{1}{n}\frac{kN}{\partial S(\cdot)/\partial r_L} = 0 \qquad (4.7')$$

Since all of the N enterprises are equal, and since N is kept constant (while n/N varies), we can equivalently evaluate the impact of monetary policy on the variable k instead of $K = Nk$. Given that we have, for symmetry, $S(\cdot) = Nk$, we can write:

$$\alpha Bk^{(\alpha-1)} - r_L - \frac{1}{n}\frac{S(\cdot)}{\partial S(\cdot)/\partial r_L} = f_1(k, r_L, n) = 0 \qquad (4.12)$$

or, solving with respect to k:

$$k = \frac{1}{B\alpha}\left(r_L + \frac{1}{n}\cdot\frac{S(\cdot)}{\partial S(\cdot)/\partial r_L}\right)^{1/(\alpha-1)} \qquad (4.13)$$

(4.12), obtained from the first-order conditions of the optimization problem of the representative firm, describes the relation between the marginal productivity of capital and r_L (or, equivalently, a relation between k and r_L), in a context characterized by oligopsonistic power of industrial firms on the market for credit.

The monetary authority

Given the level of public debt, which is assumed to be fixed and exogenous, the monetary authority implements open market operations by purchasing public bonds from households and banks. Apart from open market operations, the central bank could use another instrument of monetary policy, the level of reserve requirements. In what follows we will, for simplicity, consider only open market operations, since an analysis focused on the use of reserve requirements as an instrument of monetary policy would give similar results, and open market operations are more commonly employed as an instrument of monetary policy.

Let us assume that the characteristics of the economy are such that the payments are performed using deposits only. The money base of the economy is then given by bank reserves.

We are dealing with a partial equilibrium model, where we neglect the feedback between the real sector and wealth, and if we neglect the foreign sector, the balance sheet of the central bank can be simplified as follows:

$$B^C = R \qquad (4.14)$$

where B^C is the amount of public bonds held by the central bank and R represents the reserves of commercial banks. The reserves that the commercial banks hold at the central bank include reserve requirements and free reserves. The central bank, while varying the value of B^C, performs open market operations, and controls the money base. Therefore the money base, BM, will be equal to B^C. The balance sheet of the central bank can be regarded as a sort of budget constraint which has to be satisfied *ex post*, given the behavioural relations of the model.

The public debt BT (exogenous) will be given by

$$BT = B^P + B^b + B^C \qquad (4.15)$$

or, equivalently

$$BT = B^P + B^b + BM \qquad (4.15')$$

where B^b is the quantity of public bonds held by private banks.

Households

This model does not include labour,[4] but only capital, as a production factor owned by households, who receive all the income produced. The private sector has a wealth endowment which enters the demand functions

---

[4] We could make a *ceteris paribus* assumption, and imagine that the labour is included in the constant B which appears in the production function $y = Bk^\alpha$.

for financial assets. For simplicity, in the absence of the foreign sector, the financial wealth will be equal to the public sector debt, which is exogenous and fixed. We will limit our analysis to the impact of a variation in the degree of concentration in the industrial sector on the optimal level of investments, and on the monetary policy multiplier. The level of financial wealth is assumed to be constant.

Let us assume that households do not lend funds directly to industrial firms, but can choose only between investing in public bonds or bank deposits. This last assumption, which also appears in other versions of portfolio models *à la* Tobin and Brainard, like Hörngren (1985), is theoretically justifiable by the fact that banks enjoy scale economies in collecting information, or by the fact that the size of negotiated loans may be large with respect to the financial wealth of the single individual. This assumption could also describe the context of a bank-oriented or non-securitized financial system, such as discussed in chapters 2 and 3. The households' demand for bank deposits is the following

$$D^P = D^P(\overset{-}{r_B}, \overset{+}{r_D}, \overset{-}{r_L}, \overset{+}{W}) \text{ (demand for bank deposits)} \qquad (4.16)$$

where W is the wealth, r_B the interest rates on public bonds, r_D the interest rate on bank deposits, and r_L that on bank loans.

Consistently with the portfolio allocation theory (and with Tobin and Brainard's, 1963, model) we can now define the other demand functions for financial assets and liabilities by the public:

$$B^P = B^P(\overset{+}{r_B}, \overset{-}{r_D}, \overset{-}{r_L}, \overset{+}{W}) \text{ (demand for public bonds)} \qquad (4.17)$$

$$L^d = L^d(\overset{+}{r_B}, \overset{-}{r_L}, \overset{+}{r_D}, \overset{+}{W}) \text{ (demand for banks' loans by the public)} \qquad (4.18)$$

The budget constraint of the public is:

$$W = B^P + D^P - L^d \qquad (4.19)$$

and, as we have said, we have $W = BT$.

The banking sector

The banks finance themselves by issuing deposits. As in 'active liability management', the total amount of deposits is affected by the amount of credit that the banks are willing to supply to the industrial firms.

Once the reserve requirement has been satisfied, the funds collected can be invested in loans, unremunerated free reserves, or public bonds.

If for the sake of simplicity we neglect shares, the balance-sheet constraint of banks is given by:

$$L^s + R + B^b = D \qquad (4.20)$$

where L^s = supply of credit
R = commercial banks' liquid reserves at the central bank
D = bank deposits
The banks' demand for public bonds will depend positively on the interest rate on public bonds, and negatively on the interest rate on loans (which represents an opportunity cost) and the interest rate on time deposits. We have, therefore:

$$B^b(\overset{+}{r_B}, \overset{-}{r_D}, \overset{-}{r_L}) \qquad (4.21)$$

Public bonds, unlike loans, can be sold on a spot market. This means that public bonds held by commercial banks can be regarded both as a form of portfolio investment and a partially liquid asset, to the extent that it is traded on a 'spot' market instead of a 'customer' market.

The reserves R include the reserve requirements and free liquid reserves. Therefore, if we define:

q_0 = reserve requirements coefficient
q' = free liquidity ratio of the commercial banks

we can write:

$$R = q_0 \cdot D + q' \cdot D$$
$$= (q_0 + q') \cdot D$$

As in the 'active liability management' approach, a distinction is drawn between the 'spot' market for Government bonds and the 'customer markets' for loans, which is the result of long-run contractual relationships between lender and borrower. In such a context r_L may be regarded as the main opportunity cost for R. Furthermore, the higher the reserve requirements, the more costly it is for the bank to hold free reserves. Therefore we will assume, for simplicity, that q' behaves as follows:

$$q' = q'(\overset{-}{q_0}, \overset{-}{r_L})$$

Considering equation (4.14), we have:

$$BM = R = q(\overset{-}{q_0}, \overset{-}{r_L})D \qquad (4.22)$$

with $q = q_0 + q'$ and $0 < q < 1$
then: $D = BM/q(\cdot)$
and defining

$$q(\cdot)=1/\Phi(\cdot) \tag{4.23}$$

we have:

$$D=BM\cdot\overset{+}{\Phi(r_L)} \tag{4.24}$$

and, obviously, $\Phi>1$.

We introduce at this point a simplifying assumption on the link between r_L and r_D in order to be able to solve the simultaneous system of the market-clearing conditions.[5] Our assumption is actually less restrictive than the ones made in many models of the banking sector (as, for instance, Modigliani and Papademos, 1980, 1987), and is not very different from the one made by Hörngren (1985): having defined

$$r_D=r_D(r_L) \tag{4.25}$$

we assume, for simplicity

$$\partial r_L/\partial r_D=1 \tag{4.26}$$

In other words, we are simply assuming here that there is a generical functional link between the interest rate on bank loans r_L and the interest rate on deposits r_D. This functional link is determined on the one hand by the competition among banks, on the other by the presence of administrative costs for the banks (which prevents, in equilibrium, r_D and r_L being equal).

Therefore, concerning the non-bank agents, we have:

$$B^P=B^P(\overset{+}{r_B}, \overset{-}{r_D}(r_L), \overset{-}{r_L}, \overset{+}{W}) \text{ (demand for public bonds)} \tag{4.27}$$

$$D^P=D^P(\overset{-}{r_B}, \overset{+}{r_D}(r_L), \overset{-}{r_L}, \overset{+}{W}) \text{ (demand for bank deposits)} \tag{4.28}$$

$$L^d=L^d(\overset{+}{r_B}, \overset{-}{r_L}, \overset{+}{r_D}(r_L), \overset{+}{W}) \text{ (demand for banks' loans by}$$

$$\text{households)} \tag{4.29}$$

Concerning (4.27), (4.28) and (4.29), the sign of the partial derivatives with respect to r_L is unambiguously defined, if we consider that we have assumed that for each asset the partial derivative with respect to the own interest rate is greater, in absolute value, than the cross-derivatives, and we take into account (4.26).

Having said that there is a functional link $r_D=r_D(r_L)$ between the interest rate on loans and the interest rate on deposits, we assume that the deposits depend on the profitability of bank loans:

---

[5] Modigliani and Papademos (1980, 1987) assume that in a perfectly competitive banking sector, neglecting the administrative costs, the equality $r_D=r_L$ holds.

$$\frac{\partial D(\cdot)}{\partial r_L}=\frac{\partial \Phi(\cdot)}{\partial r_L}\cdot BM>0 \qquad (4.30)$$

In (4.30), the interest rate r_D does not appear because the bank 'recognizes' the link existing between r_L and r_D, and (4.19) expresses the amount of deposits that the banking system is willing to issue, given the fact that banks issue remunerated deposits to provide themselves with loanable funds, which are to be supplied on the loans market, remunerated at the rate r_L.

Introducing the functional relation $r_D(r_L)$ into the banks' demand for public bonds does not create any particular problem:

$$B^b(\overset{+}{r_B}, \overset{-}{r_D}(r_L), \overset{-}{r_L}) \qquad (4.31)$$

The banks' balance-sheet constraint can also be written as follows:

$$B^b+L^s=[\Phi(\cdot)-1]\cdot BM \qquad (4.32)$$

(4.32) implicitly defines the supply of banks' loans:

$$L^s=L^s(\overset{-}{r_B}, \overset{+}{r_L},\overset{+}{BM})=[\Phi(\overset{+}{r_L})-1]\cdot BM-B^b(\overset{+}{r_B},\overset{-}{r_L}) \qquad (4.33).$$

Considering (4.33) and (4.29), we can define the function $S(\cdot)$, which represents the supply of bank credit available to industrial firms:[6]

$$S(\overset{-}{r_B}, \overset{+}{r_L},\overset{+}{BM})=[\Phi(\overset{+}{r_L})-1]\cdot BM-B^b(\overset{+}{r_B}, \overset{-}{r_L})-L^d(\overset{+}{r_B}, \overset{-}{r_L}) \qquad (4.34)$$

From (4.30), we have $\partial L^d/\partial r_L<0$. This can be easily verified if we look at (4.29), and we consider two assumptions that we have made earlier: the first is that the derivatives of the demand and supply functions with respect to their own interest rates are greater, in absolute value, than the cross-derivatives; the second is that $\partial r_D/\partial r_L=1$.

Equilibrium conditions

Since the money base is exogenous, there are three relevant financial assets in our model: bank loans, public bonds and bank deposits.

Moreover, we must add (4.12) to the equilibrium conditions of the asset markets. (4.12) defines a relation between the marginal productivity of capital and interest rate on the loans market and, given the elasticity of output with respect to capital in the production function, a relation between the optimal level of investments and the interest rates. It contains the information concerning the oligopsonistic power of industrial firms in

---

[6] It might be interesting to remark that the supply of bank credit closely recalls (in the way it has been obtained) that of the model by Bernanke and Blinder (1988).

the credit market. Since the market for bank credit is described by an oligopsony 'à la Cournot', we cannot properly define a demand function for the industrial firms' capital, but we have an optimizing decision taken by the firms simultaneously with the decision of the monetary authority concerning the value of the monetary policy instrument, given the behaviour functions of the agents operating on the asset markets. Therefore, the value for k chosen by the individual enterprise (and as a consequence the aggregate value $K=Nk$, since in an oligopsony à la Cournot the behaviour of firms is symmetrical) is the level of investments resulting from the first-order conditions of the optimization problem of the firm. k can be intuitively thought of as the equilibrium value in a game describing the behaviour of the n oligopsonists, given the banks' credit supply available to industrial firms.

In our model we have three markets: loans, deposits and public bonds, and three interest rates: r_B, r_L and r_D. (4.12) determines the relation existing between k, r_L, and the other interest rates which appear in the supply of bank credit. Since the (competitive) market structure in the banking sector determines r_D through (4.18), and since W and BT are given, we actually have three unknowns: k, r_B, r_L:

$$\alpha Bk^{\alpha-1}-r_L-\frac{1}{n}\frac{S(\cdot)}{\partial S(\cdot)/\partial r_L}=0=f_1(k,r_L,r_B,n,BM) \tag{4.12}$$

Considering that the aggregate investments Nk are equal to banks' credit supply available to industrial firms $S(\cdot)$, we obtain the equilibrium condition for the market for bank loans:

$$Nk-S(\overset{+}{r_L}, \overset{-}{r_B}, \overset{+}{BM})=f_2(k, r_L, r_B, BM)=0 \tag{4.35}$$

Considering (4.27), (4.31) and (4.15′), we obtain the condition of equilibrium on the market for public bonds:

$$B^b(\overset{+}{r_B}, \overset{-}{r_L})+B^P(\overset{+}{r_B}, \overset{-}{r_L},\overset{+}{W})+BM - BT=f_3(r_L, r_B, BM)=0 \tag{4.36}$$

Combining (4.24) and (4.28) we obtain the equilibrium conditions for bank deposits:

$$D^P(\overset{-}{r_B}, \overset{+}{r_D}(r_L), \overset{-}{r_L}, \overset{+}{W}) - D(\overset{+}{r_L}, \overset{+}{BM})=f_4(r_L, r_B, BM)=0 \tag{4.37}$$

(4.12) is 'microeconomic', since it is obtained from the first-order conditions of the optimization problem for the industrial firm. (4.35), (4.36) and (4.37) are, on the contrary, 'macroeconomic' conditions.

Given (4.19), defining the wealth constraint of the private sector, (4.14), defining the budget constraint of the central bank and (4.15′), one can see, after doing some substitutions, that (4.36) and (4.37) are not independent. We will therefore drop (4.37), and we consider only the remaining three.

Comparative statics

We must now first analyse the effects of a variation of the exogenous variables BM and n (money base and number of oligopsonistic firms in the market) on the endogenous variables of the system. Then, after calculating the value of the monetary policy multiplier dk/dBM, we can see how a variation in n affects this multiplier, taking into account the direct effects of a variation of n on the money multiplier dk/dBM, as well as the 'indirect' effects induced through a modification (induced by a variation in n) in the equilibrium levels of the interest rates and in the higher-order derivatives of the functions relevant for the comparative statics.

Assuming that the vector function F, composed of the four functions f_1, f_2, f_3 and f_4, satisfies the conditions of the implicit function theorem, we may implement a comparative static analysis considering the effects of a variation in the monetary policy instrument BM and in the number of firms n, on the endogenous variables of the system. We consider (4.12), (4.35) and (4.36), and differentiating them at the equilibrium we get the following system:

$$\begin{bmatrix} \dfrac{\partial f_1}{\partial k} & \dfrac{\partial f_1}{\partial r_L} & \dfrac{\partial f_1}{\partial r_B} \\[2ex] \dfrac{\partial f_2}{\partial k} & \dfrac{\partial f_2}{\partial r_L} & \dfrac{\partial f_2}{\partial r_B} \\[2ex] 0 & \dfrac{\partial f_3}{\partial r_L} & \dfrac{\partial f_3}{\partial r_B} \end{bmatrix} \begin{bmatrix} dk \\[2ex] dr_L \\[2ex] dr_B \end{bmatrix} = \begin{bmatrix} -\dfrac{\partial f_1}{\partial BM} & -\dfrac{\partial f_1}{\partial n} \\[2ex] -\dfrac{\partial f_2}{\partial BM} & 0 \\[2ex] -\dfrac{\partial f_3}{\partial BM} & 0 \end{bmatrix} \begin{bmatrix} dBM \\[2ex] dn \end{bmatrix} \qquad (4.38)$$

We assume that (4.38) is stable; the appendix (p. 105) contains the algebraic details concerning (4.27), and an explanation of the signs of all the relevant partial derivatives. Let us define as A the matrix on the left hand side of (4.38), Δ the determinant of the matrix A, and a_{ij} the element of matrix A placed in the ith row and jth column. We have then:

$$dr_B/dn = \overset{+}{\dfrac{1}{\Delta}} \left(-\overset{-}{\dfrac{\partial f_1}{\partial n}} \overset{+}{a_{21}} \overset{-}{a_{32}} \right) > 0 \qquad (4.39)$$

$$dr_L/dn = \overset{+}{\dfrac{1}{\Delta}} \left[-\left(-\overset{-}{\dfrac{\partial f_1}{\partial n}} \right) \overset{+}{a_{21}} \overset{+}{a_{33}} \right] > 0 \qquad (4.40)$$

$$dk/dn = \frac{1}{\Delta}\left[\left(-\frac{\partial f_1}{\partial n}a_{22}a_{33}\right)-\left(-\frac{\partial f_1}{\partial n}a_{23}a_{32}\right)\right]>0 \tag{4.41}$$

(4.41) is satisfied because we have assumed that the derivatives with respect to their own interest rates are greater, in absolute value, than the cross-derivatives. As shown in the appendix, this implies that

$$|a_{22}| > |a_{23}| \text{ and } |a_{33}| > |a_{32}|$$

In the appendix (p. 105) it is also shown, given our assumptions, that $\Delta>0$. One sees from (4.39), (4.40) and (4.41) that an exogenous increase of the degree of competition (a reduction of the degree of concentration) in the industrial sector increases the interest rate on loans, public bonds and the optimal level of investments for the industrial firms. This happens because a reduction in the degree of concentration in the industrial sector, reducing the spread between marginal productivity of capital and interest rate on loans, leads to an expansionary effect.

Let us now consider the effect of monetary policy:

$$dr_L/dBM = \frac{\overset{+}{1}}{\Delta}\left\{[\overset{-}{a_{11}}(\Phi(\cdot)-1)\overset{+}{a_{33}}]+[\overset{+}{a_{13}}\overset{+}{a_{21}}(-1)]-[\overset{-}{a_{11}}\overset{+}{a_{23}}(-1)]+\right.$$
$$\left.-\left(-\frac{\overset{+}{\partial f_1}}{\partial BM}\right)\overset{+}{a_{21}}\overset{+}{a_{33}}\right\}<0 \tag{4.42}$$

$$dr_B/dBM = \frac{\overset{+}{1}}{\Delta}\left\{[\overset{-}{a_{11}}\overset{-}{a_{22}}(-1)]+\left(-\frac{\overset{+}{\partial f_1}}{\partial BM}\right)\overset{+}{a_{21}}\overset{-}{a_{32}}\right.$$
$$\left.-[\overset{-}{a_{12}}\overset{+}{a_{21}}(-1)]-[\overset{-}{a_{11}}(\Phi(\cdot)-1)\overset{+}{a_{32}}]\right\}<0 \tag{4.43}$$

$$dk/dBM = \frac{\overset{+}{1}}{\Delta}\left\{\left(-\frac{\overset{+}{\partial f_1}}{\partial BM}\right)\overset{-}{a_{22}}\overset{+}{a_{33}}+[\overset{-}{a_{12}}\overset{+}{a_{23}}(-1)]\right.$$
$$+[\overset{+}{a_{13}}(\Phi(\cdot)-1)\overset{-}{a_{32}}]-[\overset{+}{a_{13}}\overset{-}{a_{22}}(-1)]-[\overset{-}{a_{12}}(\Phi(\cdot)-1)\overset{+}{a_{33}}]$$
$$\left.-\left(-\frac{\overset{+}{\partial f_1}}{\partial BM}\right)\overset{+}{a_{23}}\overset{-}{a_{32}}\right\} \tag{4.44}$$

The sign of (4.44) is uncertain. When (4.44) is negative, the monetary policy will have perverse effects, i.e. an increase in the money base will reduce the level of investments instead of increasing it. The monetary policy will not have perverse effects when the positive addenda of (4.44) are greater than the absolute value of the negative addenda, i.e. when:

$$a_{12}a_{23}(-1)-[a_{12}(\Phi(\cdot)-1)\,a_{33}]-\left(-\frac{\partial f_1}{\partial BM}\right)a_{23}a_{32}$$

$$>\left|\left(-\frac{\partial f_1}{\partial BM}\right)a_{22}a_{33}+a_{13}(\Phi(\cdot)-1)a_{32}+a_{13}a_{22}\right| \qquad (4.45)$$

At this point, the most obvious strategy would be to perform the analysis for two different cases: effective and perverse monetary policy. However, if the monetary policy has perverse effects (i.e. if (4.45) is not met), it seems to be quite pointless to investigate how and whether market structure affects it because, in any case, a monetary policy with perverse effects is not advisable. Therefore, in what follows, the analysis will be implemented only for the case of monetary policy effectiveness, i.e. when (4.45) is true.

This means that $dk/dBM>0$, i.e. the multiplier of monetary policy (4.44) is positive.

Now let us analyse the effects on the monetary policy multiplier of an exogenous increase in the degree of competition (decrease in the degree of concentration) in the industrial sector. Differentiating (4.44) with respect to n we get the following expression, which will be positive when an increase in the number of industrial firms, keeping constant the number of enterprises, increases the effectiveness of monetary policy:

$$d(dk/dBM)/dn=\frac{\dfrac{dA1}{dn}\cdot\Delta-\dfrac{d\Delta}{dn}\cdot A1}{\Delta^2} \qquad (4.46)$$

All of the algebraic details, as well as the definitions of $A1$, $dA1/dn$, $d\Delta/dn$, and the determination of (4.46), are explained in the appendix (p. 105). The appendix also shows that (4.46) can be decomposed as follows:

$$d(dk/dBM)/dn=ED+EB+EL+ES+E\Delta \qquad (4.47)$$

As shown in the appendix, the sign of ES is uncertain, while the signs of ED, EB, EL and $E\Delta$ are unambiguously determined. In particular, we have $ED>0$, $EB<0$, $EL>0$, $E\Delta>0$. (4.47) tells us that the effect of an exogenous increase in the number of industrial firms (decrease in the degree of concentration) on the monetary policy multiplier dk/dBM can be decomposed into five parts. EB and EL can be intuitively thought of as the effect on dk/dBM induced through a variation in the equilibrium level of r_L and r_B, originated by an increase in n. ED can be thought of as a direct 'first impact' effect on the multiplier dk/dBM of a variation in n (which corresponds to the 'direct effect' $d(dk/d\theta)/dn$ of (4.11) in the preliminary and oversimplified example on p. 88). $E\Delta$ is the effect of a variation of n on the determinant of matrix A, on the left-hand side of (4.38). ES is, like $E\Delta$, a 'structural' effect of a variation in n, since they are both determined by the variations (due to a change in n) in the absolute values of derivatives and cross-derivatives of (4.38). In other words, an increase in n, by affecting the equilibrium level of the various assets and interest rates, determines a 'movement' along the functions appearing in (4.38), with (possibly) different absolute values of their first derivatives. The magnitude of ES and $E\Delta$ depends therefore on some analytic assumptions (i.e. magnitudes of the curvatures and cross-elasticities) that can be made about the functions of (4.38). Another way of interpreting these 'structural' effects is the following: having said that an increase in n affects the equilibrium values of the various assets and interest rates, to the extent that the first derivatives and cross-derivatives of the functions of (4.38) are not constant and contribute to determining the monetary policy multipliers (4.31), (4.32) and (4.33), the different values of these first derivatives associated to different equilibria correspond to different degrees of intensity of monetary policy. For instance, an increase in the values of ES and $E\Delta$ means that the modification in the equilibrium has also determined a modification in the 'intensity' of the transmission mechanism of monetary policy. ES also contains the effects of a variation of n on the marginal productivity of capital (due to the fact that a variation in n, by changing the equilibrium level of k, changes the point of the production function chosen by each enterprise) and on the elasticity of the slope of the credit supply function (since a different point on the function $S(.)$ is 'picked up' by the firms, again due to a modification of n). $E\Delta$ contains analogous effects, taking the form of modifications in the determinant of matrix A on the left-hand side of (4.38).

In other words, the direct effect on dk/dBM of an increase in n also brings some market perturbations, i.e. effects on the equilibrium values of the interest rates and other variables, as well as variations in the 'sensitivity' of the system to market signals.

Conclusions

The macroeconomic effects of an exogenous change in the oligopsonistic power of industrial firms on the credit market have been analysed by introducing a simplified industrial sector in a standard portfolio model à la Tobin and Brainard. The formal setting is meant to provide a simplified framework of analysis for the macroeconomic effects of changes in the industrial structure on the demand side of the market for credit.

The first (predictable) result is that an increase in the degree of competition (reduction in the degree of concentration) generates expansionary effects on the investments.

The same theoretical framework has been employed to analyse whether and how the transmission mechanism of the monetary policy is affected by the above-mentioned exogenous change in the oligopsonistic power of industrial firms. This part of the analysis has been performed by looking at how the monetary policy multiplier is affected by change in the industrial structure, and the results are obviously less clear-cut than in the preliminary and oversimplified example (with one asset only) contained in the Introduction to this chapter, where an increase in the degree of competition (reduction in the oligopsonistic power of the industrial firms) increases the effectiveness of monetary policy.

In the standard portfolio model à la Tobin and Brainard (1963) changes in the monetary policy multiplier caused by an increase in n have been decomposed into 'direct' (or, one could say, 'first-impact') and several 'indirect' effects. The 'direct' effect of an augmented degree of competition (decrease in the oligopsonistic power) among the industrial firms tends to increase the absolute value of the money multiplier.

The 'indirect' effects consist of the modifications in the intensity of the monetary policy multiplier given by the fact that an increase in n modifies the equilibrium level of the interest rate on Government bonds (EB), loans (EL) and other 'structural' variables of the system (ES and $E\Delta$); in this way, we 'move along' the functions of (4.38) and 'pick up' different values of the first derivatives, which implies changes in sensitiveness of the system to monetary policy measures.

If the magnitude of the 'structural' effects ES and $E\Delta$ is small, then the overall effect can be seen by comparing the direct 'fist-impact' effect ED and the indirect effect EL (determined by changes in the equilibrium level of the loans interest rate caused by an increase in the number of factories per firm): an increase in the degree of competition increases the effectiveness of monetary policy in the (more realistic case) where $|ED+EL|>EB$.

Appendix

(4.38) is obtained by differentiating at the equilibrium functions f_1, f_2, and f_3. We then consider linear approximations of the functions f_1, f_2, and f_3. This implies that the second derivatives of the behavioural functions are null. We also assume that the generical derivative $\partial f_i / \partial r_L \partial r_B$ is null:

$$-\frac{\partial f_1}{\partial BM} = \frac{\partial}{\partial BM} \left((1/n) \cdot \frac{S(\cdot)}{\partial S(\cdot)/\partial r_L} \right)$$

$$= \frac{1}{n} \cdot \frac{[\Phi(\cdot)-1] \cdot \left(\dfrac{\partial \Phi(\cdot)}{\partial r_L} \cdot BM - \dfrac{\partial B^b}{\partial r_L} - \dfrac{\partial L^d}{\partial r_L} \right) - \dfrac{\partial \Phi(\cdot)}{\partial r_L} [BM(\Phi(\cdot)-1) - B^b - L^d]}{\left(\dfrac{\partial \Phi(\cdot)}{\partial r_L} \cdot BM - \dfrac{\partial B^b}{\partial r_L} - \dfrac{\partial L^d}{\partial r_L} \right)^2} > 0$$

$$-\frac{\partial f_2}{\partial BM} = (\Phi(\cdot)-1) > 0$$

$$-\frac{\partial f_3}{\partial BM} = -1$$

$$-\frac{\partial f_1}{\partial n} = -\frac{1}{n^2} \frac{S(\cdot)}{\partial S(\cdot)/\partial r_L} < 0$$

$$\frac{\partial f_1}{\partial k} = \alpha(\alpha-1)Bk^{\alpha-2} = a_{11} < 0$$

$$\frac{\partial f_1}{\partial r_L} = -1 - \frac{1}{n} \partial \left(\frac{S(\cdot)}{\partial S(\cdot)/\partial r_L} \right) / \partial r_L$$

which can be rearranged as follows:

$$\frac{\partial f_1}{\partial r_L} = -1 - \frac{1}{n} \left(1 - \frac{E}{\epsilon} \right)$$

where $\varepsilon = [\partial S(\cdot)/\partial r_L][r_L/S(\cdot)]$ is the credit supply elasticity with respect to the interest rate; and

$$E=[\partial^2 S(\cdot)/\partial r_L^2]\left(\frac{r_L}{\partial S(\cdot)/\partial r_L}\right)$$

is the elasticity of the slope of the same function. However, since we are considering linear approximations of the functions at the equilibrium, and we further assume that the generical derivative $\partial^2 f_i/\partial r_L \partial r_B$ is null, we will have $E=0$, hence:

$$\frac{\partial f_1}{\partial r_L}=-1-\frac{1}{n}=a_{12}<0$$

Concerning the remaining signs, we will have:

$$\frac{\partial f_1}{\partial r_B}=-\frac{\partial S(\cdot)/\partial r_B}{\partial S(\cdot)/\partial r_L}\cdot(1/n)=a_{13}>0$$

$$\frac{\partial f_2}{\partial k}=N=a_{21}>0$$

$$\frac{\partial f_2}{\partial r_L}=-\partial S(\cdot)/\partial r_L=a_{22}<0$$

$$\frac{\partial f_2}{\partial r_B}=-\partial S(\cdot)/\partial r_B=a_{23}>0$$

$$\frac{\partial f_3}{\partial k}=a_{31}=0$$

$$\frac{\partial f_3}{\partial r_L}=\partial B^b/\partial r_L+\partial B^P/\partial r_L=a_{32}<0$$

$$\frac{\partial f_3}{\partial r_B}=\partial B^b/\partial r_B+\partial B^P/\partial r_B=a_{33}>0$$

Therefore, the sign pattern of matrix A on the left-hand side of (4.27) is the following:

$$\begin{bmatrix} - & - & + \\ + & - & + \\ 0 & - & + \end{bmatrix}$$

the determinant of matrix A is:

$$\Delta= (\overset{-}{a_{11}}\, \overset{-}{a_{22}}\, \overset{+}{a_{33}})+(\overset{+}{a_{13}}\, \overset{+}{a_{21}}\, \overset{-}{a_{32}})-(\overset{-}{a_{12}}\, \overset{+}{a_{21}}\, \overset{+}{a_{33}})-(\overset{-}{a_{11}}\, \overset{+}{a_{23}}\, \overset{-}{a_{32}})$$

Since we have assumed that in each demand or supply function the derivatives with respect to their own interest rate are bigger, in absolute value, than the cross-derivatives, we have:

$$|a_{22}|>|a_{23}|; \ |a_{33}|>|a_{32}|$$

and

$$|a_{12}|>|a_{13}|$$

which implies $\Delta>0$

In addition we have:

$$\partial a_{12}/\partial n=n^{-2}>0$$

$$\partial a_{13}/\partial n=n^{-2}\cdot\frac{\partial S(\cdot)/\partial r_B}{\partial S(\cdot)/\partial r_L}<0$$

$$d(\Phi(\cdot)-1)/dn=(\partial\Phi(\cdot)/\partial r_L)\cdot(dr_L/dn)$$

$$\frac{d}{dn}\left(-\frac{\partial f_1}{\partial BM}\right)=\frac{\partial}{\partial n}\left(-\frac{\partial f_1}{\partial BM}\right)+\frac{\partial}{\partial r_B}\left(-\frac{\partial f_1}{\partial BM}\right)\frac{dr_B}{dn}+\frac{\partial}{\partial r_L}\left(-\frac{\partial f_1}{\partial BM}\right)\frac{dr_L}{dn}$$

where:

$$\frac{d}{dn}\left(-\frac{\partial f_1}{\partial BM}\right)=(-1)\cdot n^{-2}\cdot(-\partial f_1/\partial BM)<0$$

$$\frac{\partial}{\partial r_L}\left(-\frac{\partial f_1}{\partial BM}\right)=[(\partial\Phi/\partial r_L)BM+(-\partial B^b/\partial r_L)$$
$$+(-\partial L^d/\partial r_L)]^{-2}[(\partial\Phi/\partial r_L)(\partial S(\cdot)/\partial r_L)$$
$$+(\partial\Phi/\partial r_L)(-\partial S(\cdot)/\partial r_L)]\cdot(1/n)=0$$

$$\frac{\partial}{\partial r_B}\left(-\frac{\partial f_1}{\partial BM}\right)=[(\partial\Phi/\partial r_L)BM+(-\partial B^b/\partial r_L)$$
$$+(-\partial L^d/\partial r_L)]^{-2}\cdot\{(\partial\Phi/\partial r_L)[(\partial B^b/\partial r_B)$$
$$+(\partial L^d/\partial r_B)]\}>0$$

At this point we are able to calculate the multiplier $d(dk/dBM)/dn$. Referring to (4.44), let us define:

$$A1=\left\{\left(-\frac{\partial f_1}{\partial BM}\right)a_{22}a_{33}+[a_{12}a_{23}\,(-1)]+[a_{13}(\Phi(\cdot)-1)a_{32}]\right.$$

$$\left.-[a_{13}a_{22}(-1)]-[a_{12}(\Phi(\cdot)-1)a_{33}]-\left(-\frac{\partial f_1}{\partial BM}\right)a_{23}a_{32}\right\}$$

Then the multiplier $d(dk/dBM)/dn$ can be written as follows:

$$d(dk/dBM)/dn=\frac{\dfrac{dA1}{dn}\cdot\Delta-\dfrac{d\Delta}{dn}\cdot A1}{\Delta^2} \tag{4.46}$$

$$d\Delta/dn=\frac{\partial a_{11}}{\partial k}\frac{dk}{dn}(a_{22}a_{33}-a_{23}a_{32})+\frac{\partial a_{13}}{\partial n}(a_{21}a_{32})-\frac{\partial a_{12}}{\partial n}(a_{21}a_{33})$$

Since we assumed that in each demand or supply function the derivatives with respect to their own interest rate are bigger, in absolute value, than the cross-derivatives, we have:

$$|\partial a_{12}/\partial n|>|\partial a_{13}/\partial n| \text{ and } |a_{33}|>|a_{32}|$$

which implies $d\Delta/dn<0$.

Having assumed $dk/dBM>0$, then we also have $A1>0$. The expression $-(d\Delta/dn)\cdot A1$, which is the second addendum at the numerator of (4.46), is therefore positive. Concerning the first addendum, we have:

$$dA1/dn=-\frac{\partial}{\partial n}\overbrace{\left(-\frac{\partial f_1}{\partial BM}\right)}^{+}(\overbrace{a_{22}a_{33}-a_{23}a_{32}}^{-})+\frac{\partial}{\partial r_B}\overbrace{\left(-\frac{\partial f_1}{\partial BM}\right)}^{+}\frac{dr_B}{dn}(\overbrace{a_{22}a_{33}-a_{23}a_{32}}^{-})$$

$$+\overbrace{\frac{\partial\Phi(\cdot)}{\partial r_L}}^{+}\frac{dr_L}{dn}(\overbrace{a_{13}a_{32}-a_{12}a_{33}}^{+})+(\partial a_{13}/\partial n)(\Phi(\cdot)-1)\overbrace{a_{32}}^{-}$$

$$-(\partial a_{12}/\partial n)\overbrace{(\Phi(\cdot)-1)}^{+}\overbrace{a_{33}}^{-}-\overbrace{(\partial a_{12}/\partial n)}^{+}\overbrace{a_{23}}^{+}+\overbrace{(\partial a_{13}/\partial n)}^{+}\overbrace{a_{22}}^{-} \qquad (4.48)$$

Let us further define:

$$ED=(1/\Delta)\frac{\partial}{\partial n}\left(-\frac{\partial f_1}{\partial BM}\right)(a_{22}a_{33}-a_{23}a_{32})>0 \qquad (4.49)$$

$$EB=(1/\Delta)\frac{\partial}{\partial r_B}\left(-\frac{\partial f_1}{\partial BM}\right)\frac{dr_B}{dn}(a_{22}a_{33}-a_{23}a_{32})<0 \qquad (4.50)$$

$$EL=(1/\Delta)\frac{\partial\Phi(\cdot)}{\partial r_L}\frac{dr_L}{dn}(a_{13}a_{32}-a_{12}a_{33})>0 \qquad (4.51)$$

$$ES=(1/\Delta)\left((\partial a_{13}/\partial n)(\Phi(\cdot)-1)a_{32}-(\partial a_{12}/\partial n)(\Phi(\cdot)-1)a_{33}\right.$$
$$\left.-(\partial a_{12}/\partial n)\,a_{23}+(\partial a_{13}/\partial n)\,a_{22}\right) \qquad (4.52)$$

$$E\Delta=(1/\Delta^2)[(d\Delta/dn)\cdot A1]>0 \qquad (4.53)$$

using definitions (4.48), (4.49), (4.50), (4.51), (4.52) and (4.53), we obtain (4.47)

$$d(dk/dBM)/dn = ED + EB + EL + ES + E\Delta \qquad (4.47)$$

The sign of ES (from (4.52)) is uncertain, while the signs of ED, EB, EL, $E\Delta$ are unambiguously determined.

5 Banks' assets and liquidity preference: an empirical investigation based on the free liquidity ratio for commercial banks

Introduction

Chapter 4 contains a model of oligopsony in the credit market and analyses the implications of an exogenous change in the market structure for the investments and the transmission mechanism of monetary policy. The analysis has been conducted within standard portfolio model à la Tobin and Brainard and not within a 'creditist' model in order to stress the fact that the issue of oligopsony in the credit market is not only relevant for the credit view, but also for more conventional modelling approaches. We begin this chapter by reversing the issue and pointing out a possible paradox: even in a completely bank-oriented financial system, without security markets, if the free liquid reserves are the mere result of unexpected shocks and the banks do not hold them as a deliberate investment (or even 'non-investment') decision, then the conventional 'money view' (and not the 'credit view') would hold. In other words, the correlation between bank credit and output would be a spurious regression determined by the banks' balance sheet constraint. This means that in a non-securitized financial system it might not be necessarily true that banks' assets are as relevant as money stock for the transmission mechanism of monetary policy, unless the investment decisions of the banking system, as well as its liquidity preference, can be modelled within an investment decision framework, where subjective valuations of profitability and risk play a precise role.

This last point is the object of the econometric analysis of the present chapter, where the free liquidity ratio for commercial banks is modelled as a 'non-investment' decision within a framework of investments with uncertainty and sunk costs and estimated for Italy, a country with a non-securitized financial system (at least definitively for the sampling period considered here: 1976Q1–1991Q4).

In Bernanke and Blinder's (1988) model and – more generally – in the 'credit view' approach, it is assumed that the banking system plays an important role in the allocation of financial funds, in contrast to the tradi-

110

tional orthodox approach that regards the banking system as a 'veil' on the economy. The main differences between the two approaches lie, of course, in the relevance of market imperfections and information asymmetries, but also in the relevance attributed to banks' autonomous financial investment and the way it affects the aggregate level of physical investment.

However here the emphasis is not on the 'special features of banks', but rather to what extent the free liquidity ratio in a non-securitized country can be empirically analysed as a 'liquidity preference' choice within an investment decision framework. In this context, the banks' loans would still reflect an 'autonomous' lending decision, independent from the stock of deposits and in spite of the aggregate balance-sheet constraint that links banks' assets and deposits in the 'creditists' macromodels (for instance, (2.8) or (2.10), see p. 37). In other words, if the non-remunerated liquid assets in the banks' portfolios reflect a non-investment decision, or a decision to postpone an investment, then a detailed empirical analysis of the banks' 'liquidity preference' could be a relevant source of information in assessing the macroeconomic relevance of the role of bank credit.

The fact of dealing with the empirical data of a non-securitized country is therefore a premise for the whole analysis, since the idea of modelling liquidity as the result of a decision of postponing investments that contain some degree of irreversibility has been developed recently in a few contributions in economic theory not at all concerned with modelling bank credit as a 'special' asset.[1]

The commercial banks' free liquid reserves were the object of a few empirical studies in the 1970s and in the early 1980s, in connection with the debate on the stability of the demand for money (for instance Cagan, 1969; Bryant, 1983; Langhor, 1981; Richter and Teigen, 1982; Wessels, 1982). Surprisingly, such empirical studies do not seem any longer to be a very central topic, although free liquid reserves play an important theoretical role for at least two reasons. First of all, the free liquidity ratio contributes to determining the money multiplier and, therefore, its behaviour directly affects the behaviour of the money stock. Endogeneity of the money supply is therefore a corollary of modelling the free liquidity ratio as a liquidity preference choice. Secondly, the free liquid reserves of commercial banks are commonly regarded as a 'shock absorber', due to their high degree of liquidity, which implies, as noted above, that the level of free liquid reserves can be regarded as a non-investment decision.

The next section briefly surveys the empirical literature on commercial

---

[1] For instance, Chamley (1993) interprets the general idea of 'liquidity preference' within a similar theoretical framework, while Messori and Tamborini (1995) show how free reserves can be explained as a 'precautionary stock' in view of the fact that an investor choses between non-marketable assets and perfectly liquid liabilities.

banks' free reserves and its theoretical foundations. The third section contains a brief non-formal description of the literature on (partially) irreversible investments under uncertainty, and some considerations on how this kind of literature might be used as an interpretative tool to describe the behaviour of free liquid reserves. The fourth section shows some empirical estimates based on a model that incorporates into a standard approach – based on the portfolio allocation theory – some theoretical aspects of the literature analysed in the third section. The fifth section draws a few conclusions. In particular, it will be argued that the empirical results presented in this chapter are broadly consistent with the idea that banks' assets are as important as banks' liabilities for the transmission of monetary shocks into the real economy, although the potential problems of observational equivalence with the conventional 'money view' mentioned earlier are not completely resolved since, as Bernanke (1993) points out, the 'credit view' and the 'money view' are not necessarily in conflict.

The appendix (p. 123) contains a detailed description of the econometric methodology.

A few comments on standard empirical works

The behaviour of the free liquidity ratio for commercial banks has often been related to the availability of liquidity and borrowing from the central bank (Langhor, 1981; Wessels, 1982; Richter and Teigen, 1982). The traditional background is provided by the portfolio allocation theory. The explanatory variables usually considered are the level of liquidity, as determined by the public and by the foreign sector (as in Richter and Teigen, 1982), some kind of opportunity cost, and the own yields on liquid assets, all of them summarized by some representative interest rate. In most empirical contributions, as often happens for the estimates of financial variables, the explanatory power of the equations describing borrowing from the central bank, or commercial banks' free liquidity ratio, is not very high. This fact is often justified by the high volatility of financial variables.

Arguing that free reserves are specially needed the more frequently the reserve requirement fluctuates, Richter and Teigen (1982) use the variance of constrained reserves as a proxy variable for the yield on free reserves. Since the required reserves ratio has in Italy been subject only to rare modifications, this solution does not seem to apply to the Italian case and in any case, the variance of liquid constrained reserves over 12 months turned out not to be significant in preliminary analyses performed with our data.

Some early studies (for example Cagan, 1969) consider the rate of interest on banks' borrowing from the central bank as a proxy for the yield on free reserves because the higher the free reserves ratio, the less likely it is that the banks need to borrow from the central bank; furthermore, the higher the interest rate on banks' borrowing, the more convenient it is to keep reserves. This point could be criticized because the same reasoning could apply to the interbank rate, or to the 'call money rate', whose behaviour is closely related to that of the Treasury bill rate which is regarded as an opportunity cost and not as a yield on reserves.

The rate of inflation and, possibly, its rate of growth, could capture some of the opportunity costs of holding free liquid reserves, especially in a context like the Italian one where the yield on free reserves has been kept constant at a very low level for a long time.

The setting of our model is partly similar to that of Richter and Teigen (1982). However, a significant difference lies in the fact that the own yield on free liquid reserves has been interpreted here according to the literature on investments with sunk costs under uncertainty, very briefly described in the next section.

A new possible interpretation of the free liquidity ratio for commercial banks

A new tool of interpretation for the free liquidity ratio of commercial banks may be provided by the recent literature on investment decisions under conditions of irreversibility and uncertainty (Bertola and Caballero, 1991; Dixit, 1992a, 1992b; Pindyck, 1991; Dixit and Pindyck, 1994), which provides a useful framework of interpretation for the decision of 'non-investing'. The purpose of the discussion of the present section is to provide an alternative theoretical interpretation of the variable employed as a proxy for the 'yield' on the free reserves of commercial banks which has always been a weak point of empirical works on this issue, given the fact that free reserves are usually non-remunerated and, therefore, the yield justifying their existence has to be defined on more theoretical grounds. Since many of the contributions mentioned at the beginning of this section provide exhaustive surveys on the literature on investments with sunk costs under uncertainty, only a brief summary of the main points of this approach will be presented here.

The literature on irreversible investments under uncertainty removes the implicit assumption of investment reversibility contained in most standard neoclassical models, which yields the familiar 'net present value' rule, stating that firms should take up a project of investment when the net present value of its cash flow is at least as large as its costs.

In the real world, though, investment decisions usually take place under the following conditions:

(a) Sunk costs, due to the fact that the investment might be firm-specific or industry-specific; in the case of bank loans and financial investments the presence of sunk costs – from the point of view of the bank – is due to the presence of a 'lemon problem': in other words, the bank invests in financial assets carrying some intrinsic risk of capital losses, due not only to the possible bankruptcy of a borrower, but also to potential unexpected changes in the market interest rates, that might determine a change in the market value of bank loans compared to other financial assets

(b) 'On-going' uncertainty concerning the future profitability of the specific investment, the latter being only inferred on the basis of probability calculus

(c) Relevance of decision timing: in other words, the investment can be delayed, allowing the firm (in our case, the bank) to collect further information on all of the variables affecting the investment profitability, before committing its resources.

These three conditions imply that the investor (in this case, the bank) has to take into account the potential positive 'value of waiting'. In this context, the investment decision has been described by using the parallel of the 'call option' in financial economics: the financial investment is not undertaken when the financial investment is 'only just in the money', while it is undertaken when the option is 'well in the money'. Therefore, the traditional 'net present value' rule could be transformed into a rule suggesting that *an investment should be undertaken if the net present value of its cash flow exceeds the purchase and installation cost by an amount at least equal to the value of keeping the option to invest the same resources elsewhere.*

The problem could be described simply as follows:

Let x_t be a variable directly affecting the level of financial profits (for instance, the price of the financial asset under consideration), let $\pi(x_t)$ be an indicator of the profitability of the financial investment, and let $F(x_{t+1}|x_t)$ be the probability distribution of $x_{t+1}|x_t$, i.e. the probability distribution of x_{t+1} given the value of x_t. Then, the value of having in hand a financial investment can be defined as follows:

$$V_1(x^*)=E_0\left\{\sum_{t=0}^{\infty}\pi(x_t)\Big|x_0=x^*\right\}$$

where β^t is the factor of discount from the (future) time to the present time t_0, and E_0 stands for 'expectation at time t_0'.

The value V_0 of having the option is given by the value of being free between choosing to invest immediately (by paying an immediate given cost, say k) and postponing the investment decision by one period. Formally, this could be described as follows.

$$V_0 = \max\{V_1(x_t) - k, \ \beta \cdot E[V_0(x_t + _1)|x_t]\}$$

With uncertainty, and for given expectations of x_{t+1}, it may be rational for the investor to postpone the investment and wait for new information. It can be proved[2] that the higher the level of 'on-going' uncertainty, the higher the value of 'keeping alive' the option to invest in the future relative to the value of 'having in hand' the investment project. In other words, an increase in the level of 'on-going' uncertainty increases the 'value of information'. Dixit (1989, 1992a, 1992b) has employed this simple idea to formally explain some empirical phenomena, such as the persistence of relatively high profit margins in the absence of barriers to entry. It has also been pointed out (in Pindyck, 1991; Dixit, 1992b) that this same theoretical framework can be applied to financial investments and bank credit, where the presence of a 'lemon premium' may cause financial investments to be partially irreversible. In many cases, the stochastic behaviour of the relevant state variable describing the 'on-going' uncertainty (in our case x_t) has been described by a geometric Brownian motion (Bertola and Caballero, 1991; Dixit, 1992a; Pindyck, 1988).

The implications of these results for our analysis are quite straightforward. To the extent that the future value of the bank assets is uncertain, the investment decision is partially irreversible because it carries certain sunk costs. Therefore, it seems reasonable to assume that for some financial investments the 'value of waiting' is greater than the value of 'having in hand' an investment project (i.e. in our case, a financial asset). In such a context, the bank needs a sort of 'buffer stock' asset; the investment into a 'buffer stock' asset could be assimilated to a 'non-investment' decision, taken in order to 'wait' for more information about those specific financial investments that contain sunk costs.

Assuming that the commercial banks' free liquid reserves play the role of temporary liquid assets, their demand will be higher the higher the 'value of waiting', i.e. the higher the degree of uncertainty about the future value of financial investments.

Since a big portion of banks' assets is constituted by direct credit to enterprises, it can be argued that the aggregate level of banks' free liquidity ratio (which is an aggregate stock of temporary liquid assets held by the banking system) might be affected by all those variables affecting the general degree of risk of the economy. An approximate measure of the risk of the economy might be given by the rate of variation of the price level, since it typically carries uncertain and asymmetric effects for the economy as a whole. This is particularly true in the Italian context where the rate of inflation has been seen (at least in economics and financial newspapers and

---

[2] See, for example, Bertola and Caballero (1991).

surveys) as a very informative variable – concerning the degree of uncertainty of the whole economy – to a larger extent than in other developed countries. Such a peculiarity might be explained by several reasons. First of all, given the structurally very high propensity to save in the Italian private sector, an acceleration of the inflation rate determines a risk of capital loss for a big portion of the population. This point is particularly relevant if we think that the Italian economy historically experienced an inflation rate not far from 20 per cent in the 1970s, until 1982. Secondly, again for structural reasons, the Italian industrial sector depends heavily on the imports of energy and oil. Therefore, whenever an acceleration of the inflation rate determines a pressure to devalue the Italian Lira, the industrial firms risk suffering a drastic and immediate increase in their costs. For these reasons, an increase of the inflation rate is often regarded by most of the press as a variable containing relevant information on the degree of risk of the whole economy.

In such a context, if the yield on the free liquid reserves is constituted by the 'value of waiting' for additional information on the financial investments, then the rate of growth of the price level should act as a proxy for the yield on the free liquid reserves and affect it positively. Therefore, the inflation rate – to the extent that it is interpreted as an indicator of the degree of uncertainty of the whole economy – should be regarded as a proxy for the 'value of waiting'.

Obviously, the size of a temporary asset (like free liquid reserves) might be affected by the volume of transactions performed by banks, and by the volume of credit intermediated. A variable that might capture the effect of such a 'transactionary' motivation on the free liquidity ratio might be the gross margin of banks' intermediation, or a proxy for it.

The model

The *free liquidity ratio* is defined as the ratio between the free reserves held by commercial banks at the central banks, and the total deposits. The estimates are based on quarterly data and have been implemented by following the 'general-to-specific' methodology. The definitions of all the variables considered and all the tables with all the estimates and diagnostic tests are shown in the appendix (p. 123).

As in Richter and Teigen (1982), it will be assumed that the free liquidity ratio for commercial banks depends on the level of the required reserves ratio, on the variations of the liquidity stock determined by the State and by the foreign sector, on the opportunity cost of holding reserves, and on the yield of liquid reserves (or on the convenience of holding them). The opportunity cost is typically described by a representative money market interest rate. The rate of interest on riskless alternative liquid assets in Italy is traditionally the rate on short-term Treasury bills. The own yield on free reserves in Italy has been kept fixed at 0.5 per cent for more than 30 years: obviously such a variable cannot properly describe the dynamics of the own yield on banks' free reserves.

Concerning the own yield of liquid reserves, while Richter and Teigen argue that the free liquid reserves are most necessary the higher the variance of the reserve requirement, in this work it will be assumed – on the basis of the literature on investment under uncertainty and with sunk costs mentioned above – that the free liquidity ratio depends positively on the degree of uncertainty of the whole economy, summarized by the rate of growth of the price level. On the other hand, the free liquidity ratio should also be positively correlated to the reallocation flow of financial resources among different financial assets. This could be positively correlated to the degree of uncertainty in the environment, but also to the margin of intermediation, given that the higher the profitability of bank intermediation, the higher the incentives to raise additional financial funds. The latter can be thought of as a transactionary component of the demand for liquid reserves.

If the bank's financial investment is regarded as partially irreversible and subject to uncertainty, and is assumed to be alternative to the choice of keeping the funds invested in liquid assets, then the free liquidity ratio should be positively correlated to the 'value of waiting' for further information about new financial investments, as argued above. If the 'value of waiting' is a concept associated to the degree of uncertainty in the economy (in the sense that the higher the degree of uncertainty, the higher the value of 'waiting for further information'), then the free liquidity ratio should be positively correlated with the rate of growth of the price level, which will be used here as a proxy for the degree of uncertainty of the whole economy. The variable employed for this purpose is the rate of variation of the implicit deflator of the gross domestic product (GDP), henceforth *DINF*. Since the growth rate of the price level is calculated with respect to two consequent periods of time, qualitatively similar information could be captured by a suitable lag structure of the price level. Therefore, in the appendix (p. 123), an alternative specification has also been implemented, with the price levels (whose suitable lag structure will again be determined by following the general-to-specific approach) instead of its rate of growth *DINF*. As shown in the appendix, the results are qualitatively very similar to those obtained with the variable *DINF*.

It must be said, however, that the validity of this empirical specification is confined to a 'high inflation regime', like Italy during the period under consideration.

The dependent variable is defined, as in Richter and Teigen (1982), as the ratio between the free bank reserves – or unconstrained bank reserves – and total bank deposits, i.e. the current account, saving deposits, *plus* the deposit certificates of the central banks. In the estimates, such a variable is defined as *L3*. As in Richter and Teigen, it has been assumed that free reserves are affected by the behaviour of reserve requirements, and that higher levels of reserve requirements would reduce the need for free reserves as a liquid asset, given that liquidity would in that case be less scarce (since the banks might be able, in case of need, to temporarily diverge from the reserve requirements by supporting some cost). Furthermore, the required reserves are relevant also because the higher their level, the more costly (in terms of opportunity cost) it is to keep free liquid reserves, because in this way banks have to waive a larger amount of potentially profitable financial investments. For these reasons, it is assumed here that the free liquidity ratio is negatively correlated with the coefficient of reserve requirements (defined as *L1*).[3]

As in Richter and Teigen, it is assumed that the free liquidity ratio is affected by variations in the aggregate liquidity determined by the public sector and the foreign sector. The two variables considered here for this purpose are quite similar to the ones employed by Richter and Teigen: the first, defined as *G*, is the ratio between the variation of the credits of the Bank of Italy with the public sector and the average level of bank deposits over the period considered; the second, defined as *FX*, is the ratio between the variation of the net foreign position of the bank of Italy and the average level of deposits over the period considered.

As mentioned earlier, and on the basis of the literature on investments irreversibility, we assume that the free liquidity ratio should be higher the higher the degree of uncertainty and risk characterizing the whole economy. Therefore, since in the present model the proxy for the 'value of waiting' is (as discussed above) *DINF*, then the dependent variable *L3* is expected to be positively correlated with *DINF*.

Finally, the variable *RDIFF3*, defined as the difference between the rate of interest on the bonds issued by special credit institutions (*RBCI*), and the rate of discount (*RD*), have been considered.[4]

---

[3] Using the levels of *L1* instead of its variance as a regressor constitutes, in our opinion, a more general approach: in fact, since we are following the general-to-specific methodology, and our general unrestricted model contains four lags, if it is the variability rather than the level of reserve requirements that matters, this should be evident from the final dynamic structure of the model which could suggest, if necessary, a re-specification of the whole model according to the results of the diagnostic tests.

[4] There are several reasons that justify a variable so defined. First of all, *RBCI* can be regarded as a representative medium–long-term interest rate, while *RD* is – obviously – a

RDIFF3 could be regarded as a proxy for banks' profitability because, being determined by the difference between a long-run and a short-run interest rate (and therefore containing information on the term structure of the interest rates), it provides information about one of the most typical roles of the banking system: transforming the maturity and degree of risk of financial assets. In addition, in Italy, for a large part of the time series here considered, many small banks operating only at a local level were investing most of their funds in assets issued by special credit institutions operating in the medium and long run. This situation gave rise to the phenomenon known in the Italian context as 'double intermediation'.

To the extent that *RDIFF3* contains information on banks' profitability, it should be regarded as an opportunity cost of holding free reserves, and should be expected to be negatively correlated with *L3*. On the other hand, if the free liquid reserves are mainly a temporary liquid asset determined by the process of funds reallocation, we should expect the variations of *RDIFF3* to be positively correlated with *L3* because changes in the term structure of the interest rate should determine reallocations of the banks' financial funds.

The time series considered for the estimates starts in 1975 in order to exclude the year of the first oil shock, 1974. Since quarterly data have been employed for the estimates, a general unrestricted model with four lags has been defined, since, as argued in econometric literature, such a number of lags is sufficient to 'capture' the dynamic behaviour of a model defined over quarterly data.

The package Microfit version 3.0 has been employed for the estimates.

The appendix p. 123 contains the definition of all the variables and the tables containing the results of the estimates and the tests in detail (tables 5A.1–5A.6, pp. 125–31).

Following the general-to-specific methodology, the following general unrestricted model with four lags has been estimated.

$$L3 = \text{const} + \sum_{i=1}^{4} \alpha_i L3_{t-i} + \sum_{i=0}^{4} \mu_i FX_{t-i} + \sum_{i=0}^{4} \tau_i G_{t-i} + \sum_{i=0}^{4} \Omega_i RDIFF3_{t-i}$$

$$+ \sum_{i=0}^{4} \theta_i DINF_{t-i} + e_t \,;\ \text{with } e \sim N(0, \sigma^2) \tag{5.1}$$

The data employed for the estimates start from 1975Q1 but, since the model employed for the estimates contains four lags, the period covered by

typical money market interest rate. Therefore *RDIFF3* contains information on the time structure of the interest rate, whose modifications may determine reallocations of the banks' assets. To the extent that the free reserves are a temporary liquid asset, their relative size should be positively correlated to the volume of funds reallocations performed by the banks.

the estimates starts in 1976Q1. The estimates have been run over the sample period 1976Q1–1991Q4.

Table 5A.1 shows the general 'unrestricted' model, while table 5A.2 shows the variable deletion test on the restrictions on the general model that determines the final parsimonious' specification, shown in detail in table 5A.3 and briefly reported here:

$$L3 = 0.023203 - 0.11475 \, L1 + 0.076871 \, FX + 0.078367 \, G$$
$$+ 0.0008509 \, RDIFF3 + 0.10131 \, DINF_{-3}$$
$$- 0.0016986 \, RDIFF3_{-4} + 0.30852 \, L3_{-4} \qquad (5.2)$$
$$R^2 = 0.68225$$

Table 5A.3 shows that the specification suggested in the restricted model yields satisfactory results for all the diagnostic tests at the 95 per cent level of confidence.

A first look at the dynamic specification obtained suggests that the behaviour of the free liquidity ratio is inconsistent with the assumption (made also by Richter and Teigen, 1982, *a priori*) of instantaneous adjustment of free liquid reserves. Such an assumption was motivated by the hypothesis of rational expectation in financial markets. This does not mean that the rational expectation hypothesis must necessarily be rejected, but it suggests that some delays in the adjustment of the variables (consistent with some form of rationality of the agents) exist.

(5.2) can be reparametrized according to the following pattern:

$$L3 = const + \beta_0 \, L1 + \beta_1 \, FX + \beta_2 \, G + \beta_3 \, RDIFF3$$
$$+ \beta_4 \, DINF_{-4} + \beta_5 \, (RDIFF3 - RDIFF3_{-4}) + \beta_6 \, L3_{-4} \qquad (5.3)$$

which can be estimated as follows:

$$L3 = 0.023203 - 0.114752 \, L1 + 0.076871 \, FX + 0.078367 \, G +$$
$$- 0.0008477 \, RDIFF3 + 0.10131 \, DINF_{-3}$$
$$+ 0.30852 \, L3_{-4} + 0.0016986 \, (RDIFF3 - RDIFF3_{-4}); \qquad (5.4)$$

$$R^2 = 0.68225$$

According to the theoretical approach presented in the previous (and partly in the present) section, the coefficient β_3 of the variable $RDIFF3$ is expected to be negative, since it may be regarded as an opportunity cost for holding liquid assets. On the other hand, the coefficient β_5 of the term $(RDIFF3 - RDIFF3_{-4})$ is expected to be positive, since it could be associated with a variation in potential bank profitability, or in the term structure of the interest rate. In fact, such phenomena would determine a reallocation of the bank financial assets which could increase the amount of liquidity necessary for transactions.

The lagged value of $L3$ appearing in all of the restricted specifications may be determined by adjustment costs.

The sign of the coefficient referred to as $DINF$ is positive. This suggests that the increase in the price level may not be regarded as an opportunity cost, but can rather be interpreted in accordance with the literature on investments with sunk costs and under uncertainty. In fact, if the bank credit and some kinds of financial assets are regarded as (partially) irreversible investments, the higher the level of uncertainty and risk of the whole economy – signalled by the rate of growth of the price level $DINF$ – and the higher the 'value of waiting', the higher the incentives for banks to keep some funds in perfectly liquid temporary (and costlessly reversible) assets, such as free liquid reserves held at the central bank.

Intuitively, one could think of a 'transactionary' component of the demand for banks' liquid reserves, positively correlated with the term $(RDIFF3 - RDIFF3_{-4})$, and a 'speculative' component positively correlated with $DINF$. However, the present level of the variable $RDIFF3$ could be regarded as an opportunity cost for holding reserves.

Conclusions

The empirical results presented here suggest that the behaviour of banks' free liquidity ratio can be interpreted according to a theoretical framework based on the implications of the recent literature on investments under uncertainty and sunk costs. Such a framework justifies – for the banks – a particular concept of 'speculative' and 'transactionary' demand for money, which shows many similarities with the Keynesian liquidity preference theory. In fact, in this context, the free liquid reserves could be interpreted as temporary and liquid assets that the banks hold in the process of collecting information on (partially) irreversible financial investments, or in the process of reallocating their funds. Therefore the amount of free liquid reserves depends on the 'value of waiting' for new information on the possible investments in (less liquid) financial assets. Increases in the 'value of waiting' may be due to the increase in the degree of uncertainty and riskiness of the whole economy as it is perceived by banks. In this model it has been assumed that the growth rate of the price level (the variable $DINF$) can be regarded as a proxy for the degree of uncertainty and risk of the aggregate economy, in the Italian context, for the period under consideration (1976Q1–1991Q4). The validity of this empirical specification is actually limited to a 'high inflation regime'.

The 'value of waiting' may also be correlated with the increase in the profitability of banks (summarized in our specific case by the difference $RDIFF3 - RDIFF3_{-4}$,), to the extent that this might generate a process of reallocation of the financial investments of banks, requiring a temporary 'transactionary' liquid asset. In our specific case, the difference $RDIFF3 - RDIFF3_{-4}$, as determined by the general-to-specific methodology, may be regarded as the variation of the banks' potential profitability, since the variable *RDIFF3* is a proxy for the banks' gross margin of intermediation.

The results are broadly consistent with the 'creditist' idea that banks' assets are as important as banks' liabilities for the transmission of monetary shocks into the real economy. In this context, particular importance is assumed by the willingness of banks to invest and by their perception of the degree of risk and uncertainty of the whole economy. These factors play a key role in the determination of the aggregate level of credit, liquidity and output. In particular, interpreting the free liquidity ratio as a decision of 'non-investing' by banks suggests a 'liquidity preference' interpretation: if the banking system perceives a high degree of risk in the whole aggregate economy, an expansionary monetary policy would yield satisfactory results only if the banking sector regarded the decision of undertaking additional financial investments as more profitable than the decision of 'waiting for new information'.

Appendix

List and description of the variables

$BLIQ$=commercial banks' free reserves held at the Bank of Italy (also defined as $BLIQ = BRES - REQRES$

$BRES = BLIQ + REQRES$

$DBITE = FBITES - FBITES_{-1}$

DEP=current account, saving deposits and certificates of deposit of commercial banks

$DEPAV = (DEP + DEP_{-1})/2$

$DFX = FXBI - FXBI_{-1}$

$DINF = (P - P_{-1})/P_{-1}$

$DBITE$=credits of the Italian Central Bank with the Italian Treasury

$G = DBITE/DEPAV$

$FXBI$=net foreign position of the Italian Central Bank

$L1 = REQRES/DEP$

$L3 = BLIQ/DEP$

P=implicit deflator of Italian GDP

$RBCI$=rate of interest on bonds of special credit institutions

RD=official rate of discount

$RDIFF3 = RBCI - RD$

$REQRES$=required reserves of the commercial banks

In all the tables the symbol $x(-n)$ defines the nth lag of the variable x. For example, the variable $L3(-2)$ is the two-period lagged variable $L3$.

The source of data is *Supplemento al Bollettino Statistico della Banca d'Italia*, with the exception of the variables P and $RBCI$ whose time series have been provided by DATASTREAM Services (at the University of Warwick) on the basis of OECD and Bank of Italy data.

Diagnostic tests

The diagnostic tests performed in all tables in this appendix are those pro-vided by the package Microfit 3.0. The references for the diagnostic test for serial correlation, functional form, Ramsey's RESET-test, normality of regression residuals, heteroscedasticity and predictive failure are the same as in chapter 3.

A few technical comments on the estimates

In some preliminary analyses, a lag polynomial of the three-months Treasury bill, which is one of the most relevant money market interest rates in the Italian context (and which had been successfully employed in a pre-vious version of the present model, estimated over a shorter sample period), turned out not to be significant in a general model including lag polynomials in $L1$, FX, G, $RDIFF3$, or in $L1$, FX, G, $RDIFF3$, or in $L1$, FX, G, $DINF$.

Other variables (such as the Treasury bill rate, the call money rate, the interbank rate, the interest rate on long-term Government bonds, and the stock market index and its variance over the last 12 months or its variation weighted with the variance over the last 12 months) that have been regarded as proxies for opportunity costs in other empirical works on banks' liquid reserves turned out to be non-significant or less significant.

Table 5A.1 contains the results of the estimates and diagnostic tests of the general unrestricted model over the sample period 1976Q1–1991Q4, which yields satisfactory results in almost all of the diagnostic tests, except the Chi-square version of the functional form test, at the 95 per cent level of confidence (while for the same test H_0 is rejected at the 99 per cent level of confidence), and the F version of the same test, at the 95 per cent level of confidence. This might be actually due to the relatively low number of degrees of freedom for the general unrestricted test, since the same test yields much better results for the 'restricted' model.

Table 5A.2 contains the variable deletion test on the restrictions in the general model that determines the final specification, shown in detail in table 5A.3, which yields satisfactory results in all of the diagnostic tests.

Since the variable $DINF$ is defined as the rate of variation of the price level, a similar kind of information – as far as the dynamic behaviour of the price level is concerned – should be obtained by introducing in an ADL model a lag polynomial in the price level P, instead of a lag polynomial in the variable $DINF$. This is done in table 5A.4. The general unrestricted model of table 5A.4 yields satisfactory results for almost all of the diag-nostic tests, excepting the functional form test. Table 5A.5 shows the vari-able deletion tests performed in order to test a restricted model containing

P_{-3} and P_{-4} instead of the three-period-lagged rate of variation of the prices ($DINF_{-3}$).

Table 5A.6 shows the final specification containing the two lagged variables P_{-3} and P_{-4} instead of $DINF_{-3}$. As for the previous specification, the restricted model yields satisfactory results for almost all the diagnostic tests. The results of table 5A.6 are actually very similar to those of table 5A.3. This suggests that the specification obtained from a model including a lag polynomial in the variable $DINF$ is analogous and consistent with the specification obtained from a general unrestricted model with a lag polynomial in the price level.

Table 5A.1

Ordinary Least Squares estimation

Dependent variable is $L3$
64 observations used for estimation from 1976Q1 to 1991Q4

Regressor	Coefficient	Std. err.	T-ratio[prob]
$CONST$	0.015878	0.019723	0.80504[0.426]
$L1$	−0.20250	0.13861	−1.4608[0.153]
FX	0.089845	0.039545	2.2720[0.030]
G	0.12392	0.053117	2.3330[0.026]
$RDIFF3$	0.4820E−3	0.6231E−3	0.77354[0.445]
$DINF$	−0.085172	0.074139	−1.1488[0.259]
$L3(-1)$	−0.015069	0.16242	−0.092777[0.927]
$L1(-1)$	0.026848	0.091035	0.29492[0.770]
$FX(-1)$	0.0063814	0.036042	0.17705[0.861]
$G(-1)$	0.034838	0.050171	0.694390[0.492]
$RDIFF3(-1)$	−0.3810E−4	0.6737E−3	−0.056555[0.955]
$DINF(-1)$	−0.046302	0.074278	−0.62337[0.537]
$L3(-2)$	0.10135	0.13861	0.73119[0.470]
$L1(-2)$	−0.022660	0.089886	−0.25209[0.802]
$FX(-2)$	0.037804	0.036066	1.0482[0.302]
$G(-2)$	−0.014769	0.051956	−0.28427[0.778]
$RDIFF3(-2)$	0.2243E−3	0.6777E−3	0.33101[0.743]
$DINF(-2)$	0.11549	0.072098	1.6019[0.118]
$L3(-3)$	0.32542	0.14593	2.2299[0.032]
$L1(-3)$	−0.035279	0.086196	−0.40929[0.685]
$FX(-3)$	−0.051524	0.034605	−1.4889[0.146]
$G(-3)$	−0.093654	0.046633	−2.0083[0.053]
$RDIFF3(-3)$	−0.9606E−3	0.6983E−3	−1.3756[0.178]
$DINF(-3)$	0.19516	0.069629	2.8028[0.008]
$L3(-4)$	0.37860	0.13897	2.7243[0.010]

Table 5A.1 (*cont.*)

Ordinary Least Squares estimation

Dependent variable is *L3*
64 observations used for estimation from 1976Q1 to 1991Q4

Regressor	Coefficient	Std. err.	*T*-ratio[prob]
L1(−4)	0.12062	0.14188	0.85014[0.401]
FX(−4)	−0.040350	0.036806	−1.0963[0.281]
G(−4)	−0.090393	0.046476	−1.9449[0.060]
RDIFF3(−4)	−0.0019906	0.6784E−3	−2.9342[0.006]
DINF(−4)	−0.014617	0.064359	−0.22711[0.822]

R-squared	0.79299	*F*-statistic *F*(29, 34)	4.4912[0.000]
R-bar-squared	0.61643	SE of regression	0.0033599
Residual sum of squares	0.3838 E−3	Mean of dependent variable	0.012533
SD of dependent variable	0.0054250	Maximum of log-likelihood	293.9631
DW-Statistic	1.8960		

Diagnostic tests

Test statistics	*LM* version	*F* version
A:Serial Correlation	*CHI-SQ*(4)=5.4641[0.243]	*F*(4, 30)=0.70009[0.598]
B:Functional Form	*CHI-SQ*(1)=5.8889[0.015]	*F*(1, 33) 3.3442[0.076]
C:Normality	*CHI-SQ*(2)=5.1442[0.076]	Not applicable
D:Heteroscedasticity	*CHI-SQ*(1)=2.2943[0.130]	*F*(1, 62)=2.3053[0.134]

A:Lagrange multiplier-test of residual serial correlation
B:Ramsey's RESET-test using the square of the fitted values
C:Based on a test of skewness and kurtosis of residuals
D:Based on the regression of squared residuals on squared fitted values

Table 5A.2

Variable deletion-test (OLS case)

Dependent variable is *L3*
List of the variables deleted from the regression:

DINF	*L3(−1)*	*L1(−1)*	*FX(−1)*	*G(−1)*
RDIFF3(−1)	*DINF(−1)*	*L3(−2)*	*L1(−2)*	*FX(−2)*
G(−2)	*RDIFF3(−2)*	*DINF(−2)*	*L3(−3)*	*L1(−3)*
FX(−3)	*G(−3)*	*RDIFF3(−3)*	*L1(−4)*	*FX(−4)*
G(−4)	*DINF(−4)*			

64 observations used for estimation from 1976Q1 to 1991Q4

Regressor	Coefficient	Std. err.	*T*-ratio[prob]
CONST	0.023203	0.0098608	2.3530[0.022]
L1	−0.11475	0.050595	−2.2680[0.027]
FX	0.076871	0.029799	2.5797[0.013]
G	0.078367	0.031487	2.4888[0.016]
RDIFF3	0.8509E−3	0.3498E−3	2.4326[0.018]
DINF(−3)	0.10131	0.048108	2.1060[0.040]
L3(−4)	0.30852	0.086850	3.5523[0.001]
RDIFF3(−4)	−0.0016986	0.3699E−3	−4.5919[0.000]

Joint test of zero restrictions on the coefficient of deleted variables:
Lagrange Multiplier-Statistic   *CHI-SQ*(22)=22.3052[0.442]
Likelihood Ratio-Statistic   *CHI-SQ*(22)=27.4245[0.196]
F-Statistic   *F*(22, 34)=0.82676[0.676]

Table 5A.3

Ordinary Least Squares estimation

Dependent variable is $L3$
64 observations used for estimation from 1976Q1 to 1991Q4

Regressor	Coefficient	Std. err.	T-ratio[prob]
$CONST$	0.023203	0.0098608	2.3530[0.022]
$L1$	−0.11475	0.050595	−2.2680[0.027]
FX	0.076871	0.029799	2.5797[0.013]
G	0.078367	0.031487	2.4888[0.016]
$RDIFF3$	0.8509E−3	0.3498E−3	2.4326[0.018]
$DINF(-3)$	0.10131	0.048108	2.1060[0.040]
$L3(-4)$	0.30852	0.086850	3.5523[0.001]
$RDIFF3(-4)$	−0.0016986	0.3699E−3	−4.5919[0.000]

R-squared	0.68225	F-Statistic $F(7, 56)$	17.1771[0.000]
R-bar-squared	0.64253	SE of regression	0.0032435
Residual sum of squares	0.5891E−3	Mean of dependent variable	0.012533
	0.0054250	Maximum of log-likelihood	280.2508
DW-Statistic	1.9467		

Diagnostic tests

Test statistics	LM version	F version
A:Serial Correlation	CHI-$SQ(4)$=6.5191[0.164]	$F(4, 52)$=1.4744[0.223]
B:Functional Form	CHI-$SQ(1)$=0.46637[0.495]	$F(1, 55)$=0.40373[0.528]
C:Normality	CHI-$SQ(2)$=5.1661[0.076]	Not applicable
D:Heteroscedasticity	CHI-$SQ(1)$=2.9345[0.087]	$F(1, 62)$=2.9794[0.089]

A:Lagrange multiplier-test of residual serial correlation
B:Ramsey's RESET-test using the square of the fitted values
C:Based on a test of skewness and kurtosis of residuals
D:Based on the regression of squared residuals on squared fitted values

Table 5A.4

Ordinary Least Squares estimation

Dependent variable is *L3*
64 observations used for estimation from 1976Q1 to 1991Q4

Regressor	Coefficient	Std. err.	*T*-ratio[prob]
CONST	−0.027609	0.035760	−0.77208[0.445]
L1	−0.13364	0.14692	−0.90961[0.369]
FX	0.062601	0.044485	1.4073[0.168]
G	0.11718	0.052976	2.2120[0.034]
RDIFF3	0.7645E−3	0.6298E−3	1.2139[0.233]
P	−0.8587E−3	0.9488E−3	−0.90501[0.372]
L3(−1)	0.0013699	0.16293	0.0084079[0.993]
L1(−1)	0.11704	0.11454	1.0218[0.314]
FX(−1)	0.0084395	0.036263	0.23273[0.817]
G(−1)	0.039619	0.053049	0.74685[0.460]
RDIFF3(−1)	0.9685E−4	0.7091E−3	0.13658[0.892]
P(−1)	0.0011425	0.0013807	0.82745[0.414]
L3(−2)	0.071539	0.13782	0.51908[0.607]
L1(−2)	0.048689	0.10574	0.46045[0.648]
FX(−2)	0.027483	0.036561	0.75171[0.457]
G(−2)	−0.0038531	0.050140	−0.076846[0.939]
RDIFF3(−2)	0.1221E−3	0.6928E−3	0.17625[0.861]
P(−2)	0.0014074	0.0014722	0.95597[0.346]
L3(−3)	0.22319	0.14767	1.5114[0.140]
L1(−3)	0.088914	0.10468	0.84938[0.402]
FX(−3)	−0.044169	0.035229	−1.2538[0.218]
G(−3)	−0.075577	0.045169	−1.6732[0.103]
RDIFF3(−3)	−0.0012158	0.7317E−3	−1.6615[0.106]
P(−3)	0.9361E−3	0.0014937	0.62666[0.535]
L3(−4)	0.31198	0.14413	2.1645[0.038]
L1(−4)	0.16089	0.15120	1.0641[0.295]
FX(−4)	−0.052233	0.038418	−1.3596[0.183]
G(−4)	−0.054721	0.045103	−1.2132[0.233]
RDIFF3(−4)	−0.0014132	0.7362E−3	−1.9197[0.063]
P(−4)	−0.0028906	0.0011715	−2.4673[0.019]

R-squared   0.77662   *F*-Statistic *F*(29, 34)   4.0762[0.000]
R-bar-squared   0.58610   SE of regression   0.0034902
Residual sum of squares   0.4142E−3 Mean of dependent variable   0.012533
SD of dependent variable 0.0054250 Maximum of log-likelihood 291.5277
DW-Statistic   1.8245

Table 5A.4 (*cont.*)

Diagnostic tests

Test statistics	LM version F version
A:Serial Correlation	$CHI\text{-}SQ(4)=$ 5.6936[0.223] $F(4, 30)=0.73237[0.577]$
B:Functional Form	$CHI\text{-}SQ(1)=11.4200[0.001]$ $F(1, 33)=7.1674[0.011]$
C:Normality	$CHI\text{-}SQ(2)=$ 1.6863[0.430] Not applicable
D:Heteroscedasticity	$CHI\text{-}SQ(1)=$ 1.7314[0.188] $F(1, 62)=1.7239[0.194]$

A:Lagrange multiplier-test of residual serial correlation
B:Ramsey's RESET-test using the square of the fitted values
C:Based on a test of skewness and kurtosis of residuals
D:Based on the regression of squared residuals on squared fitted values

Table 5A.5

Variable Deletion Test (OLS case)

Dependent variable is L3
List of the variables deleted from the regression:

P	$L3(-1)$	$L1(-1)$	$FX(-1)$	$G(-1)$
$RDIFF3(-1)$	$P(-1)$	$L3(-2)$	$L1(-2)$	$FX(-2)$
$G(-2)$	$RDIFF3(-2)$	$P(-2)$	$L3(-3)$	$L1(-3)$
$FX(-3)$	$G(-3)$	$RDIFF3(-3)$	$L1(-4)$	$FX(-4)$
$G(-4)$				

64 observations used for estimation from 1976Q1 to 1991Q4

Regressor	Coefficient	Std. err.	T-ratio[prob]
CONST	0.020968	0.0095354	2.1989[0.032]
L1	−0.050117	0.064032	−0.78269[0.437]
FX	0.081942	0.029312	2.7955[0.007]
G	0.083338	0.031282	2.6641[0.010]
RDIFF3	0.8354E−3	0.3482E−3	2.3990[0.020]
$P(-3)$	0.9413E−3	0.6880E−3	1.3681[0.177]
$L3(-4)$	0.25501	0.084727	3.0097[0.004]
$RDIFF3(-4)$	−0.0018415	0.3734E−3	−4.9314[0.000]
$P(-4)$	−0.0010241	0.7027E−3	−1.4574[0.151]

Joint test of zero restrictions on the coefficient of deleted variables:
Lagrange Multiplier-Statistic $CHI\text{-}SQ(21)=17.1962[0.699]$
Likelihood Ratio-Statistic $CHI\text{-}SQ(21)=20.0268[0.520]$
F-Statistic $F(21, 34)=0.59485[0.894]$

Table 5A.6

Ordinary Least Squares estimation

Dependent variable is *L3*
64 observations used for estimation from 1976Q1 to 1991Q4

Regressor	Coefficient	Std. err.	T-ratio[prob]
CONST	0.020968	0.0095354	2.1989[0.032]
L1	−0.050117	0.064032	−0.78269[0.437]
FX	0.081942	0.029312	2.7955[0.007]
G	0.083338	0.031282	2.6641[0.010]
RDIFF3	0.8354E−3	0.3482E−3	2.3990[0.020]
P(−3)	0.9413E−3	0.6880E−3	1.3681[0.177]
P(−4)	−0.0010241	0.7027E−3	−1.4574[0.151]
L3(−4)	0.25501	0.084727	3.0097[0.004]
RDIFF3(−4)	−0.0018415	0.3734E−3	−4.9314[0.000]

R-squared	0.69455	F-statistic F(8, 55)	15.6330[0.000]
R-bar-squared	0.65012	SE of regression	0.0032089
Residual Sum of Squares	0.5663E−3	Mean of dependent variable	0.012533
SD of dependent variable	0.0054250	Maximum of log-likelihood	281.5144
DW-Statistic	2.0484		

Diagnostic tests

Test statistics	*LM* version	*F* version
A:Serial Correlation	CHI-SQ(4)=5.2806[0.260]	F(4, 51)=1.1466[0.345]
B:Functional Form	CHI-SQ(1)=2.8426[0.092]	F(1, 54)=2.5099[0.119]
C:Normality	CHI-SQ(2)=3.1569[0.206]	Not applicable
D:Heteroscedasticity	CHI-SQ(1)=3.0690[0.080]	F(1, 62)=3.1229[0.082]

A:Lagrange multiplier-test of residual serial correlation
B:Ramsey's RESET-test using the square of the fitted values
C:Based on a test of skewness and kurtosis of residuals
D:Based on the regression of squared residuals on squared fitted values

Part III

'Inside-the-firm' interactions between finance and investments

6 Investments with firm-specific financial costs and transaction costs of adjustment

Introduction

Most empirical analyses on firms' investment decisions are based on small samples of firms issuing shares on the stock market. This is because in the empirical implementation of Tobin's q model it has become customary to use stock market data. This custom might become problematic when dealing with investment functions referring to firms operating in 'non-securitized' financial systems, in industrial sectors where the investment decision, and its modifications, might assume a strategic value, or in the presence of relevant transactions costs.

As pointed out in chapter 3, 'non-securitized' financial systems are characterized by the fact that the amount of finance raised on the stock market is negligible compared to volume of financial funds intermediated by the banking sector. An important role is played by agents competing in the activity of monitoring and collecting private information (the banks), while the stock market plays only a marginal role.[1] Since many theoretical and empirical works have shown that the stock market plays an important role as a major vehicle of information,[2] allowing firms to reduce the cost of monitoring supported by financial intermediaries,[3] the fact of operating in a securitized or in a 'non-securitized' financial system might carry very relevant qualitative implications for the investment behaviour of a firm. In particular, in an institutional context where financial markets are less developed, we could expect the speed of adjustment of investments to be affected by relevant transaction costs.

Furthermore, the solution to the 'Capital Structure Puzzle' for the firm could result in a firm-specific cost of financial capital: in the presence of

---

[1] Further details on the characteristics of 'non-securitized' financial systems can be found in Gardener (1991); Gardener and Molyneux (1990); Rybczynski (1984); Frankel and Montgomery (1991); and, concerning the ownership structure in the Italian financial markets, in Brioschi et al. (1990).   [2] See in particular Shiller (1984, 1989).
[3] See Anderson (1994); Pagano et al. (1994).

information asymmetry between suppliers and users of financial funds, when the risk of bankruptcy is explicitly taken into account, the managers' behaviour may be affected by moral hazard. In such a context, the leverage of the firm may be regarded as an indicator of risk and may consequently affect the cost of financial capital, which might then again be regarded as 'firm-specific'.

Apart from these last two points, the investment problem of the firm is formalized by using rather standard and orthodox modelling tools.

The empirical implementation is based on the relevance of transaction costs for the process of adjustment of investments, and yields a very simple specification and reasonably satisfactory results. However, in the case of investment decisions, the loss of generality caused by the need to focus on a few 'stylized facts' might be relevant, given the existence of a number of potential causal links among several different real and financial variables, as can be seen from the 'qualitative analysis' contained in chapter 7.

In Italy, as in other non-securitized financial systems, firms issuing securities in the stock market constitute only a very small minority. Among those, the ones operating in the same industry are even fewer. This justifies, even from a neoclassical point of view, the purpose of attempting to overcome a limitation of the empirical works based on Tobin's q theory, which have to rely on samples composed by firms issuing shares on the stock market: such firms usually enjoy a well established reputation, and may not always be regarded as representative for the entire population.

The use of micro data should in principle avoid the problems derived by aggregating the data of different units of observation, while the use of an unbalanced panel allows us to use the information referred to those units of observations appearing for a sub-period of the total length of time considered in the whole sample.

The source of data for the present empirical analysis is the survey provided by Mediobanca, an Italian credit institution, a reliable and commonly employed source of firms' data. The sample has been obtained from a survey of accounting data of firms operating in the chemical sector. The Mediobanca sample contains only those firms whose sales exceed a certain threshold, and this might potentially determine a slight distortion in the sample by excluding the smallest firms. However, the relevance of this potential distortion is reduced by the fact that the number of small-sized firms operating in the Italian chemical sector is less significant than in most other sectors.

The data set has been obtained from the volumes of 1988, 1989, 1990, 1991 of Mediobanca's survey on the accounting data of the main Italian enterprises. This choice is due to the fact that since 1988 the lower bound of the Mediobanca sample has been raised to 25 billion Italian Lire sales.

Since each volume contains the data of the two previous years, the observations refer to 1986, 1987, 1988, 1989, 1990, i.e. five years.

Further technical details on the data set and data processing are contained in appendix 2 (p. 153), while appendix 1 (p. 151) describes in more detail the variables under consideration and the econometric estimates.

In order to use the data from the Mediobanca sample (mainly accounting data) some restrictive assumptions are necessary. However, concerning the general issue of the use of accounting data, this chapter follows Martin (1993) who, objecting to Benston's (1982) criticism of the reliability of accounting data, argues as follows:

If this argument were correct, the consequences would be severe indeed. It would mean that industrial economists could not carry out empirical research. It would mean that a wide spectrum of government publications describing economic activity ought to be discontinued, since they are based on what is, originally, accounting data. (Martin, 1993, p. 517)

The next three sections describe the theoretical model, its empirical implementation and the use of the data. The fifth section contains the comments on the estimates, and the sixth some concluding remarks.

The theoretical model

Our theoretical framework is meant to describe the behaviour (in continuous time) of the investments of a firm operating in a context of imperfect competition. Under a *ceteris paribus* assumption, the profits of the firm $u(k(t))$ are assumed to be a function only of capital stock $k(t)$.

The problem of the firm is defined as follows:

$$\max \int_0^\infty \exp\left[-\Phi_i t\right]\left[u(k(t)|\mu_i) - A(I(t))\right] dt \tag{6.1}$$

subject to the following conditions

$$\dot{k} = I(t) - g \cdot k(t) \tag{6.2}$$

$$k(t) \geq 0 \text{ for all } t \geq \tau \text{(for some } \tau) \tag{6.3}$$

Φ_i is the (firm-specific) rate of discount; it is exogenous for the firm's dynamic optimization problem and is assumed to be the result of the optimization of the firm's financial structure in the presence of information asymmetries between insiders (managers and owners) and outsiders (lenders and other suppliers of financial funds) and transaction costs. We could rewrite it as a function of the leverage ratio:

$$\Phi_i = \Phi\,(\Omega_i) \tag{6.4}$$

where Ω_i is the leverage ratio of the ith firm.

$u(k(t)|\mu_i)$ represent profits, defined as a function of physical capital $k(t)$ and conditional on an exogenous parameter μ_i, determined by the (exogenous and constant) demand elasticity and the (exogenous) degree of collusion among the various firms.[4]

$A(I(t))$ represents the 'purely technological' adjustment costs of the investments; the qualification 'purely technological' is important because, as explained in the section on the empirical implementation of the model (p. 139), $A(I(t))$ does not include the 'non-technological' transaction costs, caused by all the transactions necessary to modify the existing level of investment, for example, the number of financial transactions required to collect all the funds to finance the investment, and losses and opportunity costs that the firm supports by performing these transactions in a short period of time.

As usual, it is assumed that $A(I(t))$ is monotonically increasing and that $A'>0$, $A''>0$.

Finally, g is the (constant) rate of capital depreciation.

$I(t)$ is the control variable and $k(t)$ is the state variable. The problem can be solved by defining the following Hamiltonian:

$$H=[u(\cdot)\text{-}A(\cdot)]\exp{(-\Phi_i t)}+z(t)[I(t)-g\cdot k(t)] \tag{6.5}$$

We assume that the Hamiltonian H is jointly concave in (k,I).

The first-order conditions for the solution of the Hamiltonian are the following:

---

[4] Alternatively, we could have assumed that since the firm operates in a context of imperfect competition, and since $u(k(t))$ is a continuous function, the functional link between k and u (i.e. the way the capital stock affects profits) 'discounts' the effects on u of the reactions of the other firms. In other words, the function $u(k(t))$ incorporates the conjectures of the other firms as well as the modifications of the capital stock (and output) of the other firms induced by a modification of k by the firm under consideration, assuming that the managers of each firm know the reaction function of the others. This does not mean that the 'outside' suppliers of funds know all the decisions and preferences of the managers, since the ability of managers to know the reactions of other competitors might be 'industry-specific' and might be acquired with long-run experience. In particular, this would be consistent with the (plausible) assumption that managers' training requires a large investment in human capital, and that the substitution of management causes a heavy loss of human capital. However, these points are obviously not included in the model, since we are working under an assumption of *ceteris paribus* concerning the labour market and the internal structure of the firm.

The purpose of all the above assumptions is define a profit function $u(k(t))$ (continuous in k and in t) that, in spite of being referred to a regime different from perfect competition, is still concave in k and is only a function of 'k' and not of the capital stock of other firms.

$$\frac{\partial H}{\partial I}=-A'(I(t))\cdot \exp\left[-\Phi_i t\right]+z(t)=0 \tag{6.6}$$

$$\dot{z}=-\frac{\partial H}{\partial k}=-u'(k(t)|\mu_i)\cdot \exp\left[-\Phi_i t\right]+g\cdot z(t) \tag{6.7}$$

The second-order conditions require the following Hessian matrix to be negative semidefinite:

$$\begin{bmatrix} u''(\cdot)\exp[-\Phi_i t] & 0 \\ 0 & -A''(\cdot)\exp[-\Phi_i t] \end{bmatrix} \tag{6.8}$$

Since we have assumed that the Hamiltonian is jointly concave in (k,I), the condition on the Hessian matrix is satisfied.

Let us now define $q(t)=z(t)\exp[-\Phi_i t]$ and let us substitute $q(t)$ in the system composed by (6.2), (6.6) and (6.7). We then obtain the following system of equations:

$$\dot{k}=I(t)-g\cdot k(t) \tag{6.2}$$

$$\dot{q}=(\Phi+g)q-u'(\cdot) \tag{6.9}$$

$$q=A'(\cdot) \tag{6.10}$$

The equilibrium point (k^*, q^*) may be obtained by setting $\dot{q}=\dot{k}=0$.
In the phase diagram of figure 6.1 SS is the saddlepath.[5]
The optimal level of investments can be defined by substituting (6.10) into equation (6.9). Solving for I we get

$$I^*=G[(\partial u/\partial k)/(\Phi+g)] \tag{6.11}$$

where $G=A'^{-1}$. The function G is monotonically increasing in I, like $A(I(t))$. I^* is conditional on the exogenous mark up which, in its turn, might depend on the demand elasticity, and market power, of the firm.

Empirical implementation

The saddlepath SS in figure 6.1 is the only path converging to the long-run equilibrium. If the managers and the decision makers of the firms are assumed to know each other's conjectures, as well as all the other 'technological' features of the industry, then they will choose to locate their firms on the stable path SS. The fact that managers are aware of competitors' reactions does not necessarily mean that there is perfect information in the

---

[5] For a proof of the optimality of the stable trajectory SS in a standard investment model, see Beavis and Dobbs (1990, pp. 326–30, 351–3).

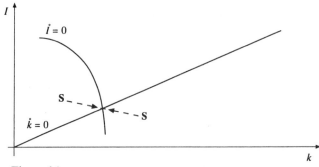

Figure 6.1

financial markets, since the ability of managers to know the reactions of the other competitors might be 'industry-specific' and might be acquired with long-run experience not necessarily shared by the 'outside' suppliers of financial funds. In particular, assuming a particular degree of 'inside' information for the firms' decision makers would be consistent with the (plausible) assumption that managers' training requires a big investment in human capital, and that the substitution of the management causes a heavy loss of human capital .

Let us start from (6.11) (p. 139). Since we have assumed that managers are rational, and since these 'rational' managers locate their firms on the path SS, the condition, $I^* = G[(\partial u/\partial k)/(\Phi + g)]$ is enough to identify the (theoretical) optimal equilibrium level of investments for the firm.

For the empirical specification we assume that for each firm the decisions are taken in continuous time, but measured at discrete intervals. In other words, the speed of adjustment of each firm to the optimal level of investments (determined by the presence of transaction costs, as assumed earlier) is measurable, and revealed only when the balance sheet and profits and losses account are issued. Nevertheless, the investment decision is taken in continuous time.

As mentioned before, the firm is assumed to face 'non-technological' transaction costs caused by all the transactions necessary to modify the existing level of investment. These can be, for example, the number of financial transaction required to collect all the funds to finance the investment, and losses and opportunity costs that the firm supports by performing these transactions in a short length of time. These 'non-technological' transaction costs will be taken into consideration in the empirical specification.

In analogy with empirical specifications in other kinds of economic literature (mainly the ones with partial adjustment, containing the lagged dependent variable among the regressors), we can think of the 'costs of being out of the optimal level of investment' as opposed to the 'transaction costs of adjustment', that, in this framework, would be proportional to the deviation of the investments at time 't' from the previous level, and at time '$t-1$'.

At this point we need a few approximations and simplifying assumptions in order to perform the empirical analysis. First of all, we will indicate analytical forms for the function $A(I)$, describing the 'purely technological' costs of investments, and formalize the functional link between the marginal profitability of capital and the average profitability of capital. Both formalizations need to be consistent with all of the assumptions of the model. What we need is simply a monotonically increasing one-to-one function between the marginal profitability of capital and the average profitability of capital. Concerning the 'purely technological' adjustment cost of investments, we need a function with the following characteristics: $A(0)=0$, $A'>0$, $A''>0$. A fairly general approximation for the function $A(I)$, could be the following, which also has the advantage of being easy to handle from an algebraic point of view:

$$A = \theta_0 \cdot I^\alpha \text{ with } \alpha > 1; \ \theta_0 > 0 \qquad (6.12)$$

Concerning the functional link between $\partial u/\partial k$ and u/k, it has to be consistent with the assumption that the *marginal* profitability of capital is always positive, even when the average profitability of capital is negative, i.e. an increase in the stock of capital will increase the profits even when they are negative. The need to relate the average to the marginal productivity of capital comes from the fact that the marginal profitability is not empirically observable, unlike the average profitability. Therefore, a condition for the latter to be employed as an approximation for the former is the existence of a one-to-one invertible functional link between them. The following analytical form shows the properties of having a positive marginal profitability of capital – even when the average profitability of capital is negative – and, at the same time, shows an invertible one-to-one functional link between the average profitability of capital and the marginal profitability of capital:

$$\partial u/\partial k = \exp(\alpha_1 \cdot u/k) \qquad (6.13)$$

Substituting (6.13) and (6.12) in equation (6.11), taking logs and rearranging, yields the following equation:

$$\ln I^* = \frac{1}{\alpha - 1} \ln(1/\theta_0 \cdot \alpha) + \frac{\alpha_1}{\alpha - 1} \cdot \frac{u}{k} - \frac{1}{\alpha - 1} \ln(\Phi + g) \qquad (6.14)$$

We have assumed that the variable Φ is a function of the leverage ratio Ω. Given that g is assumed to be constant and fixed, the leverage ratio Ω could be used as a proxy for the two variables in the bracket on the right-hand side of (6.14). In particular, we will use $\theta_1 \cdot \Omega^\beta$ as a proxy for the variable $(\Phi+g)$. Substituting then $\theta_1 \cdot \Omega^\beta$ for $(\Phi+g)$ in (6.14), we obtain the following:

$$\ln I^* = \frac{1}{\alpha-1}[\ln(1/\theta_0\alpha)+\ln\theta_1] + \frac{\alpha_1}{\alpha-1}\cdot\frac{u}{k} - \frac{\beta}{\alpha-1}\cdot\ln(\Omega) \qquad (6.15)$$

where β depends on the relation between $\theta_1 \cdot \Omega^\beta$ and $(\Phi+g)$. The size of the parameter β is not stated *a priori*, and will be determined by the data. In this way, the data themselves will specify whether the variable defined as $(\Phi+g)$ is concave or convex in $\theta_1 \cdot \Omega^\beta$. Such a formulation allows us not to rule out *a priori* either a risk-averse or a risk-lover attitude of lenders.

It is assumed that, as in the model of partial adjustment, the firm minimizes a quadratic cost function, including the *cost of being out of equilibrium*, as well as the adjustment cost of modifying the previous level of investment. The problem for the firm may be formalized as follows:

$$\min C = a(in_t - in^*)^2 + b(in_t - in_{t-1})^2 \qquad (6.16)$$

C is the total 'non-technological' cost; $in_t = \log(I_t)$; $in^* = \log(I^*)$; $in_{t-1} = \log(I_{t-1})$; a represents the 'cost of being out of equilibrium', b represents the 'non-technological transaction cost of modifying the previous level of investments'. Assuming that the second order conditions for the optimization problem described by (6.16) are satisfied, we obtain the following first-order conditions:

$$\delta C/\delta in_t = 2a(in_t - in^*) + 2b(in_t - in_{t-1}) = 0 \qquad (6.17)$$

$$in_t = [a/(a+b)]\cdot in^* + [b/(a+b)]\cdot in_{t-1} = \mu in^* + (1-\mu)in_{t-1} \qquad (6.18)$$

where $\mu = a/(a+b)$. Substituting (6.18) into (6.15), we get:

$$\ln I_t = \beta_0 + \beta_1\frac{u}{k} - \beta_2\cdot\ln(\Omega) + \beta_3 \ln I_{t-1} \qquad (6.19)$$

where

$$\beta_0 = \frac{\mu}{\alpha-1}[\ln(1/\theta_0\alpha)+\ln\theta_1]; \ \beta_1 = \frac{\mu\alpha_1}{\alpha-1}; \ \beta_2 = (\beta\cdot\mu)/(\alpha-1); \ \beta_3 = 1-\mu.$$

(6.19) represents the specification employed for econometric estimates. The value of the coefficients of (6.19) might be interpreted in economic terms. Looking at (6.18) and (6.19), it could be said that, at time t, the higher the 'transaction' cost of deviating from the $t-1$ level of investments, the lower the value of the parameter μ of (6.18), which must, in any case, be greater than 0 and smaller than 1. To give an example, in an industry characterized by a high degree of collusion among the firms, and an extremely high expected cost of breaking the collusion, the parameter μ should be positive and close to 0. In the extreme case, it should be equal to 0. This would imply that the coefficient β_3 of the lagged investments in (6.19) should be equal to 1, and (6.19) could be reformulated in the following way

$$\Delta\ln I_t = \beta_0 + \beta_1\frac{u}{k} - \beta_2 \cdot \ln(\Omega) \qquad (6.19')$$

but the regressors should be (in this extreme case) non-significant. A negative value, or a value greater than one for the coefficient β_3, would in any case contradict the theoretical framework of this model and empirical specification. No particular restrictions can be made on the value of the coefficient of (u/k) and $\ln(\Omega)$, apart from the fact that the former has to be positive, the latter negative, and their absolute value should be smaller, the larger β_3 (i.e. the closest to 1 is β_3).

The dataset and the use of the data

The data set has been constructed by using all of the available firms' data from the Mediobanca sample for the chemical sector. Appendix 2 (p. 153) contains a report on the methodology followed in processing the data.

A few comments concerning the definition of $B(t)$ and $k(t)$ are necessary at this point. Many empirical works on investments and firms' financial structure employ data obtained from the stock market, and tend not to use accounting data. Often, in those cases, the samples include only a small number of firms, usually the ones issuing securities in the stock and bond markets. It must be said, however, that these firms represent a small minority, both in terms of their number and their volume of trade, in a country with a non-securitized financial system. Since one of the purposes of this chapter is to perform estimates on a very large and representative sample of firms operating in a representative industry, a different approach has to be followed. The sample provided by Mediobanca is one of the most complete sources of information. It is therefore a natural choice for the present purpose.

For the sake of the empirical analysis, we have to consider that our data refer to an institutional context (Italy) where the overwhelming majority of finance is provided by the banking system, usually at a variable interest rate. Therefore, to the extent that the interest rate is flexible and adjusts, the balance-sheet value could be a reasonable approximation for the 'market value' of debt. In addition, if banks are regarded as institutions performing economies of scale in collecting information and monitoring the performances of the borrowers, then the information they have about the quality of their customers is not only private, but is also part of the entrepreneurial skills of banks' managers. To the extent that banks are agents seeking to maximize their profits by allocating their portfolio, the information they can get about the reliability of their customers is the main point of bank competition.

Even concerning physical capital it might be difficult to define a 'market value' for capital coming from firm-specific investments. In other words, the physical capital k might not have a market value at all if considered apart from its original production unit, while it could be extremely productive when employed within the firm's specific technology. The concept of market value of physical capital becomes even more ambiguous if we take into account strategic interaction among firms. Aoki and Leijonhufvud (1988) point out that the value of the endowment of the physical capital of a firm is not independent of the endowment of the physical capital of its competitors. Therefore, the market value of physical capital may become a very ambiguous concept in a context of imperfect competition since the various competitors are able to adjust it according to their strategic needs. These considerations could suggest that the variation of the net book value of physical capital could be a reasonable approximation, since such variation should reflect the changes in the speed of depreciation of capital goods in the period under consideration. This argument becomes stronger if we think that for a very large sample of firms, such as the one we are using here, there might not be a better approximation and measure for the investment expenditure. However, an appropriate price index of capital goods is employed when the capital stock has to be expressed at different prices from those determining the book value. Moreover, distortions constitute a problem even for alternative definitions of empirical data. In particular, empirical works where the so-called 'market value' of physical capital is properly defined (in a non-securitized country), refer only to small samples of relatively big firms, for which data determined from the stock market, or detailed surveys, usually provided by the firms themselves and only very rarely by independent institutions, are available. As is well known, the share market is subject to several distortions, for example speculative bubbles and, according to the findings of the literature on share prices excess volatility (for example, Shiller, 1981, 1984, 1989), they might not correctly reflect the net present value of dividends and as a consequence, not the proper value of the assets of the firms. Therefore, even the use of data obtained from share markets imposes some form of prior restrictive assumption, often violated by the empirical evidence, and for this reason it is argued that the kind of approximation made here might not contain more elements of distortion than the empirical works based on the usual mainstream approach. Finally, it might be worth mentioning that firms whose data appear in the Mediobanca survey are usually subject to some form of monitoring (such as official auditing), where criteria for data collecting might be no less rigorous and strict than those of the official statistical institutions.

All the above considerations lead us to conclude that, on the one hand, the models emphasizing the 'market values' of financial assets and physical capital might rely on suitable data only when they refer to very small and specific categories of firms, and on the other, the book values of the variable considered in the gearing ratio might be, in our specific case, an acceptable approximation for market values.

Since the data used here mainly concern firms not issuing securities, if we define k and B at their book values, then the leverage ratio, with regard to the balance-sheet constraint (6.1), is defined as follows:

$$\Omega = \frac{B(t)}{E(t) + R(t)} \qquad (6.20)$$

where $E(t)$ are the equities at time t, $B(t)$ the long-term debt at time t, and $R(t)$ the reserves at time t. The fact that in a 'non-securitized' financial system only very few companies issue shares on the stock market has already been mentioned. This is also the case for Italy, and almost all of the 124 firms included in our sample for the Italian chemical sector do not issue shares in the stock market. This means that we have to deal with the problem, already mentioned on p. 137, of the use of accounting data for econometric estimates. A discussion on this point is contained in appendix 2. However, it might be worth pointing out the fact that the valuation of the leverage ratio (or some analogous measure) on the basis of accounting data as an indicator of the degree of risk of a firm which is not issuing securities on the stock market, is a procedure commonly followed by financial intermediaries, especially if the reliability of the accounting data is supported by auditing.

The variable profits have been calculated, on the basis of Mediobanca data, as the value added *minus* the labour costs. Other details, such as the use of appropriate deflators for the prices of capital goods, are explained in the appendices 1 and 2. The empirical results will be considered in the next section.

The empirical results

The tables in appendix 2 contain some estimations made by following techniques of unbalanced panel data.

The data have been obtained from the Mediobanca sample and refer to the chemical sector (tables 6A.1–6A.8).

We start with (6.19) for the empirical specification of the investment function. Since the coefficient of the lagged dependent variable is close to one, the parameter restriction $\beta_3 = 1$ has been tested. Such restriction would yield (6.19') as an empirical specification :

$$\Delta\ln I_t = \beta_0 + \beta_1\frac{u}{k} - \beta_2 \cdot \ln(\Omega) \qquad (6.19')$$

The usual F-test on parameter restrictions has not been employed in this case, for two main reasons. First of all, in the case of panel data, it is necessary to make use of some testing procedure robust to heteroscedasticity, and the usual F-test based on the residual sum of squares is not robust to heteroscedasticity. Secondly, in our case there is no homogeneity among the instruments employed in the restricted and unrestricted models, as one can see in appendices 1 and 2. In fact, looking at the unrestricted model (6.19) the instruments for u/k and $\ln(\Omega)$ are their respective lagged variables, while for the lagged dependent value (i.e. $\ln I_{t-1}$) the instrument is a variable here defined as '$LNKHLAG$'. This variable corresponds to the lagged value of the book value of physical capital, gross of the accumulated depreciation (instrument for '$LAGLOGIN$', as defined below). This value includes all of the costs of purchase and installation of all of the pieces of physical capital that have not become obsolete and are still in use in the production process of the firm. Those which become obsolete earlier than expected are liquidated or eliminated from the balance sheet. The operation of liquidation originates an atypical or non-operative profit or loss. In this sense, the variable $LNKHLAG$ can be thought of as the cumulated sum of the 'purely technological' adjustment cost of investment implemented in the past and still in use in the firm. The kind of instrument employed for the lagged dependent variable is different from the one employed for the other regressors. Therefore, in comparing and contrasting the residual sum of squares of the restricted and unrestricted models, not only is there a problem of power of the test, but also a problem of homogeneity of the set of instruments employed. In fact, the 'atypical' instrument $LNKHLAG$ is only employed in the unrestricted model.

Therefore, in order to test for the parameter restriction $\beta_3 = 1$, the following procedure has been implemented. First of all, the following regression has been implemented:

$$\Delta\ln I_t = \beta_0 + \beta_1\frac{u}{k} - \beta_2 \cdot \ln(\Omega) + (\beta_3 - 1) \cdot \ln I_{t-1} \qquad (6.19'')$$

Secondly, using the 'White' (robust to heteroscedasticity) t-statistics the following null hypothesis has been tested:

$$H_0 : (\beta_3 - 1) = 0$$

When the null hypothesis is rejected, (6.19) is still regarded as the best. In the case where the null hypothesis is not rejected, then (6.19′) is adopted as an empirical specification. However, the implications of the theoretical model here adopted require that if the parameter restriction $\beta_3 = 1$ holds, then, in (6.19′) the regressors have to be non-significant, as explained on p. 143.

It might be interesting to note that the empirical specification (6.19) would be likely to yield satisfactory results even if the 'Kaleckian' inter-pretation of investment behaviour (such as formulated, for example, in Henley, 1990) is true. In fact, although the Kaleckian theory of investments is formulated in aggregated terms, it argues that the investments depend positively on the rate of profits and on the non-utilized production capac-ity. If one accepted that the leverage ratio could capture the effects of an unexpected negative shock in the profits, then it could be argued that the leverage ratio is correlated with the 'unexpectedly non-utilized' production capacity.[6]

Furthermore, by observing that the higher the level of investments at time $t-1$, the more likely is a situation of 'non-utilized' production capac-ity (especially in the presence of an 'entry-deterrence' use of investment), one could say, loosely speaking, that the explanatory power of the 'non-uti-lized' production capacity could be jointly captured by the variables $\ln I_{t-1}$ and $\ln(\Omega)$, while the rate of profits on physical capital is an explanatory cause of investment already present in the Kaleckian formulation.

The estimates have been run using the package DPD (a routine of Gauss developed by Arellano and Bond, 1988).

Concerning Italy, since the years employed for the estimates are gener-ally regarded as years of uniform economic growth without any particular shock, the estimations for all of the equations have been implemented both with and without time dummies.

Appendix 1 contains the definition of the variables.

Appendix 2 contains the estimates and a detailed description of the way the data have been processed. For the estimates in tables 6A.1, 6A.2, 6A.3

---

[6] Another observational analogy with the 'Kaleckian' investment theory lies in the presence of the leverage ratio as a regressor, and its possible connections with the literature on the 'deep pocket argument', or, in other words, the signalling use of financial structure, men-tioned in the Introduction to the chapter. According to this approach, the signalling use of financial structure leads the incumbent firms to choose a financial structure too expensive for potential entry, in order to deter it: in this way even the presence of an excessively high leverage ratio for the dominant incumbent firm might be interpreted as similar to an invest-ment in excess capacity meant to discourage (or at least reduce) entry of other firms (see Cowling, 1982, chapter 3). However, we can only talk about 'observational' similarity between the specification of the present model and these heterodox approaches, since there is not a real and explicit theoretical connection between them and the present work.

and 6A.4, the package DPD also calculates the 'White' (robust to hetero-scedasticity) tests.

The joint significance of the variables can be assessed on the basis of the (robust) Wald-test of joint significance, while the individual significance of the variables can be assessed on the basis of the (robust) t-statistics.

Table 6A.1 in appendix 2 shows the estimation of (6.19) without annual dummies. The variables are jointly significant (at the 95 per cent level of confidence), and seem to be also individually significant, although $lnmu$ is less significant than the others (the null hypothesis is only rejected with a 61 per cent level of confidence in the 'one-step estimates with robust test statistics'). Table 6A.2 shows only some descriptive statistics and the asymptotic variance matrices. Table 6A.3 shows the estimate for (6.19) with the time dummies, which are significant with only a 75 per cent level of confidence. Apart from the dummies, both the value of the coefficients and their significance are analogous to the ones shown in table 6A.1.

Table 6A.4 again shows some descriptive statistics and the asymptotic variance matrices of the equation estimated in table 6A.3.

Since in tables 6A.1 and 6A.3 the coefficient for the lagged dependent variable (lnI_{t-1}) is close to one, the parameter restriction $\beta_3=1$ for (6.19) has been tested. For this purpose, (6.19) has been reparametrized in the form of (6.19''), where the null hypothesis $H_0:(\beta_3-1)=0$ has been tested. Tables 6A.5 and 6A.7 show the estimates of (6.19'') without time dummies and with time dummies respectively. For the reasons explained at the beginning of this section, the test implemented for this purpose is the robust t-statistics on the significance of the coefficient of lnI_{t-1}. Both in the case of table 6A.5 and table 6A.7, the null hypothesis $H_0:(\beta_3-1)=0$ is rejected at the 99 per cent level of confidence. This means that the equations that better describe the behaviour of investments for the firms of the chemical sector are the ones of table 6A.1 and 6A.3, reported as follows (the numbers in brackets refer to the robust t-statistics, and the definitions of the variables are reported in appendix 1):

Estimate without time dummies

$loginv=0.777427 +0.922032\ laglogin+0.001551\ prorat-0.174732\ lnmu$
(2.98282) (29.579329)   (8.337532)   (−0.871038)

Wald (robust)-test of joint significance=1100.341505; $R^2=0.739$

Estimate with time dummies

$loginv=0.850922+0.922766\ laglogin+0.001655\ prorat-0.180182\ lnmu+$
(3.238360)(29.868663)   (8.978494)   (−0.899436)

-0.034625 D89 -0.200129 D90
(-0.383689) (-1.796919)

Wald (robust)-test of joint significance $= 1071.366471$
Wald (robust)-test of joint significance of time dummies $= 3.419619$; $R^2 = 0.743$

The results are consistent with the well known 'stylized fact' that the main source of finance for industrial firms is given by internally generated cash flow, and that the rate of profit on physical capital is strongly correlated with physical investments. On the other hand, the variable $lnmu$, proxy for the leverage ratio, is significant only at a 64 per cent evel of confidence in the one-step estimates of (6.19) with time dummies (shown in table 6A.3), and with a 62 per cent level of confidence in the one-step estimates of (6.19) without time dummies and with robust test statistic (shown in table 6A.1).

The fact that the proxy for the leverage ratio is less significant than expected might be due to the possible existence of highly complex causal links between profits and the leverage ratio. This specific point will be considered in detail in the theoretical analysis of chapter 7.

The fact that the restriction $\beta_3 = 1$ has been rejected suggests that the 'transaction' costs of adjustment do not prevail over the costs of 'being out of the optimal theoretical equilibrium'.

Conclusions

The estimates presented in this chapter are based on a very simple standard investment model, applicable to 'non-securitized' financial systems. It is assumed that the financial structure of the firm is relevant for the investment decision, and that transaction costs significantly affect the speed of adjustment of the firm's investments, since in a non-securitized financial sector financial markets and instruments are, by definition, less developed, and this might increase the relevance of the transaction costs necessary to gather financial funds.

The empirical specification of the investment function, despite being extremely simple, yields reasonably satisfactory econometric results.

The data refer to a sample of 124 firms operating in a country (Italy) whose financial system is 'non-securitized'.

The empirical analysis is performed with panel data techniques, using an unbalanced sample of 124 firms observed for the years 1987, 1988, 1989 and 1990.

The purpose of the analysis of this chapter was to run an empirical analysis (also at a 'microeconomic' level) based on a model containing two very crucial assumptions for the credit view and for the analyses of the previous chapters, namely the relevance of transaction costs and the relevance of firm's financial structure. While the latter assumption characterizes most of the recent New-Keynesian contributions, the former is identified by Williamson (1985) as one of the most relevant causes of asset specificity as opposed to 'general-purpose' contracts. Therefore, a 'non-securitized' financial system should be characterized by a higher degree of asset specificity. As explained in chapters 2 and 3, this means, from the point of credit intermediaries, higher monitoring costs and, as a consequence, higher transaction costs. The partial adjustment empirical specification employed here is in fact justified by assuming relevant transaction costs for the optimal level of investments.

The estimates confirm the significance of the rate of profits on physical capital for investment decision, while the variable *lnmu*, proxy for the leverage ratio, is less significant than expected. This might be due to the complexity and multiplicity of the potential causal links existing between profits and the leverage ratio, as discussed in the qualitative analysis of chapter 7.

Appendix 1

In what follows the symbols of the variables included in the estimations and in the equations are reported. The first section refers to the instruments, the second to the dependent variables, the third to the regressors, the fourth to the 'raw' data and variables.

Instruments

$CONST$=(constant) intercept term.

$lnkhlag$=lagged value of the book value of physical capital, gross of the accumulated depreciation (instrument for $laglogin$, as defined below). This value includes all of the costs of purchase and installation of all the pieces of physical capital that have not become obsolete and are still in use in the production process of the firm. Those which become obsolete earlier than expected are liquidated or eliminated from the balance sheet. The operation of liquidation originates an extraordinary profit or loss. In this sense, the variable $lnkhlag$ can be thought of as the cumulated sum of the 'purely technological' adjustment cost of investment implemented in the past and still in use in the firm.
$proratla$=lagged value of $prorat$, as defined below.

$lnmula$=log of the lagged value of $(1+\Omega)$, (where the debt only includes long-term financial debt). $(1+\Omega)$ has been employed instead of Ω, since Ω is often null, and could not have been calculated in logs.

Dependent variables

$loginv$=$\ln I_t$ as defined in equation (6.19)
$dloginv$=$\ln I_t - \ln I_{t-1}$
$D89$=dummy variable for the year 1989
$D90$=dummy variable for the year 1990

Regressors

$laglogin = \ln I_{t-1}$ as defined in (16.19);
$lnmu = \ln(1 + \Omega)$

$$prorat = \frac{u(t)}{k}$$

However, $u(t)/k$ determines some problems of approximation. $u(t)$ is a flow variable determined between $t-1$ and t, while k has to be defined either at time t or at time $t-1$. Again, its price has to be defined either at time t or $t-1$. Any choice would contain some degree of approximation. The choice made here, analogous to the one made by Bernstein and Nadiri (1986), is the following:

$$prorat = \frac{var.prof.(t)}{p_k(t)k(t-1)}$$

where
$var.prof.$ = variable profits, i.e. from Mediobanca data, the difference between the value-added and the labour cost. The implicit simplifying assumption here is that it is the capital stock at time $t-1$ that contributes to determine the variable profits at time t. However, the capital stock, although considered at time $t-1$ for the sake of simplification, has to be valued at a price level calculated at the same time when variable profits are calculated, i.e. time t.
p_k = implicit price deflator of capital goods (source DATASTREAM services at the University of Warwick, on the basis of OECD data).

'Raw' data and variables

$ACC.D.(t)$ = accumulated depreciations at time t
$DEPR(t)$ = depreciations at time t
$I(t)$ = gross investment (INV in the tables of the data), defined as follows:
$I(t) = K(t) - ACC.D.(t) - K(t-1) + ACC.D.(t-1) + DEPR(t)$
$u(t)$ = variable profits ($VAR.PROF.$ in the tables of the data), defined as the difference between the value added ($V.ADD.$) and the labour cost ($LAB.C.$)
EQ = equities (book value)
RES = balance-sheet reserves and accumulated profits
$LTFD$ = long term financial debt
$\Omega = (EQ + RES)/LTFD$; this ratio has been earlier defined as Ω; the variable $lnmu$ is not actually the log of mu, but its proxy.
$MU = 1 + \Omega$

Appendix 2

Table 6A.1

DPD results

Levels IV
Number of firms: 124   Sample period is 1988 to 1990
Observations: 274 Degrees of freedom: 270

Dependent variable is: *loginv*

Instruments used are:
CONST   lnkhlag   proratla   lnmula

One-step estimates
RSS=136.145185 TSS=521.925911
Estimated sigma-squared (levels)=   0.504241

   Wald-test of joint significance: 713.365013 df=3

Var	Coeff	Std. err.	*T*-Stat	*P*-Value
CONST	0.777427	0.287009	2.708721	0.006754
laglogin	0.922032	0.034794	26.499427	0.000000
prorat	0.001551	0.000695	2.230373	0.025723
lnmu	−0.174732	0.209604	−0.833627	0.404491

Note:
Standard errors and test statistics not robust to heteroscedasticity

Test for first-order serial correlation: −1.808[89]
Test for second-order serial correlation: −2.434[61]

Table 6A.1 (*cont.*)

One-step estimates with robust test statistics
Wald-test of joint significance: 1100.341505 *df*=3

Var	Coeff	Std. err.	*T*-Stat	*P*-Value
CONST	0.777427	0.260635	2.982820	0.002856
laglogin	0.922032	0.031171	29.579329	0.000000
prorat	0.001551	0.000186	8.337532	0.000000
lnmu	−0.174732	0.200602	−0.871038	0.383734

Robust test for first-order serial correlation: −1.084[89]
Robust test for second-order serial correlation: −1.621[61]

Estimated serial correlation matrix
1.000
0.013   1.000
−0.247   −0.266   1.000

Number of observations available to sample covariances
86
76   97
61   74   91
Model just identified – two-step estimates and one-step estimates coincide

Table 6A.2

Descriptive statistics

Var	Mean	Std. dev.	Min	Max
loginv	8.29173	1.38268	3.80666	11.43889
laglogin	8.18781	1.39863	2.94444	11.23452
prorat	5.60625	64.72126	−0.54212	1070.34302
lnmu	0.25076	0.25699	0.00000	1.52245

Correlation matrix

loginv	*laglogin*	*prorat*	*lnmu*
1.00			
0.86	1.00		
−0.07	−0.15	1.00	
0.11	0.12	−0.06	1.00

Asymptotic variance matrices

Non-robust AVM of one-step estimates ($\times 100000$)

CONST	*laglogin*	*prorat*	*lnmu*
8237.406			
−970.297	121.065		
−3.612	0.380	0.048	
−352.984	−92.076	0.927	4393.389

Robust AVM of one-step estimates ($\times 100000$)

CONST	*laglogin*	*prorat*	*lnmu*
6793.052			
−794.295	97.166		
−3.445	0.374	0.003	
−391.501	−42.124	0.625	4024.107

Table 6A.3

DPD results

Levels IV
Number of firms: 124 Sample period is 1988 to 1990
Observations: 274 Degrees of freedom: 268
Dependent variable is: *loginv*

Instruments used are:
CONST   lnkhlag   proratla   lnmula TIM DUMS

One-step estimates
RSS=134.188713   TSS=521.925911
Estimated sigma-squared (levels)=0.500704

Wald-test of joint significance: 718.765907   df=3
Wald-test – joint sig. of time dums: 4.080675   df=2

Var	Coeff	Std. err.	T-Stat	P-Value
CONST	0.850922	0.291546	2.918658	0.003515
laglogin	0.922766	0.034681	26.607521	0.000000
prorat	0.001655	0.000696	2.378346	0.017390
lnmu	−0.180182	0.208825	−0.862841	0.388225
D89	−0.034625	0.104818	−0.330339	0.741144
D90	−0.200129	0.106813	−1.873648	0.060979

Note:
Standard errors and test statistics not robust to heteroscedasticity

Test for first-order serial correlation: −1.813 [89]
Test for second-order serial correlation: −2.266 [61]

One-step estimates with robust test statistics
Wald-test of joint significance: 1071.366471   df=3
Wald-test – joint sig. of time dums: 3.419619   df=2

Var	Coeff	Std. err.	T-Stat	P-Value
CONST	0.850922	0.262763	3.238360	0.001202
laglogin	0.922766	0.030894	29.868663	0.000000
prorat	0.001655	0.000184	8.978494	0.000000
lnmu	−0.180182	0.200328	−0.899436	0.368421
D89	−0.034625	0.090243	−0.383689	0.701209
D90	−0.200129	0.111374	−1.796919	0.072348

Robust test for first-order serial correlation: −1.112[89]
Robust test for second-order serial correlation: −1.629[61]

Estimated serial correlation matrix
1.000
0.002   1.000
−0.233   −0.260   1.000

Number of observations available to sample covariances
86
76   97
61   74   91

Model just identified – two-step estimates and one-step estimates coincide

Table 6A.4

Descriptive statistics

Var	Mean	Std. dev.	Min	Max
loginv	8.29173	1.38268	3.80666	11.43889
laglogin	8.18781	1.39863	2.94444	11.23452
prorat	5.60625	64.72126	−0.54212	1070.34302
lnmu	0.25076	0.25699	0.00000	1.52245

Correlation matrix

loginv	*laglogin*	*prorat*	*lnmu*
1.00			
0.86	1.00		
−0.07	−0.15	1.00	
0.11	0.12	−0.06	1.00

Asymptotic variance matrices
Non-robust *AVM* of one-step estimates (×100000)

CONST	*laglogin*	*prorat*	*lnmu*	*D89*	*D90*
8499.897					
−959.771	120.275				
−3.446	0.384	0.048			
−322.892	−91.582	0.931	4360.777		
−574.327	0.062	−0.013	−34.140	1098.675	
−467.075	−12.728	−0.607	−41.846	582.659	1140.894

Robust *AVM* of one-step estimates (×100000)

CONST	*laglogin*	*prorat*	*lnmu*	*D89*	*D90*
6904.459					
−773.526	95.445				
−3.138	0.359	0.003			
−502.517	−48.320	0.404	4013.145		
−258.264	−24.767	−0.030	93.552	814.384	
−604.220	9.038	−0.592	389.434	434.822	1240.407

Table 6A.5

DPD results

First differences IV
Number of firms: 124   Sample period is 1988 to 1990
Observations: 274   Degrees of freedom: 270
Dependent variable is: *dloginv*
Instruments used are:
CONST   lnkhlag   proratla   lnmula

One-step estimates

RSS=136.145185 TSS=147.403211
Estimated sigma-squared (levels)=0.252121

Wald-test of joint significance: 20.239797 *df*=3

Var	Coeff	Std. err.	*T*-Stat	*P*-Value
CONST	0.777427	0.204538	3.800901	0.000144
laglogin	−0.077968	0.024736	−3.152046	0.001621
prorat	0.001551	0.000683	2.269625	0.023230
lnmu	−0.174732	0.159402	−1.096172	0.273004

Note:
Standard errors and test statistics not robust to heteroscedasticity
Test for first-order serial correlation: −1.882 [89]
Test for second-order serial correlation: −2.448 [61]

One-step estimates with robust test statistics
   Wald-test of joint significance: 191.495887   df=3

Var	Coeff	Std. err.	*T*-Stat	*P*-Value
CONST	0.777427	0.286724	2.711415	0.006700
laglogin	-0.077968	0.034015	−2.292135	0.021898
prorat	0.001551	0.000195	7.937991	0.000000
lnmu	-0.174732	0.172805	−1.011148	0.311946

Robust test for first-order serial correlation: −1.343 [89]
Robust test for second-order serial correlation: −1.624 [61]
   Estimated serial correlation matrix
   1.000
   0.013   1.000
   −0.247   −0.266   1.000
   Number of observations available to sample covariances
   86
   76   97
   61   74   91

Model just identified – two-step estimates and one-step estimates coincide

Table 6A.6

Descriptive statistics

Var	Mean	Std. dev.	Min	Max
dloginv	0.10392	0.73481	−3.58269	2.76505
laglogin	8.18781	1.39863	2.94444	11.23452
prorat	5.60625	64.72126	−0.54212	1070.34302
lnmu	0.25076	0.25699	0.00000	1.52245

Correlation matrix

dloginv	*laglogin*	*prorat*	*lnmu*
1.00			
−0.28	1.00		
0.16	−0.15	1.00	
−0.02	0.12	−0.06	1.00

Asymptotic variance matrices
Non-robust AVM of one-step estimates ($\times 100000$)

CONST	*laglogin*	*prorat*	*lnmu*
4183.560			
−491.340	61.186		
−2.338	0.248	0.047	
−287.520	−41.739	0.582	2540.893

Robust AVM of one-step estimates ($\times 100000$)

CONST	*laglogin*	*prorat*	*lnmu*
8221.048			
−960.425	115.705		
−3.987	0.442	0.004	
−356.808	−30.050	0.620	2986.166

Table 6A.7

DPD results

First differences IV
Number of firms: 124 Sample period is 1988 to 1990
Observations: 274 Degrees of freedom: 268
Dependent variable is: *dloginv*

Instruments used are:
CONST   lnkhlag   proratla   lnmula TIM DUMS

One-step estimates
RSS=134.188713   TSS=147.403211
Estimated sigma-squared (levels)=0.250352

   Wald-test of joint significance: 21.120679   *df*=3
   Wald-test – joint sig. of time dums: 18.490814   *df*=3

Var	Coeff	Std. err.	*T*-Stat	*P*-Value
CONST	0.850922	0.217426	3.913627	0.000091
laglogin	−0.077234	0.024657	−3.132315	0.001734
prorat	0.001655	0.000684	2.418750	0.015574
lnmu	−0.180182	0.158791	−1.134716	0.256494
D89	−0.034625	0.124695	−0.277681	0.781257
D90	−0.200129	0.106666	−1.876220	0.060625

Note:
Standard errors and test statistics not robust to heteroscedasticity
Test for first-order serial correlation: −1.888 [89]
Test for second-order serial correlation: −2.279 [61]

One-step estimates with robust test statistics
   Wald-test of joint significance: 212.232895   *df*=3
   Wald-test – joint sig. of time dums: 9.381470   *df*=3

Var	Coeff	Std. err.	*T*-Stat	*P*-Value
CONST	0.850922	0.291524	2.918873	0.003513
laglogin	−0.077234	0.033557	−2.301539	0.021361
prorat	0.001655	0.000186	8.880043	0.000000
lnmu	−0.180182	0.173496	−1.038541	0.299018
D89	−0.034625	0.090164	−0.384027	0.700958
D90	−0.200129	0.119150	−1.679641	0.093027

Robust test for first-order serial correlation: −1.367 [89]
Robust test for second-order serial correlation: −1.646 [61]

   Estimated serial correlation matrix
   1.000
   0.002   1.000
−0.233   −0.260   1.000

   Number of observations available to sample covariances
   86
   76   97
   61   74   91
Model just identified – two-step estimates and one-step estimates coincide

Table 6A.8

Descriptive statistics

Var	Mean	Std. dev.	Min	Max
dloginv	0.10392	0.73481	−3.58269	2.76505
laglogin	8.18781	1.39863	2.94444	11.23452
prorat	5.60625	64.72126	−0.54212	1070.34302
lnmu	0.25076	0.25699	0.00000	1.52245

Correlation matrix

dloginv	laglogin	prorat	lnmu
1.00			
−0.28	1.00		
0.16	−0.15	1.00	
−0.02	0.12	−0.06	1.00

Asymptotic variance matrices
Non-robust AVM of one-step estimates ($\times 100000$)

CONST	laglogin	prorat	lnmu	D89	D90
4727.385					
−493.377	60.797				
−2.265	0.249	0.047			
−259.151	−41.429	0.578	2521.450		
−882.083	9.873	0.213	−37.851	1554.877	
−598.587	3.018	−0.544	−27.834	597.461	1137.768

Robust AVM of one-step estimates ($\times 100000$)

CONST	laglogin	prorat	lnmu	D89	D90
8498.642					
−942.051	112.610				
−3.579	0.405	0.003			
−407.754	−41.518	0.455	3010.079		
−328.169	−15.461	0.037	75.519	812.951	
−1007.960	48.375	−0.384	353.130	414.646	1419.674

Data processing and the data set

The data set has been obtained from the volumes of years 1988, 1989, 1990 and 1991 of the Mediobanca survey on the accounting data of the main Italian enterprises. This choice is due to the fact that since 1988 the lower bound of the sample has been raised to 25 billion Italian Lire. Since each volume contains the data of the two previous years, the observations refer to years 1986, 1987, 1988, 1989 and 1990, i.e. five years.

Since the variable $I(t)$ has to be constructed with the stock values of K

(capital) and 'accumulated depreciations' for t and $t-1$, plus the flow variable 'depreciations' at time t, the number of available years for the estimates would be reduced to four, but since the empirical specification employed here contains the lagged dependent variable, then the number of years available is three. Furthermore, given that the dependent variable has to be constructed by using the values of consecutive stock values, and given that this same variable appears (lagged) as a regressor, then for each firm to be included in the data set, it is necessary to have at least three data referred to three consecutive years. Therefore the sample has been constructed by considering all the chemical firms appearing in the Mediobanca survey, for which at least three years of consecutive observations (between 1986 and 1990) were available. For this purpose an unbalanced panel data sample has been created. Unlike the balanced sample which includes only the 'survivors' over the sample period, and for this reason might contain some bias and lose the information referring to the firms that exit and to the new entrants during the time under consideration, the unbalanced sample yields more complete information, although at the cost of using more complex econometric methodology.

In any case, some limitations have been necessary in order to overcome a few problems.

First of all, we have to keep in mind that the purpose of this chapter is to analyse the investment in physical capital. Therefore, any kind of financial investment has not been taken into account for the estimates of the investment function. For the same reason, it has been necessary to exclude from the data set those firms that, during the period under consideration, have modified their nature from industrial firms to financial holdings. In any case, the information relative to their behaviour has been kept by including in the sample (when possible) all of the firms belonging to the old and newborn financial holdings and those operating in the industries under consideration. Obviously, each individual firm has to keep its individual nature over the time under consideration, and for this reason mergers have been regarded as events that modify the individual nature of each firm. In fact the unbalanced panel technique allows us to consider as separate individuals the firms before the mergers and the newborn firms that are determined by mergers. Such an approach has also some common sense validity, in the sense that the entity determined by the merger is actually different – in its behaviour and in its conjectures – from the different entities that contribute to determine the merger. Furthermore, a merger introduces, in general, an unpredictable piece of information in the information set of the different agents. In each different year under consideration the conjectures might be modified, and this is consistent with the argument that justifies the 'partial adjustment' empirical specification employed in this chapter for the investment function. A last point that should be mentioned is the fact that the process of liquidation that precedes mergers or failures might actually start before the merger and/or the failure of the firm under consideration takes place in legal terms. In other words, the data of the firms under consideration showed, in the years just before the liquidation or merger, the typical aspects characterizing the processes of liquidation or merger. Such processes (which in any case refer to events reported in the original volumes of the Mediobanca survey) typically involve drastic changes in the balance-sheet structure of the firm, such as a dramatic increase in the 'financial assets' or in the 'other assets' associated with a very large reduction in physical capital. Obviously, for each unity of observation, the years where such phenomena took place could not be included in the sample, while the unity of observation itself could still be considered for the rest of the period where no mergers or liquidations took place. However, the number of firms involved in the phenomena of mergers and/or liquidation is very small compared to size of the sample.[1] Mere changes of name or denomination that do not affect the structure, the main business, and the characteristics of the individual firms, will obviously not be regarded as mergers.

[1] The raw data are contained in the original volumes of the Mediobanca survey on Italian firms with more than 25 billion Lire sales (i.e. a relatively small sum).

7 Are investments and financial structure two faces of the same decision? A qualitative approach

Introduction

This chapter again deals with the interactions between industrial firms and the financial sector, but this time the analysis is focused on investments. In particular, it contains a critical discussion on a few theoretical problems raised by introducing, in a standard investment model, the assumption of simultaneity between investment and financial decisions for a firm operating in a 'non-securitized' financial system.

Obviously, introducing simultaneity between investments and financial structure dramatically increases the degree of complexity of the investment model. A qualitative discussion introduced with the help of a few simplifying assumptions, borrowed from the literature of finance, reveals some interesting similarities with the macroeconomic literature on 'excess sensitivity'.

The relevance of the firm's financial structure for investments has been the object of many contributions, both in finance and in industrial economics, although most of them do not raise the problem of simultaneity between investment and financial structure.

In industrial economics, this issue has been analysed – within the context of predatory pricing models – by the literature on the 'deep pocket argument' (Telser, 1966; Benoît, 1984; Poitervin, 1989a) and by the literature based on the assumption of 'limited liability effect' (Brander and Lewis, 1985; Poitervin, 1989b). In the former, 'strong' firms can afford a long-lasting price war because they can rely on large financial resources. In the latter, a high level of debt is regarded as a pre-commitment for an aggressive policy: a signalling game of entry deterrence yields, as a result, the optimal financial structure for both the incumbent and the entrant.

Many heterodox[1] and new-Keynesian economists[2] regard the firms'

---

[1] In particular, Kindleberger (1978); Minsky (1975, and the related literature on 'financial instability'); and Arestis (1988).

[2] In particular, Greenwald and Stiglitz (1988, 1989, 1990b); Greenwald et al. (1984); and, indirectly through the behaviour of the banking system, Bernanke (1983); Bernanke and Blinder (1992).

financial structure and its behaviour as a potential source of macro-economic instability. Some of the related literature, regarding the internally generated flow of profits as the main source of finance (because of imperfect substitutability between internal and external funds), also envisage a causal link between the flow of profits and the firm's investment decision.[3] Strong empirical evidence suggesting the existence of this causal link between financial structure and investment decision has been provided in the famous contribution by Fazzari et al. (1988). The theoretical justification for such a causal link is often based on an incentive argument suggesting that with asymmetric information 'The greater the debt–equity ratio, the more the incentives of managers who act in the interest of equity holders diverge from the interests of creditors' (Fazzari et al., 1988, p. 151). A similar 'incentive argument' has been employed in many contributions to formalize the cost of financial capital, and consequently the rate of discount of future incomes for the representative firm, as an increasing function of the leverage ratio or the gearing ratio (for example Bernstein and Nadiri, 1986; Ganoulis, 1991; Bond and Meghir, 1992), or to include managerial costs depending on the amount of borrowing in the profit function (Bernstein and Nadiri, 1993).

In chapter 6 it was pointed out that most of the empirical analyses on firms' investment decision that are based on some version of Tobin's q theory rely on stock market data and assume perfect competition on the goods market. This raises two kinds of problems: first, stock market data can refer only to a minority of firms, well reputed and 'strong' enough to bear the transaction costs necessary to have access to the stock market;[4] secondly, the simplifying assumption of perfect financial markets does not always allow us to take into account the interactions between real and financial decisions of the firm.[5]

This chapter therefore critically discusses the issue of simultaneity between investment and financial decisions of the firm. Particular attention will be dedicated to the process of information spreading and the way it might affect the investment decision in an institutional context where the market for shares is not necessarily associated with the market for firms'

---

[3] In particular, Wood (1975); Eichner (1976); Henley (1990); Çapoglu (1991).

[4] In Fama (1985) small firms rely heavily on bank credit, because they are penalized in their access to the stock market by transaction costs.

[5] A model that might be potentially adapted to describe an imperfectly competitive framework is the one by Abel and Eberly (1994), which introduces a stochastic variable in the firm's profits, and is meant to provide a framework that incorporates fixed cost investments in a stochastic context with investment irreversibility. However, the Abel and Eberly model is not explicitly designed to describe a context of imperfect competition, and is not concerned with the firm's financial decisions.

control. Since information spreading could be thought of as a continuous time process, optimal control seems to be an appropriate framework of analysis.

Given that information asymmetries seem to be so important in the determination of the cost of capital, the security market can be regarded as a vehicle of information. This interpretation, which appeared in Shiller (1984, 1989), has been reconsidered in a theoretical contribution by Anderson (1994) and in an empirical study by Pagano *et al.* (1994). Anderson (1994) suggests that securities could be complementary rather than alternative to bank credit. The argument goes as follows: since the transactions on the stock market spread information on the profitability of a firm and on the quality of its investments, they can also potentially reduce the monitoring costs for a bank or a generic lender. For these reasons, the firms issuing shares in the stock market could also borrow under better conditions from the banks. This seems to be confirmed by the empirical evidence provided by Pagano *et al.* (1994). However, in a different way, information on the firm-specific risk could be spread by other kinds of transactions, and other ways of observing the profitability of the firm (monitoring, auditing) performed by financial intermediaries in a 'non-securitized' financial sector.

For several reasons, many parts of this analysis will be deliberately conducted in a qualitative way, particularly the part concerned with the multiplicity of the potential causal links that characterize the interaction between finance and the firm's investment decision.

The next section (and its subsections), after introducing a few 'stylized facts' particularly relevant for the present study, describes a qualitative framework of analysis meant to deal with simultaneity between investments and financial structure. The third section contains a digression on how the cost of capital and the investment decision may by affected by the complex process of information spreading. The fourth section introduces a particular case characterized by a few simplifying assumptions allowing us to formalize an algebraically tractable model and the fifth section contains a few concluding comments.

A qualitative framework of analysis

In the standard models of finance, it is assumed that the market for shares is associated with a market for firms' control, acting as a mechanism of incentives and control on managers' behaviour: a management acting inefficiently would cause (in an efficient market) the firm's share price to fall, increasing the probability of a hostile take-over, and putting at risk the position of the management itself. In order for this mechanism to work, it is necessary to have a situation of highly dispersed share ownership, like the one of the British and American 'securitized' financial systems. While in the United Kingdom and in the United States hostile takeovers constitute a very frequent phenomenon, they are relatively rare in Germany (as Mayer, 1993a points out) and almost completely absent in Italy and in most of the 'non-securitized' financial systems. In non-securitized financial systems, a very low dispersion of firms' ownership is associated to the persistence of the old traditional family groups, who effectively and efficiently manage their financial holdings. Another feature of these institutional contexts is the fact that stock markets are scarcely a relevant source of financial funds, compared to intermediated credit, and the transactions in the stock market mainly concern shares of companies belonging to a small number of financial holdings.[6]

Some of the main characteristics of the 'non-securitized' financial sectors will be incorporated in the 'stylized facts' described in this and in the following sections. In particular, it is assumed that the management is directly administered by the controlling group, while the individual shareholder herself is regarded as an external supplier of funds.[7] Nevertheless, 'informal' financial markets are assumed to exist for those firms whose shares are not traded on the official stock market; this means that the outsiders can attribute a value to a share even though it is traded only informally.

General assumptions

The main assumptions of the present analysis may be summarized as follows:

(i)   The market for goods is assumed to be imperfectly competitive, although perfect competition can be a particular case.

(ii)   The management is composed of members of the controlling group of the firm and acts in the interest of the controlling group of the firm.

(iii) The stock market is not associated with a market for the firm's control; in other words, takeovers, mergers, and any transaction having as an object the firm's control are performed by means of private negotiations among the managements of the different firms.

(iv)   On the basis of assumptions (ii) and (iii), the controlling group of shareholders finances the physical capital by retaining profits, or by raising external funds, which can be debts or shares allocated to non-

---

[6] In 1987, according to the data provided by Brioschi *et al.* (1990), 29 larger financial groups issued 94 per cent of the shares traded on the Italian stock market.

[7] In Italy, such a situation applies not only to small or average-sized firms, but also to most of the giant firms that issue shares on the stock market.

controlling shareholders. In other words, the following balance-sheet constraint must always hold:

$$k = E + R + B \qquad (7.1)$$

where k=value of the physical capital (net of the accumulated depreciation); $E = p_{sub} N$, i.e. equities defined at their 'subscription' price; R=reserves; B=financial debt. The expression '$E + R + B$' is then the financial capital of the firm. Following the finance literature, its cost is the discount factor for the future streams of income.

(v) The decisions of the firm are assumed to be taken in continuous time, but are made known to outsiders only at discrete intervals (i.e. when the accounting data are available to outsiders).

Concerning assumption (i), we define the variable profit function as follows:

$$u(k, w | v_i) \qquad (7.2)$$

where k is the physical capital, w the cost of variable inputs, and v_i is a parameter that summarizes the (exogenous) market power of the firm: we assume v_i to be determined by the demand elasticity, the degree of collusion, the degree of product differentiation, and all the other aspects affecting the market power. $u(k, w | v_i)$ is assumed to be a maximum value function: in other words, the firm is at any given moment assumed to maximize profits (conditional on the parameter v_i), given the variables w and k. While w is assumed exogenous in our analysis (and we also assume that the markets for variable inputs are perfectly competitive), k will be the state variable in the optimal control problem describing the investment decision of the firm.

Concerning assumption (ii), it might be worth mentioning an empirical study by Blanchard et al. (1993) on the behaviour of managers with cash windfalls, that shows evidence that contrasts with the assumption of perfect capital markets models, while it 'needs to be stretched considerably to fit the asymmetric information model in which managers act in the interest of shareholders, . . . and supports the agency model of managerial behaviour'. However, in those institutional contexts (i.e. non-securitized financial systems) which have not experienced the structural and institutional phenomenon of the dispersion of firms' ownership, the persistence of controlling groups and the lack of a market for firms' control might take the appearance of a self-sustaining mechanism, if one assumes that the insiders are better informed on the quality of the firm's investments than the potential outsider buyers of the shares. In fact, the assumption of highly dispersed share ownership may raise the 'radical economics' objection as to why the original controlling groups should have decided to give up their control and switch to a configuration of highly dispersed ownership.[8] The relatively higher share ownership dispersion (and higher frequency of hostile take-overs) which characterizes the 'securitized' financial systems (i.e. mainly the United States and the United Kingdom) can certainly find reasonable economic justification. However, the 'radical' objection mentioned above could be considered at least in a weak form, accepting that the economic conditions that would induce the original controlling groups to gradually disperse their controlling shares might not have occurred in all institutional contexts.

The shareholders who do not belong to the controlling group cannot interfere either in the strategic choices of the firm, or in the decision concerning the distribution of dividends, and their motivation lies entirely in the remuneration (dividends *plus* capital gains) of their shares. The stock market in this framework provides a constraint only on the behaviour of managers, compelling them to distribute dividends in order to remunerate the shareholders at the market rate of return.[9]

Assumptions (ii) and (iii) do not imply that the financial control of a firm cannot be the object of a transaction: they say only that the existence of a stock market does not necessarily imply that the stock market be associated with a market for firms' control, since the ownership structure in a 'non-securitized' financial system tends to be extremely stable (and, of course, 'outsiders' are excluded from the control of the firm). The transactions involving the firm's control are in general the object of private negotiations among the various controlling groups. They could be modelled as individual episodes of bargaining, or described as modifications of coalitions among a (small) number of 'insiders', but they will be considered exogenous for the purposes of this analysis.

---

[8] For a discussion, see Cowling (1982), chapter 4.

[9] The individual's decision on whether to invest in financial assets or physical assets is intrinsically characterized by a situation of information asymmetry. If we interpret the investment decisions of agents in terms of traditional portfolio allocation theory, the distinction between insiders and outsiders introduces a sort of discontinuity in the portfolio analysis because the fact of being an 'insider' is normally associated with being a member of the majority coalition and/or having invested an amount of wealth greater than a certain threshold. The traditional assumption that managers act on behalf of the generic shareholder removes this discontinuity in the portfolio decision because it allows us to regard the single share as a portion of ownership of the firm. But this may imply a loss of relevant information, if the level of wealth needed to buy the control of a firm is high compared to the wealth that an individual might be willing to invest in a diversified portfolio of financial assets. In other words, in the absence of a market for control associated with the stock market and the decision of buying the asset denominated 'control of the firm' could be comparable to a decision of entry.

On the basis of assumptions (ii) and (iii), the asset denominated 'control of the firm' can be defined as follows:

$$V(0) = \int_0^\infty \exp\left[\int_0^t \Phi(t)dt\right] \{u(k,w|v_i) - A[I(t)]\} \, d\tau \tag{7.3}$$

where $\Phi(t)$ is the (instantaneous) cost of firm's financial funds, and $A(I(t))$ is the 'purely technological' adjustment cost function of investment. This function is twice continuously differentiable, with $A(0)=0$; $A'>0$; $A''>0$. (7.3) simply expresses the fact that, by definition, the controlling group has the right to choose how to allocate the flow of variable profits; therefore, the value of the asset denominated 'control of the firm' is given by the present value of the future profits. Furthermore, the value of the asset denominated 'control of the firm X' might not be the same for the controlling group of firm X and the controlling group of another firm, say Y. In fact, since the variable profits $u(k,w|v_x)$ of firm X are conditional on the profit rate (which, in its turn can be thought of as a function of the conjectures and the market share of firm X), it might be the case that, because of the strategic market interactions, if the management of firm Y bought the control of firm X, the increase in the present value of the variable profits of firm Y could be bigger than $V(0)$, as defined in (7.3).

In other words, due to market strategic interactions, the value attributed to the asset denominated 'control of firm X' by the management of firm X might not necessarily coincide with the value attributed to the same asset by the management of firm Y. Thus, a non-hostile takeover might take place when the management of firm Y offers the controlling group of firm X a price for the control of firm X larger that the present value of the future variable profits. In this way, an element of indeterminacy is introduced concerning the value of the firm's financial capital. In such a context it might be difficult to identify a (unique) market price of a given share and associate it with the value of the physical capital of the firm in question, even if one assumes (following the efficient financial markets hypothesis) that the price of shares is determined by the present value of the firm's future profits.[10] Furthermore, serious objections to the equality between stock prices and the present value of future dividends have been raised by the empirical studies on excess volatility, begun by Shiller (1981, 1984) and Summers (1986).[11]

[10] At this point, an obvious objection is that a situation of different value attributed to the firm's control by the managements of two different firms would be unstable and temporary, since it would cause mergers and takeovers, and would ultimately disappear. However, the managers of a firm might have incentives not to reveal the impact of a merger on its conjectures, while some of the advantages of a merger could be obtained by a collusive strategy.

[11] For an exhaustive analysis of some of the main contributions in this regard see Shiller (1989).

Since we assume here that the market for shares is not associated with the market for control (and given that the market for firms' control is considered exogenous in our formalization), the problem for the managers is just to raise, in the cheapest way, the financial funds necessary to cover the optimal physical capital, according to (7.1). The price of the shares of their company is relevant to the managers only to the extent that it allows the possibility of raising financial funds in the future by issuing new shares. The yield on shares is defined as follows:

$$r_s^*(t) = \frac{D(t)}{p_s(t)N(t)} + \frac{\dot{p}_s(t)}{p_s(t)} \tag{7.4}$$

If the managers are concerned only with remunerating the shareholders at the expected *ex ante* rate of return on shares r_s^*, the higher the rate of growth of the share price, the lower the dividends that the managers need to pay in order to keep the remuneration of the shares of their company at the market level. If we identify the managers with the controlling group, we can regard the decision of profits retention as a redistribution of income internal to the firm that makes a portion of the income produced by the firm unavailable to the shareholders not belonging to the controlling group. Such a portion of income could increase the value of the firm (and, as a consequence, the value of the firm's control), or it could be reallocated in the future, on the basis of a decision taken by the controlling group. The dividend distribution can therefore be thought of as the cost that the management has to support in order to raise external finance on the stock market.

For given values of r_s^*, $\dot{p}_s(t)$, $p_s(t)$, $N(t)$, (7.4) yields the dividend policy that the managers are compelled to apply in order to keep the shareholders happy (or not too unhappy). If we assume a stable functional link (on the basis of the information available for investors) between r_s^* and the risk-free interest rate r_f, r_s^* also represents an opportunity cost for the controlling group's wealth invested in the asset defined as 'control of the firm'.

Therefore, the dividends will be:

$$D(t) = r_s^*(t)p_s(t)N(t) - \dot{p}_s(t)N(t) \tag{7.5}$$

Managers are constrained to choose their dividend policy in order to remunerate the shareholders at the market yield on shares.[12] Once such a 'market' constraint is satisfied, the managers retain the remaining profits on behalf of the controlling group. In this case, if the cash flow is not sufficient

---

[12] We can imagine that if the elements affecting the time path of $p_s(t)$ act, for a sufficient length of time, in such a way that the capital gain element prevails to the extent that

$$D(t) = r_s^*(t)p_s(t)N(t) - \dot{p}_s(t)N(t) < 0$$

then this situation of 'negative dividends' would correspond to a situation where the firm finds it convenient to issue new shares on the stock market.

to pay for the required level of dividends, the firm could pay the shareholders by reducing the accumulated profits (reserves), or the shares. However, on the basis of the balance-sheet constraint of (7.1), such a reduction of the reserves has to be financed by issuing new debt, or new shares, or by reducing the level of physical capital. The reduction in the level of physical capital may bring about the liquidation of the firm. On the other hand, the liquidation of the firm may happen not only in cases of bankruptcy, but also when the controlling group finds the opportunity cost of keeping its wealth endowment invested in physical capital higher than the net present value of the right to dispose of the future flows of variable income of the firm.

We now define the cost of the firm's own capital as the negative cash flow that the firm has to pay in order to provide itself with this source of capital. Therefore:

$$c(t) = r_s^*(t)p_s(t)N(t) - \dot{p}_s(t)N(t) \tag{7.6}$$

where $c(t)$ stands for cost of own capital. Hence, the unit cost of own capital will be:

$$i(t) = \frac{c(t)}{E(t) + R(t)} \tag{7.7}$$

where $E(t)$ and $R(t)$, are respectively the *subscription* value of the shares and the reserves originating either from past accumulated profit retention, or, again, from shareholders' subscriptions. Therefore, the cost of the firm's own capital could be defined as follows:

$$i(t) = \frac{r_s^*(t)p_s(t)N(t) - \dot{p}_s(t)N(t)}{E(t) + \int_0^t [\pi(t) - (r_f + \phi(\Omega))B(t) - D(t)]dt} \tag{7.8}$$

where $\pi(t) = u(\cdot) - A(I(t))$ $\tag{7.9}$

(7.9) defines the variable profits, net of 'purely technological' adjustment costs of investments, at time t. $D(t)$ are the dividends such as defined in (7.5), r_f the interest rate on risk-free assets, and $\phi(\Omega)$ a risk premium on borrowing which is assumed to be, as in the model of chapter 6, an increasing function of the leverage ratio Ω such that $\phi(0) = 0$ and $\phi' > 0$. The denominator of (7.8) shows that own capital is increased by past accumulated profits, which are in their turn determined by the profits (net of the 'purely technological' adjustment costs of investments and of the remuneration of borrowed capital) as well as own capital. If the remuneration of debt and own capital entirely exhausts π, then the firm does not

accumulate profits. If the remuneration of debt and own capital leads to
financial flows greater than π (when, for example, $p_s(t)$ not only instantaneously adjusts, but also overshoots to variations in π), then the numerator
of (7.8) increases more than the denominator, and the cost of own capital
also increases. This kind of mechanism obviously needs more detailed
explanation which will be given on p. 179, concerned with the financial
decisions of the firm.

The firm, which at any moment is assumed to be maximizing the level of
variable profits $u(k,w|v_i)$, chooses the financial structure that minimizes the
cost of financial capital and the optimal stock of capital k that maximizes
the net present value of future profits. The managers have to remunerate the
shareholders at the *ex ante* expected yield, and have to pay the lenders'
interest rate on borrowing. The minimization of the cost of financial capital
determines the rate of discount of future profits for the (more general and
intertemporal) problem of maximization of the value of the asset denominated 'control of the firm', defined as follows:

$$\max V(0) = \int_0^\infty \exp[-\Phi(t)t]\{u(k,w|v_i) - A[I(t)]\}\, dt \qquad (7.10)$$

subject to the following constraints (apart, obviously, from the balance-
sheet constraint (7.1):

$$\dot{k} = I - gk,\ k(0) > 0\ and \lim_{t\to\infty} k(t) \geq 0 \qquad (7.11)$$

$$u(k,w|v_i) - A[I(t)] - [r_f(t) + \phi(\Omega(t))]\cdot B(t) + \dot{B}(t)$$
$$- \dot{R}(t) - D(t) = 0 \qquad (7.12)$$

where r_f is the interest rate on risk-free assets, ϕ (Ω) a risk premium on
borrowing defined earlier, $A[I(t)]$ the function of (purely technological)
adjustment costs of investments (with $A(0) = 0$, $A' > 0$, $A'' > 0$), $D(t)$ the dividends, $B(t)$ the level of borrowing, $R(t)$ the reserves, $S(t)$ the shares, and
a dot over the variables indicates differentiation with respect to time. All
of the above equations could remind the reader of an optimal control
model, but in this case the framework of analysis is complicated by the
assumption that the firm is assumed to be optimizing the financial structure. This means that in each and every moment the value of Φ is determined in a way consistent with the fact that the firm is equating the
marginal cost of borrowing to the marginal cost of the own capital i. In
particular, the following part of this section will define a generic system of
equations determining i and Ω conditional on the share price and its time
differential.

The optimal financial structure

Let us regard – for the moment only – the optimization of the firm's financial structure as a separable problem.

We will define Φ^o as that specific value of Φ which is consistent with the firm's optimal financial structure. Let us define the gearing ratio as

$$\mu = \frac{B(t)}{k(t)}$$

Then, given the balance-sheet constraint (7.1), we have:

$$\frac{B(t)}{k(t)} = 1 - \frac{1}{\dfrac{B(t)}{E(t)+R(t)}+1} \tag{7.13}$$

which can be written as

$$\mu = 1 - \frac{1}{\Omega+1} = h(\overset{+}{\Omega}) \tag{7.14}$$

where $h(\Omega)$ is a monotonically increasing function of Ω.[13] Hence, if we define a risk premium on the gearing ratio, we can identify an equivalent risk premium ratio defined on the leverage ratio. In fact, if $\theta(\mu)$ is the risk premium defined on μ, then we have $\theta(\mu) = \theta(h(\Omega)) = \phi(\Omega)$. In particular $\theta(0) = 0$, $\theta' > 0$, and , $\phi(0) = 0$, $\phi' > 0$.

We can then define the optimization of the firm's financial structure as follows:

$$\Phi^* = \min_{\mu} \{(1-\mu)i(t) + [r_f(t) + \phi(\mu)] \, \mu\} \tag{7.15}$$

(7.15) is the weighted average of the cost of financial funds, including borrowing and own capital.

In each and every moment the firm is optimizing the financial structure by choosing the optimal leverage ratio (which, as we will see later, is determined simultaneously with the cost of own capital, given the flow of funds condition in (7.12)). The optimized financial structure contributes to determine the rate of discount appearing in the intertemporal problem. However, the optimal rate of discount is conditional on the flow of profits, net of the 'purely technological' adjustment costs of investments. This will determine, in the next sub-sections, an intertemporal optimization problem for investments where the rate of discount is going to be a function of both the state and the control variables.

---

[13] In particular, we have $\Omega = h^{-1}(\mu) = \mu/(1-\mu)$. $h(\Omega)$ is defined for Ω not equal to -1 (which is always met, since $\Omega > 0$ by definition), and $h^{-1}(\mu)$ is defined for μ not equal to 1 (i.e. the situation where the firm finance its stock of physical capital only with debt is not permitted).

Considering (7.15), and assuming that the second-order conditions are satisfied, the first-order condition will be:

$$d\Phi^*/d\mu = r_f + \theta(\mu) + \mu\theta'(\mu) - i = 0 \tag{7.16}$$

(7.16) states that the firm is equating the marginal cost of borrowing to the marginal cost of the own capital i. Let us assume that $\theta(\mu)$ is homogeneous of degree 1, such that

$$\mu\theta'(\mu) = c\theta(\mu) \tag{7.17}$$

where c is a constant, then (7.16) becomes:

$$i - r_f = \theta(\mu)(1+c) \tag{7.16'}$$

then:

$$\mu = \theta^{-1}((i-r_f)/(1+c)) \tag{7.18}$$

assuming that $\theta(\cdot)$ is monotonically increasing and invertible, then (7.18) shows that μ is a monotonically increasing function of $(i-r_f)$, i.e. the difference between the cost of own capital and the interest rate on a risk-free asset. Since we have $\Omega = h(\mu)$, with $h(\cdot)$ monotonically increasing in μ, then Ω is a monotonically increasing function of the difference $(i-r_f)$. We can then define :

$$\Omega = h(\mu) = h(\theta^{-1}((i-r_f)/(1+c))) = b(\overset{+}{i-r_f}) \tag{7.19}$$

The leverage ratio is an increasing function of the difference between the cost of own capital and the interest rate on risk-free assets because, for a given r_f, the higher the cost of own capital, the higher the incentive for the firm to borrow and increase the leverage ratio.

However, (7.19), which derives from the equality, at the margin, between the cost of own capital and the cost of debt, has to be considered together with the fact that the determination of dividends (which depends on a few variables containing information on the financial markets) contributes to determining the cost of own capital.

It is important to point out that (7.16) may be solved in order to determine $\Phi(t)$ as a function of $\mu(t)$. In fact, solving (7.16) for $i(t)$ and substituting it into (7.15), we get (omitting, for simplicity, the symbol (t))

$$\Phi = r_f + \theta(\mu) + \mu\theta'(\mu) - \mu^2\theta'(\mu) = \Phi^*(\mu) \tag{7.20}$$

If we further assume that $\theta''(\mu)$ is null or negligible, and keeping in mind that by definition we have $0 < \mu < 1$, then Φ is monotonically increasing in μ (or in Ω):

$$\Phi^* = \Phi^*(\overset{+}{\mu}) = \Phi^*(\overset{+}{h}(\overset{+}{\Omega})) \tag{7.21}$$

Now let us consider jointly (7.19), (7.8) and (7.12). (7.12) may be significantly simplified with the following notations and definitions:

$$u(k,w|v_i) - A[I(t)] = \pi(k(t),I(t)|v_i) \tag{7.22}$$

$$\dot{B}(t) - \dot{R}(t) = -f(\dot{\Omega}) \tag{7.23}$$

(7.22) is simply a redefinition of (7.9), while (7.23) comes from the definition of the leverage ratio Ω, by observing that an increase in the debts and a reduction in the reserves (accumulated profits) reduces the leverage ratio. Therefore, the difference between the time derivative of the debt stock $B(t)$ and the accumulated reserves $R(t)$ is a (negative) function $-f(d\Omega/dt)$ of the time derivative of the leverage ratio. Hence, we can define:

$$\pi(k(t),I(t)|v_i) - [r_f(t) + \phi(\Omega(t))] \cdot B(t) - D(t) = -f(\dot{\Omega}) \tag{7.12'}$$

Now, considering (7.8), and substituting in it (7.12'), we get

$$i(t) = \frac{r_s^*(t)p_s(t)N(t) - \dot{p}_s(t)N(t)}{E(t) + \int\limits_0^t [-f(\dot{\Omega})]dt} \tag{7.8'}$$

Keeping in mind that (7.12') is simply a rearrangement of (7.12) on the basis of (7.21), then $i(t)$ and $\Omega(t)$ are simultaneously determined by the following system:

$$\begin{cases} i(t) = \dfrac{r_s^*(t)p_s(t)N(t) - \dot{p}_s(t)N(t)}{E(t) + \int\limits_0^t [-f(\dot{\Omega})]dt} & (7.8') \\[4ex] \Omega = b(\overset{+}{i} \overset{-}{-} r_f) & (7.19) \end{cases}$$

The above system will be analysed only qualitatively, and with the help of a few simplifying assumptions.

By substituting (7.8') into (7.19), one gets a non-linear differential equation in Ω such as the following (where b is the function defined in (7.9)):

$$\Omega = b \left[\frac{r_s^*(t)p_s(t)N(t) - \dot{p}_s(t)N(t)}{E(t) + \int\limits_0^t [-f(\dot{\Omega})]dt} - r_f \right] \tag{7.19'}$$

Obviously (7.19') might have or not have (one or more) real solutions, depending on the analytical form of the functions appearing in it. What we need for the sake of our qualitative analysis is to be able to focus on one possible causal link at a time, i.e. on a relevant solution at a time only. This would be the case, for example, if we assumed (as we are going to do) that among the solutions (if any) of (7.19′), only one is real.[14] Such a solution would yield a value for Ω conditional on $p_s(t)$, its time derivative, and $r_s^*(t)$. Let us have an intuitive look at this possible solution.

Two forces act on Ω: on the one hand, the non-distributed profits (which, from (7.12′) are a negative function of the time derivative of the leverage ratio) that have been accumulated in the past contribute to reducing the cost of own capital (as shown in (7.8)). On the other hand, an increase in $p_s(t)$ would cause the firm to accumulate fewer profits (i.e. reduce the denominator of (7.8′)) and increase the dividends (i.e. increase the numerator of (7.8′)), increasing in this way the cost of own capital.

By considering the above system together with (7.20) (or, equivalently, together with (7.14) and (7.15)), one can note a causal link going from i (in (7.8′)) to Ω (in (7.19), reminding us that r_f is exogenous) and to the (optimized) cost of financial capital Φ^*. In fact, an increase in i, by increasing the cost of own capital, would increase the comparative convenience to borrow, determining an increase in the leverage ratio Ω, which would, in its turn, cause an increase in the cost of the financial capital Φ^*. Therefore, for the sake of our analysis it is crucial to discuss whether and how $p_s(t)$ is a function of the (present and future) value of π, i.e. whether, and how, the information on the profitability of the firm spreads into the financial markets, and whether and how the expected yield on share $r_s^*(t)$ might also be affected by the profitability of the firm (i.e. how things would change if we assumed that $r_s^*(t)$, instead of being exogenous, contained a risk premium correlated with the profitability of the firm).

To give an example, an increase in $\pi(t)$ associated with an increase with overshooting in $p_s(t)$[15] would force the firm to decumulate its reserves and increase the dividends: the numerator of (7.8′) would increase and the denominator would decrease. This would cause $i(t)$ and (from (7.19)), the leverage ratio to increase. On the other hand, if an increase in $\pi(t)$ takes place without affecting the share price $p_s(t)$ (possibly because the management might have incentive or strategic reasons not to reveal the increases in the cash flow), the firm would be able to accumulate more reserves (non-distributed profits): the denominator of (7.8′) would increase, and this would reduce the cost of the own capital $i(t)$ and (from (7.19)) the leverage ratio.

---

[14] The assumption of unicity of the solution is indeed very strong. It is very usual and commonly accepted in neoclassical and rational expectation literature, where linear functions, or other simply tractable analytical forms are assumed *a priori*.

[15] The literature on 'excess volatility' (for instance, Shiller, 1981, 1984, 1989) suggests that this may happen frequently.

The system comprising (7.8') and (7.19) has been defined only in very general terms: its qualitative behaviour would significantly vary according to the assumption that one can make about the links (if any) between the variables $\pi(t), p_s(t), r_s^*$ and $\Omega(t)$. All these functional links will be briefly discussed in the next two sections. Before doing that we still need to anticipate a few considerations.

First of all, a few points can be made on the relevance and implications of the system comprising (7.8') and (7.19) for the more general investment decision problem described by (7.10) (subject to the constraints (7.1), (7.11) and (7.12)). Even if we assume that the firm operates in a 'non-securitized' financial system (and therefore in an institutional context where financial funds are mainly supplied by the banking system, i.e. by financial intermediaries involved in long-run contractual relationships and monitoring), the rate of discount in the intertemporal investment decision problem should not be regarded as constant, but rather as firm-specific, being the result of all the transaction costs, incentive mechanisms and information asymmetries that typically characterize the choice of the optimal financial structure for the firm. However, having assumed a firm-specific rate of discount of future profits, its behaviour and characteristics critically depend on a number of implicit assumptions concerning – for example – financial market efficiency, and a number of institutional factors, such as the relevance of transaction costs, information asymmetries, and contractual features that characterize interactions between firms and suppliers of financial funds.

Our qualitative discussion on the interaction between investments and financial structure could end here. Having pointed out, however, that several causal links could exist between the profits of the firm and the rate of discount of their future values, we might still wonder how such causal links would qualitatively affect the behaviour of a standard intertemporal investment model. To do that we must make our general framework algebraically tractable, even at the cost of some restrictive assumptions.

The problem of simultaneity between investments and financial structure

By anticipating a few hypotheses that will be justified and discussed in more detail in the next section, let us then assume that the system comprising (7.8') and (7.19) yields a unique real simultaneous solution for $\Omega(t)$ and $i(t)$. Such a solution is conditional on $\pi(t)$, and its behaviour would be strongly affected by the (possible) presence of a functional link between the variables $\pi(t), p_s(t), r_s^*$ and $\Omega(t)$. Conditionally on the relations existing among $\pi(t)$, $r_s^*(t)$ and $p_s(t)$ (that will be discussed in the next section), the system comprising (7.8') and (7.19) could result in some kind of causal link between π

and $i(t)$. Given that the cost of financial capital $\Phi^*(t)$ is defined as a function of Ω, which, in its turn, is a function of the difference between $i(t)$ and the exogenous interest rate on a risk-free asset $r_f(t)$, then a possible causal link between π and $i(t)$ would determine a causal link between $\pi(t)$ and $\Phi^*(t)$.

If we further assume that such a causal link can be approximated by a function $\Phi^*(\pi)$, the investment decision problem of our firm would still be rather complex. Considering (7.10), subject to the constraint (7.11), the Hamiltonian of the problem can be defined as follows:

$$H = \exp\left[-\Phi^*(\pi(t))t\right]\left[u(\cdot) - A(I(t))\right] + z(t)\cdot[I(t) - gk(t)] \qquad (7.24)$$

Since the discount factor is a function of π which is, in its turn, a function of both the state variable $k(t)$ and of the control variable $I(t)$, the system is time dependent. Again, it might not have a solution and, in any case, the determination of a solution requires extremely complex procedures. Some simplifying assumptions on the causal link between Φ^* and π, meant to avoid the problem of time dependency (and to make the model easily tractable), will be introduced on p. 187 by following the implications of some recent results in literature on finance and industrial economics.

However, before dealing with the solution of the Hamiltonian (7.24), we must digress to say a few words on the nature of the possible causal links between the variables $\pi(t)$, $p_s(t)$, r_s^* and $\Omega(t)$.

A digression on the cost of capital and the 'financial side of the firm'

Many empirical studies on the behaviour of the stock market have seriously questioned the assumption of market efficiency,[16] in particular, the literature on 'excess volatility' (Shiller, 1981, 1984, 1989; Summers, 1986) and other recent contributions concerned with the interaction between managers and shareholders, such as the empirical evidence provided by Blanchard *et al.* (1993) showing that firms tend to accumulate cash windfalls without distributing them to shareholders.

Some of the main issues in the debate on market efficiency are relevant for our analysis, such as the question of whether or not share prices reflect the net present value of dividends, and whether or not dividend payments adjust completely to changes in the flow of profits.

Any hypothesis on the relation between $\pi(\cdot)$ and p_s should (at least implicitly) rely on some assumptions concerning the diffusion of information about the profits and the profitability of the firm. In fact, by looking at (7.8), one could say that the effects of an increase in $\pi(\cdot)$ on the cost of

---

[16] In a completely different context, this has also been done recently by the theoretical approach denominated as 'rational beliefs' (Kurz, 1993, 1994a, 1994b, 1994c, 1994d).

financial capital might be ambiguous and depend on the assumptions on how p_s reflects the information on profits, and whether, and how, the *ex ante* yield on the generic share, when regarded as an external source of finance, contains some risk premium.

Still considering (7.8), let us assume that p_s only imperfectly reflects the net present value of the future dividends, and that the information about π only gradually spreads and affects p_s. For a given exogenous value r_s^*, a persistent increase in profits associated with a less than complete adjustment of $p_s(t)$ to the new level of profits would enable the firm to retain more profits, reducing steadily further the denominator of (7.8), since an increase in the accumulated reserves would result in a negative cumulated variation of the leverage ratio Ω. Since (from (7.21)) the cost of financial funds is an increasing function of the leverage ratio, then the cost of financial capital for the firm would be increasingly reduced. In other words, if $p_s(t)$ only partially adjusts to variations in the net present value of the sum of the future profits $\pi(\cdot)$ (or, more generally, if $p_s(t)$ is weakly and very imperfectly correlated with π), then an increase in π would determine a reduction in the cost of financial capital.

Obviously the situation would be totally different in a world of perfect and efficient financial markets. In particular, if the managers acted in the interest of the shareholders, they should pay out all of the available flow of profits (net of the 'purely technological' adjustment cost of investments and of the interest payments on borrowing) as dividends. If this increase in dividends is perceived as permanent, a corresponding adjustment of the expected future dividends should take place. This would cause an increase in $p_s(t)$ and in the numerator of (7.8'). The final effect would be an increase in the cost of own capital $i(t)$, and as a consequence (by considering simultaneously (7.8'), (7.12') and (7.19)), increase in the leverage ratio Ω and in the overall cost of financial capital. An increase in the profits would simply determine an increase in the cost of financial capital through one of its components: the dividends and, as a consequence, the remuneration of the own capital.

For r_s^* exogenous, we can summarize this first part of our digression by identifying two extreme cases:

Case A1: $p_s(t)$ adjusts imperfectly and only partially to changes in the future values of $\pi(t)$

This case would correspond to a negative functional link between the profits $\pi(t)$ and the cost of own capital $i(t)$. This would imply in its turn (given (7.19) and (7.21)) a negative causal link between the profits $\pi(t)$ and the cost of financial capital Φ, as explained already. It might be interesting to note that when the managers act in the interest of the controlling group, they may have strong incentives to pay out (as dividends) as little profits as possible, because in this way they may increase the value of the asset defined as 'control of the firm' in (7.10) by reducing the cost of financial capital and the rate of discount of future profits. This point seems to be consistent with the results of the empirical work by Blanchard *et al.* (1993), showing that the firms tend to accumulate cash windfalls without distributing them to shareholders.

Case B 1: $p_s(t)$ adjusts perfectly and instantaneously to $\pi(t)$, and profits (net of 'purely technological adjustment costs of investments') are entirely exhausted in interest and dividends payments.

In this case, which is consistent with the efficient markets hypothesis and with the assumption that the management acts in the interest of the generical shareholder (without a distinction between minority and majority shareholders), an increase in $\pi(t)$ would not determine any accumulation of reserves and the denominator of (7.8') would not change, while the numerator would increase because of the increase in $p_s(t)$ determined by the increase in $\pi(t)$. This would determine an increase in the cost of own capital which would determine, in its turn, an increase in the leverage ratio. Therefore we would have in this case a positive correlation between the cost of financial capital, the leverage ratio, and the profits.

In the case of 'excess volatility' (Shiller, 1981, 1984, 1989), the share prices would overshoot with respect to the expected level of dividends determined by the original increase in $\pi(t)$. *Ceteris paribus*, the increase in the numerator of (7.8') would be larger than in the case of complete exhaustion of profits into dividends, and complete and proportional adjustment of $p_s(t)$ to changes in $\pi(t)$: in other words, we would have a positive and strong correlation between the profits and the leverage ratio. However, the case of excess volatility is very unlikely to apply to firms not issuing shares on the official stock markets.

Let us now remove the assumption that $r_s^*(t)$ is exogenous and constant, and let us assume that $r_s^*(t)$ contains some kind of risk premium negatively correlated to $\pi(\cdot)$. In this case an increase in $\pi(\cdot)$ would make the numerator of equation (7.8) smaller, and the denominator larger. All of these possible cases could be summarized by assuming some kind of functional link between $\pi(\cdot)$, p_s and $r_s^*(t)$, whose quantitative effects have to be determined simultaneously with the firm's financial decision and the flow of funds equation.

The nature of a possible functional link between $\pi(\cdot)$, p_s and $r_s^*(t)$ could be discussed with the help of the implications of some relevant results of finance and industrial economics literatures, which will now be briefly summarized.

(a) 'Signalling and profit retention' argument: As Leland and Pyle (1977) point out, with information asymmetry and signalling on a stock market, the proportion of investment 'owned' by insiders is a signal of the good quality of the investment. If the firm has to choose between financing new investments by issuing new shares or by retaining profits, then the decision to retain profits to finance new investments and to give up dividends may be equivalent to the insiders' decision to keep a high proportion of their investment. In this way, the decision concerning profits retention and dividends distribution enables the firm to send a signal. However, firms operating in a context close to perfect competition, or not enjoying a significant margin of profits, may not send such a signal. Therefore, the firms enjoying a certain degree of monopoly power and, as a consequence a high margin of profits, are enabled to send a signal that perfectly competitive firms (or firms with low market power) cannot send. The immediate consequence of this argument would be a sort of binary discrimination between the firms able to reduce the 'lemon premium' on their external finance by issuing a costly signal, and those unable to do so. However, if we assume that lenders also detect the *intensity* of the signal (i.e. how large the dividends that the insiders are giving up are, and what their magnitude is compared to the capital invested in the enterprise), it could be assumed that the higher the profit rate, the more successful the firm could be in reducing the risk premium on $r_s^*(t)$. If we assume that there is a risk premium on $r_s^*(t)$, this could be 'captured' by defining a negative functional link between the risk premium on external finance and the profits π, i.e. the profits net of the 'purely technological' adjustment costs of investments.[17]

(b) 'Transactions and information spreading' argument: Let us assume that the transactions concerning the liabilities of the firm (i.e. equities and debt) are a major vehicle of information for the quality of firms' investments. This is equivalent to the rather orthodox assumption that prices are the main vehicle of information spreading. This assumption can be formalized following the 'general epidemic model' (Bailey, 1957, quoted in Shiller, 1984, 1989).

It is assumed, first, that new carriers of news (as of a disease) are created at a rate equal to an 'infection rate' β times the number of carriers times the number of susceptibles and, second, that carriers cease being carriers at a 'removal rate' τ. (Shiller, 1989, p. 15)

---

[17] The specification 'purely technological' depends on the fact that we are assuming that the rate of profit is exogenous and constant. However, a brief discussion on this specific point is provided later in this section.

This model is quoted by Shiller as a possible tool for interpreting phenomena of information spreading. It could be extended to the interpretation of the diffusion of information concerning the profitability of the firm. In particular, let us assume that the 'infection rate' β is constant, the removal rate τ depends on the maturity of the financial assets (and, for simplicity, could be assumed to be constant, as a first approximation), the 'number of carriers' of information correspond to the individuals who have been involved in the negotiations of assets issued by the firm, and the 'number of susceptibles' corresponds to all of the potential buyers of the firm's assets (i.e. at least potentially, the entire population). We might now discuss what kind of transactions might be considered 'information carriers': only the transactions concerning the financial assets of the firms (whose price should be associated with the net present value of the future yields) or *just any transaction* (since we can assume that details such as the amount of sales and the time required to pay the creditors could carry relevant information on the profitability of the firm). In this regard, one could argue that in a 'non-securitized' financial system only a very small minority of firms is interested in the negotiations of their assets on the financial markets, while the large majority raise funds from banks, who often tend to assess the risk of their customers on the basis of accounting data, auditing and on the basis of the information provided by the departments who have been charged with collecting information on the sales, profitability and risk of the various industries.[18]

All these considerations could again suggest the existence of a negative functional link between the profits π and the risk premium on $r_s^*(t)$.[19]

Since it has been specified earlier that the analysis of this chapter ideally refers to firms operating in an imperfectly competitive goods market, a few comments on the nature of the profits is appropriate. As Aoki and Leijonufvud (1988) point out, when we are dealing with investments even only in the context of stock-flow analysis, we have to keep in mind that the value of the physical capital of a firm depends on the value of the stock of capital of its other competitors. In other words, to the extent that the degree

---

[18] On the other hand, even for those firms whose shares are negotiated on the securities markets, one can easily imagine that the volume of assets transactions *per se* does not contain complete information unless it is associated with the level of profits (or with some measure of profitability). In fact, a firm with a very large outstanding stock of securities negotiated on the financial markets could also suffer the consequences of a sudden and very wide diffusion of 'bad news' coming form a possible negative shock on its profits or even its potential profitability.

[19] The idea of considering prices as a vehicle of information is quite common in the orthodox literature.

of collusion among the different firms affects the profit rate of the firm x and the profits $u(\cdot)$ (and noting that the profits $u(\cdot)$ are gross of the adjustment costs $A(\cdot)$)), then an exogenous change in the degree of collusion would modify the profit rate, the variable profits $u(\cdot)$ and (on the basis of the functional link of definition (7.2)), the value of the stock of capital k. This is precisely what happens when, due to the modified conditions of the market (possibly caused by changes in the degree of collusion among the different firms), the firms need to rectify the book value of their stock of physical capital. However, the degree of collusion among the different firms and the rate of profit on physical capital have been considered exogenous (although such an assumption could be criticized on the basis of the literature on industrial economics that emphasizes the endogeneity of market structure as opposed to the traditional 'structure conduct performance' approach), because the analysis of the possible causal links between $r^*_s(t)$, $p_s(t)$, $\pi(\cdot)$, the cost of financial capital $\Phi^*(\cdot)$, and the investment decision is already extremely complex in itself. However, we wanted to point out here that a possible (and very likely) origin of exogenous shock in the profits could be an exogenous change in the degree of collusion.[20]

Finally, it is important to note that in the process of diffusion of information on firm-specific risk, the relevant variable under consideration is $\pi(\cdot)$, i.e. profits net of the adjustment costs $A(\cdot)$. This is because $\pi(\cdot)$ and not $u(\cdot)$ is the relevant variable for the definition of the risk of bankruptcy, moral hazard and adverse selection in a context of asymmetric information in the financial markets.

(c) **'Strategic use of financial structure' argument:** Loosely speaking, the literature on entry deterrence with strategic use of financial structure (Benoît, 1984; Poitervin, 1989a 1990), would suggest that higher profit margins could be associated with a higher leverage ratio and, more generally, a more costly financial structure. In fact, as suggested by Poitervin (1990), a costly financial structure is a signal that the incumbent with low costs (high profit margins) conveys to the potential entrant.

On the basis of this argument, one could define (but only for the incumbent firm) a causal link among the risk premium ϕ, the leverage ratio Ω, and the profits π, such as the following:

$$\phi = \phi(\overset{+}{\Omega}(\overset{+}{\pi}))$$

---

[20] On the other hand, even the literature that emphasizes the endogeneity of market structure (except for the contributions by Telser, 1966; Benoît, 1984; Brander and Lewis, 1985; Poitervin, 1989a, 1989b, 1990, dealing with very specific problems of signalling), has the limit of not identifying the fundamental role of financial markets as a strategic vehicle of diffusion of information, since the investments are in general defined as a 'real' decision which takes place in the goods market.

This functional link could be thought of as an effect of the persistence of an equilibrium in a strategic financial signalling game analogous to the one described in Poitervin (1990).

Alternatively, if there is common knowledge of this particular use of financial structure for entry deterrence purposes, banks could be aware that the use of a more costly financial structure is needed to preserve a high market power and, therefore, high profit margins. For this reason they could allow more profitable firms to have a higher leverage ratio without charging them with a higher risk premium on borrowing. In other words, one could imagine a trade off between leverage ratio and profits such as the following:

$$\phi = \phi(\overset{+}{\Omega}, \overset{-}{\pi})$$

Argument c ('strategic use of financial structure') above will not be considered in the following part of this study because it deals with very specific problems of signalling and entry deterrence that would not apply to the generality of the firms acting in a big industry, quantitatively relevant at a macroeconomic level. Furthermore, it would require a detailed analysis of the characteristics of the equilibrium in a financial signalling game, which is beyond the purpose of this chapter.

At this point it might be convenient to summarize the last part of the discussion on the cost of the financial capital of the firm by formulating two more cases.

Case A 2: The ex ante *yield on shares $r_s^*(t)$ contains a 'risk premium' negatively correlated with profits $\pi(\cdot)$.*

Case B 2: The ex ante *yield on shares $r_s^*(t)$ is exogenous and if it contains some 'risk premium' the risk premium is also exogenous.*

Case A2 would be true if the 'Signalling and profit retention' argument and/or the 'transactions and information spreading' argument applied. Case B2 would be true if neither the 'signalling and profit retention' argument nor the 'transactions and information spreading' argument applied.

Assuming, as we did on p. 177, that the system composing (7.8'), (7.12') and (7.19) yields a unique solution for Φ and Ω conditional on π, we can now summarize the whole discussion of this section.

When case A1 alone, or case A1 associated with case A2, or case A1 associated with case B2 applies, then $i(t)$ is negatively correlated with π. Such a negative correlation would also imply, given (7.19) and (7.21), a negative causal link going from π to the cost of financial capital Φ.

Inspired by Blanchard's (1981) terminology, let us define this as the 'good news case'.

When case B1 alone, or case B1 associated with case B2 applies, then the profits π are positively correlated with $i(t)$. This would imply a positive correlation between the profits π and the cost of financial capital Φ^*. Let us define this as the 'bad news case'.

When case B1 associated with case A2 applies, then the sign of the correlation, between $i(t)$ and $\pi(t)$ is ambiguous, since we cannot say *a priori* whether in the correlation between $i(t)$ and π the negative sign of case B1 or the positive sign of case A2 would prevail. This would render ambiguous also the sign of the causal link between π and Φ^*. Let us define this as the 'ambiguous case'.

Generally (and loosely) speaking, the connection between $\pi(t)$ and $p_s(t)$ looks indeed ambiguous. In fact, if an increase in $\pi(t)$ determines only with delay an increase in $p_s(t)$ (because the process of information spreading takes time and because the management might have incentives not to reveal immediately the increase in profits in order to accumulate reserves, or even because the observability of profits is founded on accountancy data, while the accumulation of profits takes place in continuous time), from (7.8) or (7.8′) we see that after an initial reduction in $i(t)$ (when π increases but $p_s(t)$ has not yet adjusted to it), the increase of $p_s(t)$ to its value, consistent with the new value of $\pi(t)$, would determine a gradual reduction in i.

The ambiguity would increase if we assumed that the variable $r_s^*(t)$, instead of being exogenous (and defined as the *ex ante* market rate of return on shares) is the *ex ante* expected firm-specific rate of return on shares: in this last case we could assume $r_s^*(t)$ to contain some risk premium negatively correlated with the instantaneous profits $\pi(t)$. The fact that $r_s^*(t)$ contains some risk premium is consistent with the *ex ante* expected negative correlation between risk and return: if a firm is more risky, and if the market perceives such a riskiness, then the *ex ante* expected return $r_s^*(t)$ on the firm's shares is higher, since it has to contain some risk premium. Now, if the profits π increase, and this increase is only gradually made known to outside observers, then we can expect that the information spreading will affect at the same time both $p_s(t)$ (by increasing it) and the risk premium contained in the *ex ante* expected return on shares $r_s^*(t)$ (by causing a reduction in $r_s^*(t)$). As we see from (7.8) and (7.8′) the effect on $p_s(t)$ and the effect on $r_s^*(t)$ of the diffusion of the information of an increase in π, are opposed: an increase in $p_s(t)$ would increase $i(t)$ and (as a consequence) Φ^*, while a reduction in $r_s^*(t)$ would cause a reduction in $i(t)$ and in Φ^*.

In the next section a few specific hypotheses are introduced in order to make the Hamiltonian (7.24) algebraically tractable. In particular, we assume that the system comprising by (7.8′) and (7.19) yields a unique solution $(i(t), \Omega(t))$. The assumptions of the 'good news case' are assumed to apply and, finally, we assume that the causality from π to Φ^*, such as determined by (7.21) and by the system comprising (7.8′) and (7.19), can be approximated by a function, say

$$\Phi^* = \Phi^*(\pi(t),t). \qquad (7.25)$$

All these assumptions might cause some loss of generality. However, as we will see below, these assumptions can be justified on the basis of a few recent results in the literature of financial economics. The purpose of the next section is to get some qualitative hint on which additional causations would be introduced in the investment problem of the firm if we accepted the idea of a correlation between profits π and the cost of own capital 'i', which determines, in its turn (from (7.21)), a correlation between the profits π and the cost of financial capital Φ^*.

A special solution

The simplifying assumptions that will be introduced in the model of this section are meant to capture two 'stylized facts': the first one is that young and newborn firms meet less favourable conditions in the credit market than existing firms with a consolidated reputation. The second is that the *ex ante* expected return on shares $r_s^*(t)$ contains some risk premium negatively correlated with the performance and profitability of the firm. To reach an intuitive rationale for the second 'stylized fact', we can imagine that the risk valuation of the external investor reacts to any information (for example, new agreements with particularly important customers, or other forms of collusive agreement) susceptible to increasing the profitability and performance of the firm *as soon as such information is known and spreads into the market*.[21]

As anticipated on p. 178, a functional link like that of (7.25) is assumed to hold. In what follows, a few qualitative explanations for the existence of such a functional link are provided.

Let us come back to the system comprising (7.8′) and (7.19), and let us assume that the 'good news case' and the considerations introduced at the end of the last section apply. What we are describing here is the investment decision of a generic firm operating in a 'non-securitized' financial system, where only very large firms issue securities on the stock market and the most relevant source of external finance is constituted by bank credit. As we pointed out in the analysis of chapter 3, another feature of non-securitized financial sectors is the fact that hostile takeovers are extremely rare, and the change in ownership and controlling groups is performed through

---

[21] When the firm in consideration has issued shares on the stock market, the effects of the new information spreading can be associated with day-to-day fluctuations of share prices.

private negotiations between the controlling groups of different firms. We try to capture this feature by assuming that the market for firms' control is not associated with the market for shares. In this context the generic shareholder is regarded as an external supplier of finance: this allows us to keep the representation of the financial decisions of the firm such as shown on p. 176 and summarized by the system comprising (7.8') and (7.19).

When the firm is taking the step of issuing shares on the stock market, we assume that this determines a gradual process of information spreading from π to $r_s^*(t)$. This process of information spreading takes place according to the 'epidemic models' described in Shiller (1984, 1989). We can further assume that this process can be conceptually sub-divided into two qualitative elements: first, the availability of a very long series of observations on the behaviour and the share prices of a firm may allow the outsiders to make inferences on the characteristics and riskiness of the firm under consideration (i.e. in the very long run the 'degree of information asymmetry may be reduced), second, a process of information spreading concerning the short-run performance of a firm may be reflected by the short-run behaviour of its stock prices. In particular, concerning the second point, we assume that an hypothetical increase (decrease) in π is perceived by the market only with a delay, when the data on the profitability of the firm's investments become available to outsiders. Such a process will determine – in case of an increase (decrease) in profits – a gradual increase (decrease) in $p_s(t)$ and a gradual reduction (increase) in $r_s^*(t)$ (since it has been assumed in the last section that $r_s^*(t)$ contains a risk premium negatively correlated with profits). However, if the effect on $r_s^*(t)$ is more powerful than the effect on $p_s(t)$, the process of information spreading associated with an increase (decrease) in π determines a gradual reduction (increase) in Φ^*: this would result in a negative causal link between π and Φ^*, since it has been assumed on p. 176 that the system comprising (7.8') and (7.19) yields a unique solution for Φ and Ω conditional on π. On the other hand, if the effect on $r_s^*(t)$ is less powerful than the effect on $p_s(t)$, the process of information spreading associated with an increase (decrease) in π determines a gradual increase (reduction) in Φ^*, i.e. a positive causal link between π and Φ^*. We could again consider two different cases, according to whether a positive or a negative causation between π and Φ^* applied. However, given that the only qualitative difference between the two cases would be the sign of the functional link $\Phi^*(\pi)$, only the case of a negative causation from π to Φ^* will be considered here. Therefore, the value of Φ^* is assumed to be a function of $\pi(t)$ and of the time t, since even just the short run process of information spreading is a function of time. Furthermore, the causal link going from the variables $\pi(t)$ and t, to the variable $r_s^*(t)$ will be approximated by a function whose behaviour has to be consistent with the 'epidemic' models of information spreading described in Shiller (1984, 1989).

To describe the fact that firms with a consolidated reputation tend to be considered less risky, we assume that the expected *ex ante* yield on shares $r_s^*(t)$ contains a 'risk' parameter a that tends to disappear asymptotically (it will be assumed later that the parameter a contains the elements of the process of information spreading):

$$r_s^*(t)=r_s^o+a(t) \tag{7.26}$$

where r_s^o is the *ex ante* theoretical rate of return on shares with perfect information, and a is a risk parameter associated with the lack of information (available to outsiders) on the quality of management and on the quality of investments of the firm under consideration:

$$a=\begin{cases} \xi^* \text{ (constant) for } t<1 \\ (1/t)\cdot a_1(\bar{\xi}) \text{ for } t\geq 1 \text{ with } d(a_1)/d\xi<0 \end{cases} \tag{7.27}$$

The conditions on the variable t reflect the fact that the phenomena of information spreading and processing, that asymptotically reduce and remove the risk parameter a, do not take place immediately (i.e. at the exact time $t=0$ where the firm materially issues shares on the stock market), but after a length of time required by the outside observers to collect and process the data on which they may base their valuations of riskiness, i.e. after the outsiders have been able to observe the daily behaviour of the stock prices for long enough and after a relevant amount of accounting data have been available. For these reasons, a depends on a parameter ξ reflecting the process of information spreading only when $t\geq 1$, while for $t<1$ the firm is still regarded as 'risky' and charged with the constant parameter ξ^* for risky investments. The assumption contained in (7.27) and in its justifications is consistent with the results of the theoretical model by Anderson (1994), showing that the process of information spreading associated with stock negotiations can reduce the monitoring costs for agents lending money to firms issuing shares on the stock markets, and with the empirical results by Pagano *et al.* which confirm Anderson's (1994) theoretical predictions.

(7.27) tells us that the risk factor a (and the function $a_1(\xi)$) tends to disappear when t tends to infinity: the rationale for such an assumption is that when the available amount of information on the behaviour of a given firm becomes very high, outsiders increase their ability to make inferences on the quality and characteristics of the firm's behaviour (profitability of investments, dividend policies, skills of the decision makers, etc.). In a sense, one could say that asymptotically the degree of information asymmetry is reduced and $r_s^*(t)$ tends to the value $r_s^o(t)$.[22]

In what follows, referring to (7.21) and the system comprising (7.8'), (7.12') and (7.19), we will associate, for convenience, the variables $\Omega^*(t)$ and $\Phi^*(t)$ with $r_s^*(t)$, and the variables $\Omega^o(t)$ and $\Phi^o(t)$ with $r_s^o(t)$. This means that when t tends to infinity, the variable $\Omega(t)$ tends to the value Ω^o and the variable $\Phi(t)$ tends to the value Φ^o, both corresponding to a situation of 'perfect' financial markets and 'absence' of the risk parameter a.

Having suggested that the effects of the risk parameter a and the risk premium on shares ξ tend to disappear when t becomes infinite, it might be reasonable to ask ourselves what happens to ξ when t is not infinite. It seems natural to assume that in these circumstances ξ depends on the qualitative characteristics of the process of information spreading. It also seems natural to assume that the information spread by such a process must reflect the performances of the firm under consideration. We thus will define a parameter β which reflects the diffusion in time of the information concerning the profits π. For the sake of simplicity, we also assume that the risk premium charged to 'risky' firms will be the same for the firms having 'not significantly positive' profits and for those not issuing shares on the stock market (since the available information concerning the latter is generally considered much lower than for firms issuing shares on the stock market). In other words, both the firms with 'not significantly positive' profits and those not issuing shares on the stock markets will be charged with maximum (constant) risk premium ξ^*. All the others enjoy the advantages of the 'process of information spreading', but this process of information spreading could be suddenly interrupted whenever the performance of a firm worsens, causing the profits π to be 'not significantly positive'. By 'not significantly positive' profits, we could simply mean a condition such as

$$\pi > 0 \tag{7.28}$$

However, since for the sake of algebraical tractability of the model, logarithmic functions will be used, we will assume the following condition (that could be qualitatively equivalent to (7.28) if we imagine that we measure the profits with a sufficiently small unit of measure, like, for example, the Italian Lira):

$$\pi > 1 \tag{7.29}$$

On the basis of the previous discussion, we will define the risk parameter a as follows:

[22] This applies obviously if the firm 'exists' when $t \to \infty$ i.e. the firm is a 'survivor', it does not go bankrupt, and belongs to the category of reliable and therefore 'risk-free' borrowers.

$$a = \begin{cases} a_1(\bar{\xi})/t \text{ for } \pi > 1 \text{ and (as in (7.27))} t > 1 \text{ with } d(a_1)/d\xi < 0 \\ \xi^* \text{ for } \pi \leq 1 \text{ and/or } t < 1 \end{cases} \qquad (7.30)$$

(7.30) implies that the firm can take advantage of the process of information spreading only if its performances is good enough ($\pi > 1$) and after the length of time required by the outsider to collect and process enough data ($t \geq 1$, i.e. after the first accounting data after issuing shares on the stock market become public). If at any time the profits of the firm fall below the level $\pi > 1$, then the firm is charged the maximum (constant) risk premium ξ^*. The virtuous circle of information spreading may begin again (by setting again $t = 0$) if and only if the profits increase again to the point where $\pi > 1$. Furthermore, for $\pi > 1$ and $t \geq 1$, we assume that the process of information spreading does not only detect when the profits are 'significantly positive' ($\pi > 1$) but will also show 'how good the performance' of the firm is, i.e. 'how high' the profits are. Therefore, for $\pi > 1$ and $t \geq 1$, we assume:

$$\xi = \xi(\pi(t), t) \qquad (7.31)$$

The function $\xi(\pi(t), t)$ is meant to 'capture' and qualitatively 'describe' the process of information spreading; the variable t appears in (7.31) since the intensity of the process of information spreading is obviously affected by time. It is assumed that the behaviour of (7.31) is qualitatively consistent with the 'epidemic' models of information spreading described by Shiller (1989) and briefly summarized on pp. 182–4. Since in the 'epidemic' models the 'new carriers of news . . . are created at a rate equal to an "infection rate" ß times the number of carriers times the number of susceptibles and . . . carriers cease being carriers at a removal rate τ' (Shiller, 1989, p. 15), we will assume that the 'infection rate' is in our case the 'object of the epidemic' or, in our case, the main piece of news (i.e. the performance of the firm, summarized by the profits π). The number of carriers and susceptibles are individuals interested in transactions in the stock market, and the 'removal rate can be thought of as a parameter depending on the structural characteristics of the stock market on which the firm is issuing its shares. For the sake of simplicity, the number of carriers, the number of susceptibles and the rate of removal are assumed to depend on the time t and on a generic parameter β which captures the structural characteristics of the financial market under consideration. Furthermore, again according to the hypotheses of the 'epidemic' models, the process of diffusion must reach a maximum at some point in time, and subsequently decrease.

Therefore, the function $\xi(\pi(t), t)$ of (7.31) can be better specified as follows:

$$\xi(\pi(t),t)=(\beta/t)\log(\pi t) \tag{7.32}$$

In (7.32), with an appropriate value for the constant parameter β, a dynamic behaviour can be reproduced where the function $\xi(\cdot)$ is monotonically increasing in π and has a point of maximum in t^o concerning the variable t. When t further increases after the point of maximum t^o (i.e. when the 'removal rate' prevails over the process of diffusion determined by the 'information carriers'), the function is decreasing in t (while still increasing in π). The phenomenon described by (7.32) is qualitatively different from the simple asymptotic reduction of risk premium described in (7.30), since (7.32) could reproduce the effects of an exogenous negative shock in the profits π, which would increase the variable a_1.

If we assume that the system comprising (7.8') and (7.19) yields a unique real solution for Ω and i that can be approximated by a monotonic continuous and differentiable function $\Omega(i)$, and if (considering (7.21) together with (7.26), (7.27), (7.30) and (7.32)) we assume that the causal links between i and π can be approximated (for $\pi>1$ and $t>1$) by monotonic, continuous and differentiable functions – say $i(\pi)$ and $\Phi(\Omega(i(\pi)))$ – then we return to the problem of optimal investment of p. 173. Now, however, the link between the variable π and Φ has been specified in more detail with the help of the assumptions contained in the present section. Let us consider then (7.10'), (7.11) and (7.24) describing the intertemporal optimization problem of the firm and the Hamiltonian associated to it. The transversality conditions are the following:

$$\lim_{t\to\infty} z(t)\geq 0,\ [k^*(t)-k(t)]=0$$

where k^* is the optimal level of physical capital. Remembering that

$$\pi(t)=u(k(t)|v_i)-A[I(t)]$$

it is assumed, in what follows, that the transversality conditions are satisfied for $\pi>1$ and $t\geq1$. Assuming that the second-order conditions are satisfied, the first-order conditions will be:

$$\partial H/\partial I=0=-e^{-\Phi(\pi(t))t}\cdot A'-e^{-\Phi(\pi(t))t}\cdot\left[t\frac{d\Phi}{d\pi}\cdot(-A')\right]\cdot\pi+z(t) \tag{7.33}$$

where, on the basis of (7.30) and (7.32), and assuming that a differentiable function $\Phi(\Omega(i(\pi)))$ exists, we have:

$$d\Phi/d\pi=(d\Phi/d\Omega)\cdot(d\Omega/di)\cdot(di/d\pi)=\frac{\beta}{t^2\pi} \tag{7.34}$$

hence

$$\partial H/\partial I=0=-e^{-\Phi(\pi(t))t}\cdot A'-e^{-\Phi(\pi(t))t}\cdot(\beta/t)\cdot(-A')+z(t) \tag{7.33'}$$

and solving for z

$$z = A' [1 - (\beta/t)] e^{-\Phi(\pi(t))t} \tag{7.35}$$

The condition for the state variable is the following:

$$dz/dt = -\frac{\partial H}{\partial k} = -\frac{\partial u}{\partial k} e^{-\Phi(\pi(t))t} + t \left[\frac{d\Phi}{d\pi} \cdot \frac{\partial u}{\partial k} \right] e^{-\Phi(\pi(t))t} \cdot \pi(t) + z(t) \cdot g$$

Hence, substituting in it (7.34) we get:

$$\frac{dz}{dt} = e^{-\Phi(\pi)t} \left[-\frac{\partial u}{\partial k} \right] [1 - (\beta/t)] + z \cdot g \tag{7.36}$$

By putting together (7.35), (7.36) and (7.11) we determine the following system:

$$\begin{cases} z = A'[1 - (\beta/t)] e^{-\Phi(\pi(t))t} & (7.35) \\[2mm] \dfrac{dz}{dt} = e^{-\Phi(\pi)t} \cdot \left[-\dfrac{\partial u}{\partial k} \right] [1 - (\beta/t)) + z \cdot g & (7.36) \\[2mm] \dot{k} = I - gk & (7.11) \end{cases}$$

Time differentiating (7.35) we get the following:

$$\dot{z} = e^{-\Phi(\pi)t} A''[1 - (\beta/t)] \cdot \dot{I} - \Phi \cdot e^{-\Phi(\pi)t} A'[1 - (\beta/t)] + e^{-\Phi(\pi)t} A'[1 - (\beta/t^2)] \\ + e^{-\Phi(\pi)t}(-t) \{(-\beta/t^3) \cdot \log(\pi t) + (\beta/\pi t^3)[\pi + t(-A') \dot{I}]\} \tag{7.37}$$

where, for simplicity, the arguments of π have been omitted. In (7.37), for $t \to \infty$, the last two addends, i.e.

$$e^{-\Phi(\pi)t} A'[1 - (\beta/t^2)]$$

and

$$e^{-\Phi(\pi)t}(-t) \{(-\beta/t^3) \cdot \log(\pi \cdot t) + (\beta/\pi t^3)[\pi + t(-A') \dot{I}]\}$$

tend to zero, and the term $[1-(\beta/t)]$ tends to 1.

Therefore, for $t \to \infty$, by substituting (7.35) into (7.36) and equating the right-hand side of the equation obtained in this way with the right-hand side of (7.37), we would obtain a model analogous to the standard neo-classical investment model, i.e.:

$$\begin{cases} \dfrac{dI}{dt} = \dfrac{1}{A''} \cdot \left[-\dfrac{\partial u}{\partial k} + (\Phi^o + g)A' \right] [1 - (\beta/t)] + z \cdot g & (7.38) \\[2mm] \dot{k} = I - gk & (7.11) \end{cases}$$

which yields the conditions

$$I^* = A'^{-1}[\partial u/\partial k)/(\Phi + g)] \text{ for the locus } \dot{I} = 0 \text{ and}$$

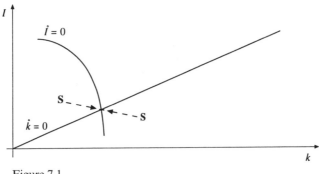

Figure 7.1

$I=g \cdot k$ for the locus $\dot{K}=0$.

Therefore, the system composed by (7.38) and (7.11) yields a result which looks at a first sight very similar to that of the standard neoclassical investment model. However, some relevant qualitative difference can be found in the long-run dynamics in the presence of an exogenous shock in the profits.

In figure 7.1, SS is the stable saddlepath. In this case $\partial u/\partial k$ is the 'marginal profitability' of capital (and not the marginal productivity of capital), which depends on the profit rate. A few significant qualitative differences from the standard neoclassical model appear if we look at the effects of a perturbation in $u(t)$, given the interaction existing between this variable, the rate of discount and the leverage ratio.

Let us assume that $A'>0$, that $A''>0$, and that the profit function $u(t)$ is homogeneous in k, so that an increasing monotone and differentiable function $f(\cdot)$ exists such that $\partial u/\partial k=f(u/k)$. This means that a disturbance in u(t) would also imply a disturbance in $\partial u/\partial k$. Let us consider a medium-sized firm which does not issue securities on the stock market. The cost of financial capital for this firm will be Φ^*, which includes a risk premium such as described in (7.26)–(7.32).

If this firm does not issue any shares on the stock market, our investment model would be exactly identical to a standard neoclassical investment model. The same would happen for $\pi \leq 1$. These cases are not very interesting, and will therefore not be taken into consideration.

On the other hand, if the firm decides to issue shares on the stock market, it will take advantage of the process of information spreading (described in this and in the previous section) that reduces asymptotically the risk premium. According to our assumptions, however, this process of information spreading generates a link between profits and the cost of financial capital. If, for example, an exogenous shock in the profits $u(k,w|v_i)$ takes place, two effects on the long-run equilibrium can be detected. First, by

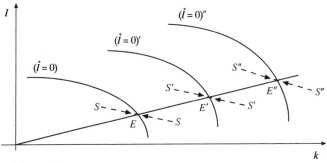

Figure 7.2

affecting $\partial u/\partial k$, the shock moves the locus $dI/dt=0$ to a new position $(dI/dt)'$. Second, when t is not infinite, a causal (time dependent) link between π and Φ exists, so that the initial exogenous shock in $u(k,w|v_j)$ would generate effects in the cost of financial capital and in the 'financial side' of the firm decision. The asymptotic equilibrium E'' (in figure 7.2) is determined by the 'real shock' (from E to E') and by the 'financially induced shock' (from E' to E'') determined by the process of information spreading (described in the present and in the previous sections) which allows the (profitable) firm to consolidate its reputation and reduce the risk premium and the cost of financial capital until the (asymptotic) level Φ^o.

An initial unexpected disturbance in $\partial u/\partial k$ would shift the locus $dI/dt=0$ away from the initial equilibrium E to E'. However, to the extent that $\Phi^o(\pi)$ is affected by $u(t)$ (since $\Phi^o(\pi)$ is a function of $\pi=[u(t)-A(I(t))]$), the initial disturbance may also affect the financial variables of the problem (altering the 'slope' of dI/dt) and determining (asymptotically) the new equilibrium E''.

Obviously, in the short run, any element that exogenously modifies financial variables such as stock prices would contribute to make the optimal investments I^* more unstable because of the 'financial channel' determined by the functional link $\Phi(\pi)$.

Furthermore, an exogenous negative shock in $u(\cdot)$ would affect I^* through two channels: the 'real one', which is captured by the link between $u(\cdot)$ and $\partial u(\cdot)/\partial k$, and the 'financial one', which is captured by the functional link $\Phi(\pi)$.

If (for $t\geq 1$) at some point the condition $\pi>1$ is violated (on the basis of assumptions (7.26)–(7.32)), the risk premium on the yield on shares $r_s(t)$ reaches the constant value ξ^* attributed to risky firms. The expected *ex ante* yield on shares reaches the level $r_s^*(t)$, associated with the cost of financial capital Φ^*. In this case, given that ξ^* is constant, the functional link between the profits π and the rate of discount Φ would disappear, and we would have again the common (and less interesting for our purposes) standard neoclassical investment model.

The fact of acting in a 'securitized' financial system, or the fact of issuing shares on the stock market, determines the existence of an additional channel of transmission of real exogenous shocks in $u(\cdot)$. This additional channel of transmission can amplify the fluctuations in the optimal level of investments generated by the original exogenous shock. This last result is consistent with the implications of the 'excess sensitivity' literature.

Conclusions

The qualitative analysis of investment decision contained in this chapter applies to financial markets characterized by imperfect competition, asymmetric information, and by the assumption that transactions on the stock market do not affect the control of firms, which is firmly in the hands of controlling groups. This last assumption is meant to capture a feature of non-securitized financial systems, where hostile takeovers are very rare (or in some cases, such as Italy, almost absent), and changes in the ownership and control are the result of private negotiations among the controlling groups of the various firms.

The investment and financial decisions of the firm are assumed to be simultaneous, and in this context an attempt has been made to qualitatively describe the transition between non-securitized and securitized financial systems, by modelling the discontinuous change that takes place for a firm issuing shares on the stock market for the first time. This discontinuous change has been described by introducing a few assumptions (deriving form theoretical and empirical results of the literature of finance and industrial economics) that determine a negative functional link between profits and cost of financial capital.

The discussion developed on these grounds suggests a feedback mechanism among profits, financial structure, the cost of capital and firm's investments. The nature and characteristics of this feedback are extremely complex and depend critically upon the assumption one makes about the relationship between future profits, the price of the firm's shares and the yield on shares.

By simplifying the feedback mechanism between profits and the cost of financial capital (and eliminating time dependence from it, although at the cost of some loss of generality), it has been shown that the interaction between financial and investment decisions introduces an additional 'financial' channel of causation between profits and real investments. This 'financial' channel can potentially amplify the effects on the investments of an exogenous shock in the profits of the firm. This last result is consistent with the implications of the 'excess sensitivity' literature.

Furthermore, the existence of a causal nexus (determined by the process of information spreading associated with the negotiation of securities on the spot financial markets) between profits and cost of external capital also accounts for the different credit price conditions granted by the banks to heterogeneous firms. Such a heterogeneity among different firms in their ability to borrow is also a typical assumption of the macroeconomic 'creditist' models.

Summing up . . .

This study contains several investigations on a few causal links (partly neglected by the literature) between credit, financial markets and industry. The interactions between industrial firms and financial institutions have been analysed here in several contexts: relevance of securitization for the behaviour of macroeconomic credit aggregates (chapter 3), effects of the market power of industrial firms in the credit market (chapter 4), relevance of liquidity preference of the banking system (chapter 5), relevance of firms' financial structure and transaction costs for the investment decision (chapter 6) and simultaneity of financial and investment decisions for the (microeconomic) firm's investment decision (chapter 7).

The work is related to the debate on 'credit and the macroeconomy', and since one of the most characteristic assumptions of the 'Credit View' is the intrinsic qualitative difference between securities and bank credit, the phenomenon of 'securitization' is likely to carry significant macroeconomic implications for the behaviour (i.e. empirical identification of theoretical functions, stability and predictability) of some of the most important credit aggregates. In particular, it is shown in chapter 3 that a stable supply function for bank credit to industry can be identified and estimated for a securitized financial system, because of the substitutability between bank credit and securities. On the one hand this result weakens the 'creditist' position, since one of the main criticisms of the supporters of the conventional 'money view' is the fact that financial innovation is going to generate an increasing number of highly substitutable financial instruments (ideally a 'continuum' of financial instruments). On the other it is consistent with the idea of high heterogeneity among firms (a typical creditist statement), since only the largerst and most reputable can afford the transaction costs associated with issuing securities. The issues of securitization and firms' heterogeneity are also taken into account in the empirical analysis of investments in chapter 6.

To the extent that stability is a desirable and informationally relevant property, then banks' credit to the industrial sector should be regarded as an important source of information for economic policy and targeting. On the other hand, since in 'non-securitized' financial sectors the volume of transactions that takes place on the stock markets is not quantitatively relevant compared to the intermediated credit the monetary policy has to be transmitted through the banking sector: the role of banks' 'investments' and liquidity preference (object of the empirical analysis in chapter 5) for the macroeconomic equilibrium becomes an interesting object of analysis. In fact, even in a non-securitized financial system it is not necessarily true that banks' assets are as relevant as money stock for the transmission mechanism of monetary policy, unless the investment decisions of the banking system, as well as its liquidity preference, can be modelled within an investment decision framework, where subjective valuations of profitability and risk play a precise role. The free liquidity ratio of commercial banks has been analysed in chapter 5 within this theoretical framework.

Chapter 4 deals with the fact that exogenous changes in the oligopsonistic power of industrial firms on the credit market affect the macroeconomic equilibrium and the transmission mechanism of monetary policy. In particular, an increase in the degree of concentration in the industrial sector reduces the equilibrium level of investments and affects the transmission mechanism of monetary policy by a direct 'first-impact' effect that tends to reduce the effectiveness of monetary policy and various 'indirect effects' whose sign and intensity depends on the analytical form (i.e. curvature and cross-elasticities) of the various excess demand functions for the various financial assets. These effects can modify the link between the different interest rates, and the functional link(s) existing between the equilibrium level of aggregate income and the interest rate of relevant financial assets such as State bonds and/or banks' assets. In this sense, they could be interpreted as a source of instability in macroeconomic models.

Part III looks inside the 'black box' of the macroeconomic causality between credit and investments suggested by the credit view, and investigates the interactions between firms' finance and investments decisions. The empirical analysis of the firms' investments contained in chapter 6 relies on three assumptions. First, in a non-securitized financial system, financial markets and instruments are – by definition – less developed than in a world of perfect financial markets; this implies that relevant transaction costs might significantly affect the speed of adjustment of the optimal investments. The presence of such transaction costs is also one of the starting points of Williamson's (1985) contractual framework, and is one of the crucial variables in explaining the intrinsic evolution and differences between the 'transaction-specific' contracts (between banks and industrial firms) and the 'general-purpose' contracts that generate transactions in the securities markets. In particular, various forms of transaction costs are among the main components of the monitoring costs that the financial intermediaries have to bear when undertaking long-run contractual relationships with their customers. Second, the cost of the firm's financial capital, in a world characterized by asymmetric information in financial markets, reflects a problem of optimization of the firm's financial structure, and can be summarized by a (firm-specific) leverage ratio. Third, in a non-securitized financial system, transaction costs and 'firm-specific' costs of financial capital are relevant factors for interpreting the behaviour of physical investments. In fact, the phenomenon of securitization can be interpreted (as suggested in chapter 5) on the basis of Williamson's (1985) contractual framework, which emphasizes the differences between 'general-purpose' or 'standardized' contracts (associable with the impersonal transactions characterizing the security markets) and 'specific' contracts, which involve higher monitoring and transaction costs for the financial intermediary. In a country characterized by a non-securitized financial system, since financial markets and financial instruments are by definition less developed, the transaction costs necessary to raise financial funds are likely to be more significant and to affect the speed of adjustment of investments and capital stock. Chapter 6 contains an empirical analysis (based on a sample of Italian chemical firms, i.e. firms operating in a country with a non-securitized financial system) where the specification of the firms' investments is based on the assumptions of transaction adjustment costs and firm-specific cost of financial capital.

The assumption of simultaneity between financial and investment decisions of the firms may result in a theoretical functional link between the marginal profitability of capital and the cost of financial capital. The interaction with institutional factors is again relevant for this point, analysed in chapter 7, which contains an attempt to qualitatively describe the transition from a non-securitized to a securitized financial system, by modelling the discontinuous change that takes place for a firm issuing shares on the stock market for the first time. This discontinuous change has been described by introducing a few assumptions (derived from theoretical and empirical results of the literature of finance and industrial economics) that determine a negative functional link between profits and the cost of financial capital. In this context, an exogenous change in the level of profits affects the optimal level of investments through two channels: a 'real' channel (i.e. via the 'marginal profitability of capital' assumed to depend on the level of variable profits), and a 'financial' channel (i.e. via the cost of financial capital, assumed to depend also on the level of variable profits). The 'financial' channel amplifies the 'real' effects of an exogenous disturbance in the profits if the level of profits is negatively correlated to the cost of financial capital. This result is consistent with that part of the New-Keynesian Macroeconomics concerned with financial markets imperfections

The macroeconomic statement of the credit view on the relevance of banks' assets for the transmission of monetary shocks can be decomposed into a number of microeconomic 'stylized' facts describing the interactions between credit and industry. This work has attempted to 'isolate' some of them, often 'neglected' by the mainstream and more conventional models. Some of them are potentially relevant and should be explicitly taken into account, if not in macroeconomic models, at least in policy analyses, or even just in our picture of the economic world.

Bibliography

Abel, A.B. and Eberly, J.C. (1994) 'A Unified Model of Investment Under Uncertainty', *American Economic Review*, 84, pp. 1369–84

Akerlof, G. (1970) 'The Market for Lemons: Quality Uncertainty and the Market Mechanism', *Quarterly Journal of Economics*, 84 August, pp. 488–500

Anderson, R.W. (1994) 'An Exploration of the Complementarity of Bank Lending and Securities Markets', Ente 'Luigi Einaudi', Roma, mimeo

Angeloni, F. (1984) 'Il mercato degli impieghi bancari in Italia: Un'analisi econometrica (1974–1982)', *Banca d'Italia, Temi di Discussione*, 41

Angeloni, F., Buttiglione, L., Ferri, G. and Gaiotti, E., (1995) 'The Credit Channel of Monetary Policy Across Heterogeneous Banks: The Case of Italy', *Banca d'Italia, Temi di Discussione*, 256

Aoki, M. and Leijonhufvud, A. (1988) 'The Stock-Flow Analysis of Investments' in Kohn, M. and Tsiang, S. (eds.), *Financial Constraints, Expectations and Macroeconomics*, Oxford, Oxford University Press

Ardeni, P.G. and Messori, M. (1996) *Il razionamento del credito*, Roma, Laterza

Ardeni, P.G., Boitani, A., Delli Gatti, D. and Gallegati, M. (1996) 'La nuova economia keynesiana: risultati e problemi aperti', in Messori, M. (ed.), *La Nuova Economia Keynesiana*, Bologna, Il Mulino

Arellano, M. and Bond, S.R. (1988) 'Dynamic Panel Data Estimation Using DPD – A Guide for Users', *Institute for Fiscal Studies Working Paper*, 88/15

Arestis, P. (1988) 'Post-Keynesian Theory of Money, Credit and Finance', in Arestis, P. (ed.), *Post-Keynesian Monetary Economics*, Aldershot, Edward Elgar

Arrow, K.J. (1963) 'Uncertainty and the Welfare Economics of Medical Care', *American Economic Review*, 53, pp. 941–73

(1968) 'The Economics of Moral Hazard: Further Comment', *American Economic Review*, 58, pp. 537–9

Bailey, N.T. (1957) *The Mathematical Theory of Epidemics*, London, C. Griffin

Baltensperger, E. (1980) 'Alternative Approaches to the Theory of the Banking Firm', *Journal of Monetary Economics*, 6, pp. 1–37

Banca d'Italia (1986) 'Modello trimestrale dell'economia italiana', *Banca d'Italia, Temi di Discussione*, 80

(1989) *Atti del seminario ristrutturazione economica e finanziaria delle imprese*, Rome, Banca d'Italia

Beavis, B. and Dobbs, I.M. (1990) *Optimization and Stability Theory for Economic Analysis*, Cambridge, Cambridge University Press

Benassy, J.P. (1989) 'Microeconomic Foundations and Properties of a Macroeconomic Model with Imperfect Competition', *CEPREMAP*, 8927 (September), Paris

Benoît, J.-P. (1984) 'Financially Constrained Entry in a Game with Incomplete Information', *RAND Journal of Economics*, 15, pp. 490–9

Benston, G.J. (1982) 'Accounting Numbers and Economic Values', *Antitrust Bulletin*, 21, pp. 161–215

Bera, A.K. and Jarque, C.M. (1981) 'An Efficient Large-Sample Test for Normality of Observations and Regression Residuals', *Working Paper in Econometrics*, 40, Canberra, Australian National University

Bernanke, B.S. (1983) 'Non-Monetary Effects of the Financial Crisis in the Propagation of the Real Depression', *American Economic Review*, 73, pp. 257–76

(1990) 'On the Predictive Power of Interest Rates and Interest Rates Spread', *New England Economic Review* (November/December), Federal Reserve Bank of Boston, pp. 51–68

(1993) 'Credit in the Macroeconomy', *Federal Reserve Bank of New York Quarterly Review*, Spring, pp. 50–70

Bernanke, B.S. and Blinder, A.S. (1988) 'Is it Money or Credit, or Both, or Neither? – Credit Money and Aggregate Demand', *American Economic Review*, 78, pp. 435–51

(1992) 'The Federal Funds Rate and the Channels of Monetary Transmission', *American Economic Review*, 82, pp. 901–27

Bernanke, B.S. and Campbell, J. (1988) 'Is there a Corporate Debt Crisis?', *Brookings Papers on Economic Activity*, 1, pp. 83–125

(1990) 'US Corporate Leverage Developments in 1987 and 1988', *Brookings Papers on Economic Activity*, 1, pp. 255–78

Bernanke, B.S. and Gertler, M. (1987) 'Banking and Macroeconomic Equilibrium', in Barnett, W.A. and Singleton, K.J., *New Approaches to Monetary Economics*, New York, Cambridge University Press.

(1989) 'Agency Costs, Net Worth and Business Fluctuations', *American Economic Review*, 79, pp. 14–31

(1990) 'Financial Fragility and Economic Performance', *Quarterly Journal of Economics* (February), pp. 87–114

(1995) 'Inside the Black Box: the Credit Channel of Monetary Policy Transmission', *NBER Working Paper*, 5146 (June)

Bernanke, B.S., Gertler, M. and Gilchrist, S. (1994) 'The Financial Accelerator and the Fligh to Quality', *NBER Working Paper*, 4789 (July)

Bernanke, B.S. and James, H. (1991) 'The Gold Standard, Deflation and Financial Crisis in the Great Depression: An International Comparison', in Hubbard, G.H. (ed.), *Financial Markets and Financial Crises*, Chicago, University of Chicago Press

Bernanke, B.S. and Lown, C. (1992) 'The Credit Crunch', *Brookings Papers on Economic Activity*, 2, pp. 205–39

Bernanke, B.S. and Mishkin, F. (1992) 'Central Bank Behaviour and the Strategy of Monetary Policy: Observations from Six Industrialized Countries', *NBER Working Paper*, 4082 (May)

Bernstein, J.I. and Nadiri, M.I. (1986) 'Financing and Investment in Plant and Equipment and Research and Development', in Peston, M.H. and Quandt, R.E., *Prices, Competition and Equilibrium*, Oxford, Philip Allan

(1993) 'Production, Financial Structure and Productivity Growth in US Manufacturing', *NBER Working Paper Series*, 4309

Bertocco, G. (1987) 'Per un'analisi degli effetti della politica monetaria nel periodo del controllo del credito totale interno', *Rivista di Politica Economica*, 77, pp. 4–32

(1989) 'Il ruolo del credito in un recente modello macroeconomico', *Note Economiche*, 2, pp. 231–45

(1991) *Teoria e politica monetaria nell'analisi della banca d'italia*, Turin, Giappichelli

(1995) 'Teorema di Modigliani–Miller, imperfetta informazione e meccanismo di trasmissione della politica monetaria', *Moneta e Credito*, 191 (September), pp. 391–420

(1996) 'Il governo della moneta e del credito in italia – un'analisi del meccanismo di trasmissione della politica monetaria nel periodo 1960–95', *Quaderni del Dipartimento di Economia Politica e Metodi Quantitativi*, Università di Pavia

Bertola, G. and Caballero, R.J. (1991) 'Irreversibility and Aggregate Investment', *NBER Working Paper*, 3865

Bester, H. (1985) 'Screening vs. Rationing in Credit Markets with Imperfect Information', *American Economic Review*, 75, pp. 850–5

Blanchard, O.J. (1981) 'Output, the Stock Market and Interest Rates', *American Economic Review*, 71, pp. 132–43

Blanchard, O.J. and Fischer, S. (1989) *Lectures on Macroeconomics*, Cambridge, MA, MIT Press

Blanchard, O.J. and Kiyotaki, N. (1987) 'Monopolistic Competition and the Effects of Aggregate Demand', *American Economic Review*, 77, pp. 647–66

Blanchard, O.J., Lopez-de-Silanez, F. and Shleifer, A. (1993) 'What do firms do with Cash Windfalls?', *NBER Working Paper*, 4258

Blinder, A.S. (1987) 'Credit Rationing and Effective Supply Failure', *Economic Journal*, 97, pp. 327–52

Blinder, A.S. and Stiglitz, J.E. (1983) 'Money, Credit Constraint and Economic Activity', *American Economic Review*, 73, pp. 297–302

Blundell, R., Bond, S. and Meghir, C. (1992) 'Econometric Models of Company Investments', in Matyas, L. and Sevestre, P. (eds.) *The Econometrics of Panel Data – Handbook of Theory and Applications*, Dordrecht, Kluwer Academic Publishers

Bond, S. and Meghir, C. (1992) 'Dynamic Investment Models and the Firm's Financial Policy', *UCL Discussion Papers in Economics*, 92–14, Department of Economics, University College London

Bradley, J.A., Jarrel, G.A. and Kim, H.E. (1984) 'On the Evidence of the Optimal Capital Structure, Theory and Evidence', *Journal of Finance*, 39, pp. 857–78

Brander, J.A. and Lewis, T.R. (1985) 'Oligopoly and the Financial Structure – The Limited Liability Effect', *American Economic Review*, 75, pp. 956–70

Brennan, M. and Kraus, A. (1987) 'Efficient Financing under Asymmetric Information', *Journal of Finance*, 42, pp. 1225–43

Brennan, M. and Schwartz, E. (1978) 'Corporate Income Taxes Valuation and the Problem of Optimal Capital Structure', *Journal of Business*, 51, pp. 103–14

Brioschi, F., Buzzacchi, L. and Colombo M.G. (1990) *Gruppi di imprese e mercato finanziario*, Roma, La Nuova Italia Scientifica

Bryant, R.C. (1983) 'Controlling Money: The Federal Reserve and its Critics', Washington DC, Brookings Institution

Buttiglione, L. and Ferri, G. (1994) 'Monetary Policy Transmission via Lending Rates in Italy: Any Lessons From Recent Experience?', *Banca d'Italia, Temi di Discussione*, no. 224

Cagan, P. (1969) 'Interest Rates and Bank Reserves – A Reinterpretation of the Statistical Association', in Guttentag, J.M. and Cagan P. (eds.), *Essays on Interest Rates*, New York, NBER, pp. 223–72

Calomiris, C. and Hubbard, R.G. (1990) 'Firm Heterogeneity, Internal Finance and Credit Rationing', *Economic Journal*, 100, pp. 90–104

Çapoglu, G. (1991) *Prices, Profits and Financial Structures: A Post–Keynesian Approach to Competition*, Aldershot, Edward Elgar

Carpenter, R.E., Fazzari, S.M. and Petersen, B.C. (1994) 'Inventory Investments, Internal-Finance Fluctuations, and the Business Cycle', *Brookings Papers on Economic Activity*, 2, pp. 75–138

Chamley, C. (1993) 'Liquidity Trap', University of Warwick (July), mimeo

Chick, V. (1983) *Macroeconomics after Keynes: A Reconsideration of the General Theory*, Oxford, Philip Allan

Christiano, L. and Eichenbaum, M. (1992) 'Liquidity Effects and the Monetary Transmission Mechanism', *American Economic Review, Papers and Proceedings* (May), pp. 346–53

Coase, R.H. (1960) 'The Problem of Social Cost', *Journal of Law and Economics*, 3, pp. 1–44

Conigliani, C. (1990) *La concentrazione bancaria in Italia*, Bologna, Il Mulino

Conti, V. (1991) 'Concorrenza e redditività nell'industria bancaria: un confronto internazionale', *Banca d'Italia, Temi di Discussione del Servizio Studi*, 149 (February)

Corradi, V., Galeotti, M. and Rovelli, R. (1988) 'Il Sistema bancario e il meccanismo di trasmissione', in Cesarini, F., Grillo, M., Monti, M. and Onado, M. (eds.), *Banca e Mercato*, Bologna, Italy, Il Mulino

Cottarelli, C. and Kourelis, A. (1994) 'Financial Structure, Bank Lending Rates and the Transmission Mechanism of Monetary Policy', *IMF Staff Papers*, 41 (4), pp. 587–623

Cottarelli, C., Ferri, G. and Generale, A. (1995) 'Bank Lending Rates and Financial

Structure in Italy: A Case Study', Università Cattolica del S. Cuore, Milano, mimeo

Cowling, K. (1982) *Monopoly Capitalism*, London, MacMillan

Cowling, K. and Waterson, M. (1976) 'Price–Cost Margins and the Market Structure', *Economica* (May)

Cuthbertson, K. (1985) 'Banking Lending to UK Industrial and Commercial Companies', *Oxford Bulletin of Economics and Statistics*, 47, pp. 91–118

(1988) 'The Demand for M1: A Forward-Looking Buffer Stock Model', *Oxford Economic Papers*, 40, pp. 110–31

Davidson, J.E.H., Hendry, D.F., Srba, F. and Yeo, S. (1978) 'Econometric Modelling of the Aggregate Time-Series Relationship Between Consumers' Expenditure and Income in the United Kingdom', *Economic Journal*, 88, pp. 661–92

Davidson, P. (1982) *International Money and the Real World*, London, MacMillan

(1994) *Post Keynesian Macroeconomic Theory – A Foundation for Successful Economic Policies for the Twenty-first Century*, Aldershot, Edward Elgar.

Debreu, G. (1974) 'Excess Demand Functions', *Journal of Mathematical Economics*, I, pp. 15–21

De Felice, G. and Esposito, M. (1995) 'Il comportamento dei tassi d'interesse interbancari e la trasmissione della politica monetaria', Università Cattolica del Sacro Cuore, Milan, (February) mimeo

Delli Gatti, D. and Gallegati, M. (1989) 'Financial Instability, Income Distribution and the Stock Market', *Journal of Post-Keynesian Economics*, 11, pp. 356–74

(1991) 'Informazione asimmetrica, accumulazione del debito e ciclo economico', in Kregel, J. (ed.), *Nuove Interpretazioni dell'Analisi Monetaria di Keynes*, Bologna, Il Mulino

(1995) 'Financial Constraints, Aggregate Supply and the Monetary Transmission Mechanism', Università Cattolica del S. Cuore, Milan, (February) mimeo, forthcoming in *Manchester School of Economics and Social Studies*

Delli Gatti, D., Gallegati, M. and Gardini, L. (1990) 'Real Accumulation and Financial Instability: A Model of Profit Flows, Debt Commitments and Capital Asset Prices', *Studi Economici*, 41, pp. 101–26

(1993) 'Investments, Confidence, Corporate Debt and Income Fluctuations', *Journal of Economic Behaviour and Organization*, 22 (2), pp. 161–87

De Meza, D. and Webb, D.C. (1987) 'Too Much Investment: A Problem of Asymmetric Information', *Quarterly Journal of Economics*, 102, pp. 281–92

Deshmukh, S., Greenbaum, S.I. and Kanatas, G. (1983) 'Bank Forward Lending in Alternative Funding Environments', *Journal of Finance*, 38, pp. 873–86

Diamond, D.W. (1984) 'Financial Intermediation and Delegated Monitoring', *Review of Economic Studies*, 51, pp. 393–414

(1989) 'Reputation Acquisition in Debt Markets', *Journal of Political Economy*, 97 pp. 828–62

Dixit, A.K. (1989) 'Entry and Exit Decision under Uncertainty', *Journal of Political Economy*, 97, pp. 620–38

(1992a) 'Investment and Hysteresis', *Journal of Economic Perspectives*, 6, pp. 107–32

(1992b) 'Irreversible Investment with Uncertainty and Scale Economy', Princeton University, (April) mimeo

Dixit, A.K. and Pindyck, R.S. (1994) *Investment Under Uncertainty*, Princeton, New Jersey, Princeton University Press

Dotan, A. and David, A. (1985) 'On the Interaction of Financial Decisions of the Firm under Uncertainty', *Journal of Finance*, 50, pp. 178–94

Duca, J.V. and VanHoose, D.D. (1990) 'Loan Commitments and Optimal Monetary Policy', *Journal of Money, Credit and Banking*, 22, pp. 178–94

Dufour, J.M. (1980) 'Dummy Variables and Predictive Tests for Structural Changes', *Economic Letters*, 6, pp. 241–7

Eichner, A.S. (1976) *The Megacorp and Oligopoly: Micro Foundations of Macro Dynamics*, Cambridge, Cambridge University Press

Fama, E. (1980) 'Banking in the Theory of Finance', *Journal of Monetary Economics*, 6, pp. 39–57

(1985) 'What's Different about Banks?', *Journal of Monetary Economics*, 15, pp. 29–40

Fazzari, S.M., Hubbard, G.R. and Petersen, B.C. (1988) 'Financing Constraints and Corporate Investment', *Brookings Papers on Economic Activity*, 1, pp. 141–206

Fischer, E.O., Heinkel, R. and Zechner, J. (1989) 'Dynamic Capital Structure, Theory and Tests', *Journal of Finance*, 44, pp. 19–40

Fischer, S. (1983) 'A Framework for Monetary and Banking Analysis', *Economic Journal*, 93, pp. 1–16

Fisher, I. (1933) 'The Debt–Deflation Theory of the Great Depression', *Econometrica*, 1 (October), pp. 1–16

Frankel, A.B. and Montgomery, J.D. (1991) 'Financial Structure: an International Perspective', *Brookings Papers on Economic Activity*, 1, pp. 257–97

Frasca, F. and Marotta, G. (1988) 'La ristrutturazione finanziaria delle grandi imprese', in Banca d'Italia, *Atti del seminario Ristrutturazione economica e finanziaria delle imprese*, Rome

Freimer, M. and Gordon, M.J. (1965) 'Why Bankers Ration Credit', *Quarterly Journal of Economics*, 79, pp. 397–410

Friedman, B.M. (1990) 'Targets and Instruments of Monetary Policy', in Friedman, B. and Hahn, F.H. (eds.), *Handbook of Monetary Economics*, vol. 2, Amsterdam, North-Holland

(1993) 'The Role of Judgment and Discretion in the Conduct of Monetary Policy: Consequences of Changing Financial Markets', *NBER Working Paper*, 4599

Friedman, B.M. and Kuttner, K.N. (1992) 'Money, Income, Prices and Interest Rates', *American Economic Review*, 82, pp. 472–92

(1993) 'Economic Activity and the Short-Term Credit Markets: An Analysis of Prices and Quantities', *Brookings Papers on Economic Activity*, 2, pp. 193–266

Friedman, M. and Schwartz, A.J. (1963a) 'Money and Business Cycle', *Review of Economics and Statistics*, 45 (1) part 2, Supplement (February), pp. 32–64

(1963b) *A Monetary History of the United States*, Princeton, Princeton University Press for the National Bureau of Economic Research

(1982) *Monetary Trends in the United States and the United Kingdom. Their*

Relation to Income, Prices and Interest Rates, 1867–1975, Chicago, University of Chicago Press

Fuerst, T. (1992) 'Liquidity, Loanable Funds and Real Activity', *Journal of Monetary Economics* (February), pp. 3–24

Ganoulis, I. (1991) 'Stock Market Prices and Investment when Financial Markets are not Strongly Efficient', *Applied Economics Discussion Paper Series*, 128, Institute of Economics and Statistics, Oxford University

Gardener, E.P.M. (1991) 'Nuove strategie per le banche europee', *Banca Impresa, Società*, Anno X, 1 (April), pp. 19–39, Bologna, Il Mulino

Gardener, E.P.M. and Molyneux, P. (1990) *Changes in Western European Banking*, London, Unwin Hyman

Gertler, M. (1988) 'Financial Structure and Aggregate Economic Activity: An Overview', *Journal of Money, Credit and Banking*, 20, pp. 559–88

(1992) 'Financial Capacity and Output Fluctuations in an Economy with Multi-Period Financial Relationships', *Review of Economic Studies*, 59, pp. 455–72

Gertler, M. and Gilchrist, S. (1991) 'Monetary Policy, Business Cycles and the Behaviour of Small Manufacturing Firms', *NBER Working Paper*, 3892

(1993) 'The Role of Credit Market Imperfections in the Monetary Transmission Mechanism: Arguments and Evidence', *Scandinavian Journal of Economics*, 95 (1), pp. 43–64

Giannini, C., Papi, L. and Prati, A. (1991) 'Politica di offerta e riallocazione del credito bancario negli anni ottanta', *Banca d'Italia Temi di Discussione* (February)

Godfrey, L.G. (1978a) 'Testing Against General Autoregressive and Moving Average Error Models when the Regressors Include Lagged Dependent Variables', *Econometrica*, 46, pp. 1293–301

(1978b) 'Testing for Higher Order Serial Correlation in Regression Equations When the Regressors Include Lagged Dependent Variables', *Econometrica*, 46, pp. 1303–10

Graziani, A. (1984) 'The Debate on Keynes' Finance Motive', *Economic Notes*, 13, pp. 5–32

Greenwald, B.C. and Stiglitz, J.E. (1988) 'Imperfect Information, Financial Constraints, and Business Fluctuations', in Kohn, M. and Tsiang, S. (eds.), *Financial Constraints, Expectations and Macroeconomics*, Oxford, Oxford University Press

(1989) 'Financial Market Imperfections and Productivity Growth', *NBER Working Paper*, 2945

(1990a) 'Asymmetric Information and the New Theory of the Firm: Financial Constraints and Risk Behaviour', *NBER Working paper*, 3359

(1990b) 'Macroeconomic Models with Equity and Credit Rationing', in Hubbard, R.G. (ed.), *Information, Capital Markets and Investments*, Chicago, University of Chicago Press

(1993a) 'Financial Market Imperfections and Business Cycles', *Quarterly Journal of Economics* (February), pp. 77–115

(1993b) 'New and Old Keynesians', *Journal of Economic Perspectives*, 7 (1), pp. 23–44

Greenwald, B.C., Stiglitz, J.E. and Weiss, A. (1984) 'Informational Imperfections in the Capital Market and Macroeconomic Fluctuations', *American Economic Review*, 74, pp. 194–9

Gurley, J. and Shaw, E. (1955) 'Financial Aspects of Economic Development', *American Economic Review*, 45, pp. 515–38

Harris, M. and Raviv, A. (1990) 'Capital Structure and the Informational Role of Debt', *Journal of Finance*, 45, pp. 321–49

Harvey, A.C. (1989) *The Econometric Analysis of Time Series*, Oxford: Philip Allan

Hayashi, F. (1982) 'Tobin's Marginal q and Average q: A Neoclassical Interpretation', *Econometrica*, 50, pp. 213–24

Heinkel, R. (1982) 'A Theory of Capital Structure Relevance Under Imperfect Information', *Journal of Finance*, 37, pp. 1141–50

Heinkel, R. and Zechner, J. (1990) 'The Role of Debt and Preferred Stock as a Solution to Adverse Investment Incentives', *Journal of Financial and Quantitative Analysis*, 25, pp. 1–24

Hendry, D.F. (1979) 'Predictive Failure and Econometric Modelling in Macroeconomics: The Transactions Demand for Money', in Ormerod, P. (ed.), *Economic Modelling*, London, Heineman

(1985) 'Monetary Economic Myth and Economic Reality', *Oxford Review of Economic Policy*, 1, pp. 72–84

(1988) 'The Encompassing Implications of Feedback versus Feedforward Mechanisms in Econometrics', *Oxford Economic Papers*, 40, pp. 132–49

Hendry, D.F. and Mizon, G.E. (1978) 'Serial Correlation as a Convenient Simplification, not a Nuisance: A Comment on a Study of the Demand for Money by the Bank of England', *Economic Journal*, 88, pp. 549–63

Henley, A. (1990) *Wages and Profits in the Capitalist Economy – The Impact of Monopolistic Power on Macroeconomic Performance*, Aldershot, Edward Elgar

Hicks, J.R. (1937) 'Mr Keynes and the Classics: A Suggested Interpretation', *Econometrica*, reprinted in Hicks, J.R., *Critical Essays in Monetary Theory*, Oxford, Oxford University Press (1967)

Hillier, B. and Ibrahimo, M.V. (1993) 'Asymmetric Information and Models of Credit Rationing', *Bulletin of Economic Research*, 45, pp. 271–304

Hite, G.L. (1979) 'Leverage Output Effects and the M-M Theorem', *Journal of Financial Economics*, 4, pp. 177–202

Hodgman, D. (1960) 'Credit Risk and Credit Rationing', *Quarterly Journal of Economics*, 74, pp. 258–78

Hörngren, L. (1985) 'Regulatory Monetary Policy and Uncontrolled Financial Intermediaries', *Journal of Money, Credit and Banking*, 17, pp. 203–19

Hsiao, C. (1986) *Analysis of Panel Data*, Cambridge, Cambridge University Press

Huang, C.-F. and Litzenberger, R.H. (1988) *Foundations for Financial Economics*, Amsterdam and New York, North-Holland.

Jaffee, D. and Modigliani, F. (1969) 'A Theory and Test of Credit Rationing', *American Economic Review*, 59, pp. 850–72

Jarque, C.M. and Bera, A.K. (1980) 'Efficient Tests for Normality, Homoscedasticity and Serial Independence of Regression Residuals', *Economic Letters*, 6, pp. 255–9

Jensen, M. and Meckling, W. (1976) 'Theory of the Firm: Managerial Behaviour, Agency Costs and Ownership', *Journal of Financial Economics*, 3, pp. 305–60

Kaldor, N. (1982) *The Scourge of Monetarism*, Oxford, Oxford University Press

Kalecki, M. (1971) *Selected Essays on the Dynamics of the Capitalist Economy*, Cambridge, Cambridge University Press

Kashyap, A.K. and Stein, J.K. (1993) 'Monetary Policy and Bank Lending', *NBER Working Paper*, 4317

Kashyap, A.K., Stein, J.K. and Wilcox, D.W. (1993) 'Monetary Policy and Credit Conditions: Evidence from the Composition of External Finance', *American Economic Review*, 83, pp. 78–98

Keynes, J.M. (1930) *A Treatise On Money*, London, Macmillan
    (1936) *The General Theory of Employment, Interest and Money*, London, Macmillan

Kindleberger, C. (1978) *Manias, Panic and Crashes*, New York, Basic Books

King, S.R. (1986) 'Monetary Transmission – Through Bank Loans or Bank Liabilities?', *Journal of Money, Credit and Banking*, 18, pp. 290–303

Kose, J. (1987) 'Risk-Shifting Incentives and Signalling through Corporate Capital Structure', *Journal of Finance*, 42, pp. 622–41

Kurz, M. (1993) 'General Equilibrium with Endogenous Uncertainty', in Chichilnizky, G. (ed.), *Challenge of Economic Theory*, Cambridge, Cambridge University Press
    (1994a) 'On the Structure and Diversity of Rational Beliefs', *Economic Theory*, 4, pp. 877–900
    (1994b) 'On Rational Beliefs Equilibria', *Economic Theory*, 4, pp. 859–76
    (1994c) 'Explaining Volatility and Excess Returns', Stanford University (May) mimeo
    (1994d) 'Asset Prices with Rational Beliefs', *CEPR Discussion Paper* 375, Stanford University

Langhor, H. (1981) 'Banks Borrowing from Central Bank and Reserve Position Doctrine: Belgium 1960–1973', *Journal of Monetary Economics*, 7 pp. 107–24

Lavoie, M. (1984a) 'Un modèle post-Keynesien d'économie monétaire fondé sur la théorie du circuit', ISMEA, *Série Monnaie et Production*
    (1984b) 'The Endogenous Flow of Credit and the Post Keynesian Theory of Money', *Journal of Economic Issues*, 18, pp. 771–97

Leland, H. and Pyle, D. (1977) 'Information Asymmetries, Financial Structure, and Financial Intermediation', *Journal of Finance*, 32, pp. 371–98

Litner, J. (1956) 'The Distribution of Incomes of Corporations Among Dividends, Retained Earnings and Taxes', *American Economic Review*, 46, pp. 97–113

Maddaloni, G. (1996) 'Il credito commerciale in italia, aspetti teorici e verifiche empiriche', *ICER Working Paper*, 4/96

Malécot, J.-F. (1992) 'Modeling Companies' Dividend Policy Using Account Panel Data', in Matyas, L. and Svestre, P. (eds.), *The Econometrics of Panel Data – Handbook of Theory and Applications*, Dordrecht, Kluwer Academic

Mantel, R. (1974) 'On the Characterization of Aggregate Excess Demand', *Journal of Economic Theory*, 7, pp. 348–53

Marotta, G. (1995) 'Il credito commerciale in Italia: una nota su alcuni aspetti strutturali e sulle implicazioni di politica monetaria', Dipartimento di Economia Politica, Università di Modena, *Materiali di Discussione*, 121

Marris, R. (1991) *Reconstructing Keynesian Economics with Imperfect Competition – A Desktop Simulation*, London, Macmillan

Martin, S. (1993) *Advanced Industrial Economics*, Oxford, Basil Blackwell

Mattesini, F. (1993) *Financial Markets, Asymmetric Information and Macroeconomic Equilibrium*, Aldershot, Dartmouth

Mayer, C. (1989) 'The Influence of the Financial System on the British Corporate Sector', prepared for the conference *The Separation of Industry and Finance and the Specialization of Financial Intermediaries*, Bocconi University, Milan, mimeo

(1990) 'Financial Systems, Corporate Finance and Economic Development', in Hubbard, G. (ed.), *Asymmetric Information, Corporate Finance and Investment*, Chicago, University of Chicago Press

(1993a) 'Corporate Finance', in Eatwell, J., Milgate, M. and Newman, P. (eds.), *The New Palgrave Dictionary of Money and Finance*, London, Macmillan

(1993b) 'Ownership', University of Warwick, mimeo

Messori, M. (1996) 'Introduzione', in Messori, M. (ed.), *La nuova economia keynesiana*, Bologna, Il Mulino

Messori, M. (ed.) (1988) *Moneta e Produzione*, Turin, Einaudi

Messori, M. and Tamborini, R. (1995) 'Fallibility, Precautionary Behaviour and the New Keynesian Monetary Theory', *Scottish Journal of Political Economy*, 42, pp. 443–64

Miller, M.H. (1962) 'Credit Risk and Credit Rationing: Further Comments', *Quarterly Journal of Economics*, 76, pp. 1–48

Minsky, H.P. (1975) *John Maynard Keynes*, New York, Columbia University Press

(1982) *Can 'it' Happen Again? Essays on Instability and Finance*, Armonk, NY, M.E. Sharpe

(1986) 'The Evolution of Financial Institutions and the Performance of the Economy', *Journal of Economic Issues* (June)

Modigliani, F. (1944) 'Liquidity Preference and the Theory of Interest and Money', *Econometrica*, 12, pp. 45–88

Modigliani, F. and Miller, M.H. (1958) 'The Cost of Capital, Corporation Finance and the Theory of Investment', *American Economic Review*, 48, pp. 261–97

(1963) 'The Cost of Capital, Corporation Finance and the Theory of Investment – A Correction', *American Economic Review*, 53, pp. 433–43

Modigliani, F. and Papademos, L. (1980) 'The Structure of Financial Markets and the Monetary Mechanism', in *Controlling Monetary Aggregates III*, Conference Series, 23, Federal Reserve Bank of Boston

(1987) 'Money, Credit and the Monetary Mechanism', in De Cecco, M. and Fitoussi, J.-P. (eds.), *Monetary Theory and Economic Institutions*, London, Macmillan

Monti, M. (1971) 'A Theoretical Model of Bank Behaviour and its Implications for Monetary Policy', *L'Industria*, 2, pp. 3–29

Muscatelli, V.A. (1989) 'A Comparison of the "Rational Expectations" and "General-to-Specific" Approaches to Modelling the Demand for M1', *Oxford Bulletin of Economics and Statistics*, 51, pp. 353–75

Myers, S.C. (1984) 'The Capital Structure Puzzle', *Journal of Finance*, 39, pp. 575–92

Myers, S.C. and Majluf, N.S. (1984) 'Corporate Financing and Investment Decisions when Firms have Information that Investors do not have', *Journal of Financial Economics*, 13, pp. 187–221

Narayanan, M.P. (1988) 'Debt Versus Equity under Asymmetric Information', *Journal of Finance and Quantitative Analysis*, 23, pp. 38–51

Okun, A.M. (1981) *Prices and Quantities: A Macroeconomic Analysis*, Washington, DC, Brookings Institution

Pagano, M., Panetta, F. and Zingales, N. (1994) 'Why Companies Go Public? An Empirical Analysis' (December), Ente 'Luigi Einaudi', Roma, mimeo

Patinkin, D. (1956) *Money, Interest and Prices*, New York, Harper & Row

Peterson, P.P. and Benesh, G.A. (1983) 'A Reexamination of the Empirical Relationship Between Investment and Financial Decisions', *Journal of Finance and Quantitative Analysis*, 18, pp. 439–53

Pindyck, R. (1988) 'Irreversible Investment, Capacity Choice and the Value of the Firm', *American Economic Review*, 78, pp. 969–85

(1991) 'Irreversibility, Uncertainty and Investment', *Journal of Economic Literature*, 29, pp. 1110–48

Poitervin, M. (1989a) 'Financial Signalling and the "Deep Pocket" Argument', *Rand Journal of Economics*, 20, pp. 26–40

(1989b) 'Collusion and Banking Structure of a Duopoly', *Canadian Journal of Economics*, 22 (2), pp. 263–77

(1990) 'Strategic Financial Signalling', *International Journal of Industrial Organization*, 8, pp. 499–518

Precious, M. (1987) *Rational Expectations, Non-Market Clearing and Investment Theory*, Oxford, Clarendon Press

Ramey, V. (1993) 'How Important is the Credit Channel in the Transmission of Monetary Policy?', *Carnegie–Rochester Conference Series on Public Policy*, 39, pp. 1–45

Ramsey, J.B. (1969) 'Tests for Specification Errors in Classical Linear Least Squares Analysis', *Journal of the Royal Statistical Society*, series B, 31, pp. 350–71

(1970) 'Models, Specification Error and Inference: A Discussion of Some Problems in Econometric Methodology', *Bulletin of the Oxford Institute of Economics and Statistics*, 32, pp. 301–18

Richter, R. and Teigen, R.L. (1982) 'Commercial Bank Behaviour and Monetary Policy in an Open Economy: West Germany 1960–1980', *Journal of Monetary Economics*, 10, pp. 383–405

Romer, C.D. and Romer, D.H. (1989) 'Does Monetary Policy Matter? A New Test in the Spirit of Friedman and Schwartz', in O. Blanchard and S. Fisher (eds.), *NBER Macroeconomic Annual*, Cambridge, MA, MIT Press, pp. 121–69

(1990) 'New Evidence on the Monetary Transmission Mechanism', *Brookings Papers on Economic Activity*, 1, pp. 149–98

Ross, S. (1977) 'The Determination of the Financial Structure: The Incentive-Signalling Approach', *Bell Journal of Economics*, 8, pp. 23–40

Rybczynski, T. (1984) 'The Financial System in Transition' *National Westminster Bank Quarterly Review* (November)

Salkever, D.S. (1976) 'The Use of Dummy Variables to Compute Prediction Errors and Confidence Intervals', *Journal of Econometrics*, 4, pp. 393–400

Santomero, A.M. (1984) 'Modeling the Banking Firm', *Journal of Money, Credit and Banking*, 16, pp. 576–602

Shiller, R. (1981) 'Do Stock Prices Move too much to be Justified by Subsequent Changes in Dividends?', *American Economic Review*, 71, pp. 421–36

(1984) 'Stock Prices and Social Dynamics', *Brookings Papers on Economic Activity*, 2, pp. 457–510

(1989) *Market Volatility*, Cambridge, MA, MIT Press

Sims, C. (1980) 'Comparison of Interwar and Postwar Business Cycles: Monetarism Reconsidered', *American Economic Review*, 70, pp. 250–7

Sonnenschein, H. (1972) 'Market Excess Demand Functions', *Econometrica*, 40, pp. 549–63

(1974) 'Do Walras' Identity and Continuity Functions Characterize the Class of Community Excess Demand Functions?' *Journal of Economic Theory*, 6, pp. 345–54

Starz, R. (1989) 'Monopolistic Competition as a Foundation for Keynesian Macroeconomic Models', *Quarterly Journal of Economics* (November), pp. 737–52

Stiglitz, J.E. (1974) 'On the Irrelevance of Corporate Financial Policy', *American Economic Review*, 64, pp. 851–66

(1987) 'The Causes and Consequences of the Dependence of Quality on Price', *Journal of Economic Literature*, 25, pp. 1–47

(1991) 'Alternative Approaches to Macroeconomics: Methodological Issues and the New Keynesian Economics', *NBER Working Paper* 3580

(1992) 'Methodological Issues and New Keynesian Economics', in Vercelli, A. and Dimitri, N. (eds.) *Macroeconomics*. Oxford, Oxford University Press

Stiglitz, J.E. and Weiss, A. (1981) 'Credit Rationing in Markets with Imperfect Information', *American Economic Review*, vol. 71, pp. 393–410

(1986) 'Credit Rationing and Collateral', in Edwards, J., Franks, J., Mayer, C. and Shleifer, S. (eds.), *Recent Developments in Corporate Finance*, New York, Cambridge University Press, pp. 101–35

(1992) 'Asymmetric Information in Credit Markets and its Implications for Macroeconomics', *Oxford Economics Papers*, 44, pp. 694–724

Summers, L.H. (1986) 'Do Market Prices Accurately Reflect Fundamental Values?', *Journal of Finance*, 41, pp. 591–601

Tamborini, R. (1992) *Il trasferimento mondiale delle risorse – un approccio finanziario ai pagamenti internazionali*, Rome, La Nuova Italia Scientifica

(1995) 'A General Equilibrium Analysis of the Credit View', *Quaderno*, 46–95, University of Padua, Department of Economics

(1996a) 'An Investigation into the New Keynesian Macroeconomics of Imperfect Capital Markets', University of Padua, Department of Economics, mimeo

(1996b) 'C'è (o ci sarà) una Nuova Teoria Monetaria Keynesiana?', in Messori, M. (ed.), *La Nuova Economia Keynesiana*, Bologna, Il Mulino

Taylor, L. and O'Connell, S.A. (1985) 'A Minsky Crisis', *Quarterly Journal of Economics*, 100, pp. 871–86

Telser, L.G. (1966) 'Cutthroat Competition and the Long Purse', *Journal of Law and Economics*, 20, pp. 26–40

Thornton, D.L. (1994) 'Financial Innovation, Deregulation and the "Credit View" of Monetary Policy', *Federal Reserve Bank of St Louis Review* (January/February), pp. 31–49

Titman, S. and Wessels, R. (1988) 'The Determinants of Capital Structure Choice', *Journal of Finance*, 43, pp. 1–19

Tobin, J. (1961) 'Money, Capital and Other Stores of Value', *American Economic Review, Papers and Proceedings*, 51 (2), pp. 26–37

(1969) 'A General Equilibrium Approach to Monetary Policy', *Journal of Money, Credit and Banking*, 1, pp. 15–29

Tobin, J. and Brainard, W.C. (1963) 'Financial Intermediaries and the Effectiveness of Monetary Control', *American Economic Review*, 53, pp. 383–400

Townsend, R.M. (1979) 'Optimal Contracts and Competitive Markets with Costly State Verification', *Journal of Economic Theory*, 21, pp. 265–93

Van Hoose, D.D. (1983) 'Monetary Policy under Alternative Market Structure', *Journal of Banking and Finance*, 7, pp. 383–404

(1985) 'Bank Market Structure and Monetary Control', *Journal of Money, Credit and Banking*, 17, pp. 298–311

Vercelli, A. and Dimitri, N. (eds.) (1992) *Macroeconomics*, Oxford, Oxford University Press

Wallis, K.F. (1974) 'Seasonal Adjustment and Relations between Variables', *Journal of the American Statistical Association*, 69, pp. 18–31

Wessels, R.E. (1982) 'The Supply and Use of Central Bank Advance Facilities', *Journal of Monetary Economics*, 10, pp. 89–100

Williamson, O. (1985) *The Economic Institutions of Capitalism*, New York, The Free Press

Williamson, S. (1987) 'Financial Intermediation, Business Failures, and Real Business Cycle', *Journal of Political Economy*, 95, pp. 1196–1216

Wood, A. (1975) *A Theory of Profits*, Cambridge, Cambridge University Press

Wood, J.H. (1974) 'A Model of Commercial Bank Loan and Investment Behaviour', in Johnson, H.G. and Nobay, A.R. (eds.), *Issues in Monetary Economics*, Oxford, Oxford University Press

Index